HOW TO GET A
MORTGAGE

HOW TO GET A MORTGAGE

A COMPLETE, NO-NONENE

GUIDE TO FINDING THE MONEY TO BUY, REFINANCE OR REMODEL YOUR HOME

DIXIE·LEE·BUTLER

PROBUS PUBLISHING COMPANY
Chicago, Illinois

© 1991, Dixie Lee Butler

ALL RIGHTS RESERVED. No part of this publication may be reproduced, stored in a retrieval system, or transmitted by any means, electronic, mechanical, photocopying, recording or otherwise, without the prior written permission of the publisher and the copyright holder.

This publication is designed to provide accurate and authoritative information in regard to the subject matter covered. It is sold with the understanding that the publisher and author are not engaged in rendering legal, accounting or other professional service.

   Library of Congress Cataloging-in-Publication Data
Butler, Dixie Lee.
   How to get a mortgage: a complete, no-nonsense guide to finding the money to buy, refinance or remodel your home/ Dixie Lee Butler.
   p.   cm.
   ISBN 1-55738-193-3 $12.95
   1. Mortgage loans.   I. Title.
HG2040.15.B88   1991
332.7'22—dc20   91-3349

Printed in the United States of America

1 2 3 4 5 6 7 8 9 0

Contents

Preface xii

Section I

Chapter 1: **Prepare for this Major Transaction 3**

Types of Loans *7*
  FHA Insured Loans *7*
  VA Guaranteed Loans *8*
  Conventional Loans *8*
Prequalify Yourself Before You Shop *8*
Qualifying Guidelines *11*
The Loan Package *15*
  The Appraisal Package *16*
  The Credit Package *16*
  How to Calculate Your Income *18*
  What Are Your Continuing Expenses? *19*
  Ratios and Residuals *21*
  Calculating Your Loan Amount *23*

Chapter 2: **How Much Will Be Enough? 27**

Closing Costs — Normal vs. Abnormal *28*
Types of Closing Costs *29*
  Impounds, Prepaids, or Escrows *29*
  Prepaid or Per Day Interest (Per Diem) *32*
  FHA Mortgage Insurance Premium (MIP) *33*
Closing Costs That You Can Control *34*
  Attorney's Fees *34*
  Flood Insurance *35*
  Inspection Fees *35*
  Title Company or Escrow Company Fees *37*
  Discount Points and Loan Orgination Fees *38*

Chapter 3: **Shopping for a Mortgage Loan 41**

Choosing a Realtor *41*
For Sale By Owner *43*
Types of Lenders *45*
  Your Local Banker *45*
  Your Local Savings Bank (Alias Savings and Loan Association) *45*
  The Local Mortgage Banker vs. the Not-So-Local Mortgage Banker *46*
  The Mortgage Broker and Other Lending Sources *47*

vi *How to Get a Mortgage*

The Role of the Lender *48*
  The Loan Officer *48*
  The Loan Processor *50*
  The Underwriter and the Closer *51*
  After the Closing: Servicing Your Loan *52*

Chapter 4: Types of Loans Available *55*

Loans Insured by the FHA *55*
  FHA Maximum Mortgage Amounts *56*
  Purchase Owner-Occupied Maximum Loan to Value Ratio (LTV) *57*
  Refinance Owner-Occupied *58*
  Mortgage Insurance Premium (MIP) *58*
  Prepayment Penalty *59*
  Assumability *59*
  Multiple FHA Loans *59*
  Property Requirements *60*
  Credit Requirements *62*
  Bankruptcy *62*
  Collections *63*
  Stability and Adequacy *65*
  Negotiated Discount Points *65*
Loans Guaranteed by the Veterans Administration *66*
  Eligibility *66*
  Loan Guaranty Funding Fee *69*
  Assumability *70*
  Property Requirements *71*
  Credit Analysis *71*
  Residual Income *72*
  Income Stability *73*
Conventional Loans *74*
  Maximum Number of Properties Financed *74*
  Loan-to-Value Ratios *75*
  Sales Concessions, or Contributions by the Seller *76*
  Private Mortgage Insurance *77*
  Property Requirements *78*
  Credit Requirements *79*
  Income Stability *79*
  Buyer and Seller Fees *80*
  Reduced Documentation, Timesaver and Timesaver Plus *80*
  Assumability *81*
  Prepayment Penalty *82*

Contents **vii**

Chapter 5: The Loan Interview and Application 83

How to Prepare, What to Expect *83*
   The Loan Application Forms *85*
      What to Bring and Say — What Not to Bring and Say *86*
      The Residential Mortgage Loan Application Checklist *86*
The Property Appraisal (Or, It's Worth What?!!) *87*
Creditworthiness (Or It's in the Mail!) *90*
   Credit Problems *90*
   Credit Reporting and Your Rights *91*
Types of Acceptable Income *92*
   Wage Earners *92*
   Overtime *92*
   Second Job *93*
   Bonuses and Commission Income *93*
   Tips and Gratuities *94*
   Interest and Dividends *94*
   Note Receivable Income *94*
   Real Estate Income *94*
   Child Support and Alimony *95*
   VA Benefits *96*
   Unemployment or Public Assistance Income *96*
   Trust Income *97*
   Retirement Income *97*
   Social Security and Military Retirement Income *98*
   Part-Time or Seasonal Employment *98*
   Income from Boarders and Relatives Residing in the Home *99*
Self-Employed Borrowers *99*
Assets Verification (or, It's 11 p.m., Do You Know Where Your Assets Are? *101*
   Secondary Financing *102*
   Gifts *102*
   Borrowed Funds *103*
   Time Deposits *103*
   Stocks and Bonds *104*
   Sale of Previous Home *104*
   Co-borrowers and Co-signers *105*

Chapter 6: Loan Approval and the Closing 107

If Your Application Is Rejected *108*
After the Approval *110*
The Closing *111*
Servicing Your Loan *112*

Section II

Chapter 7: The Types Of Loans Available For Purchases Or Refinance *117*

Fit the Loan to Your Lifestyle *118*
  Income *118*
  Expenses *120*
  Age and Future Housing Needs *121*
Features of Loan Types *124*
  Fixed Rate Mortgage *124*
  Adjustable Rate Mortgages (ARMS) *127*
  Graduated Payment Mortgages (GPM) *133*
  The Twenty-Year Mortgage *134*
  Fifteen-Year Equal Program *135*
  The Thirty-Year Due In Seven Program 136
  Reverse Annuity Mortgages (RAMS) *137*
  Portable Mortgages *138*

Chapter 8: Refinancing Your Home *141*

Before You Shop *141*
Refinance Guidelines *143*
  FHA One-To-Four Unit Properties *144*
  VA One-To-Four Unit Properties *144*
  Closing Costs and Fees Required *145*
Comparison of Your Old and New Loans *146*
  Mortgage Insurance and Funding Fee *148*
  Prepaids or Impounds *149*
  Prepaid Interest *150*
  Prepayment Penalty *150*
  Cash-out Refinances *151*
  Secondary Financing *151*

Chapter 9: Secondary Financing *153*

Home Rich, Cash Poor *153*
Second Mortgages and Installment Loans *154*
Home Equity Line of Credit *158*
  Minimum/Maximum Advances *159*
  Terms for Repayment *160*
  Interest Rates *161*
  Concluding the Line of Credit *162*

Contents ix

Section III

Chapter 10: Buying and Financing A Second (Vacation) Home *167*

Shopping for the Mortgage Loan *168*
Programs Available *170*
   Tax Advantages *170*
   Types of Units *173*
   Timeshares *173*
   Qualifying *174*
Comparisons Before Buying a Second Home *175*

Chapter 11: Buying or Refinancing a Rental Property *179*

Shopping for Financing *179*
Taxes, Taxes, Who Pays the Taxes *181*
The Downside of Being A Landlord *185*

Chapter 12: Building Your Own Home *189*

Construction Financing *189*
Preparing Your Loan Package *194*
   Building Contract *194*
   Fire Insurance *195*
   Description of Materials *195*
   Construction Cost Breakdown *196*
   The Permanent, or Take-Out, Loan *196*
   Construction Steps *197*
FHA And VA New Construction Loans *199*

Appendix *201*

FHA Prequalifying Worksheet *203*
Factor Sheet *204*
VA Prequalifying Worksheet *205*
Conventional Prequalifying Worksheet *206*
Mortgage Insurance Premium Refund Calculations *207*
FHA Assumption Policy *208*
Closing Costs Worksheet *209*
Types of Closing Costs *210*
Residential Mortgage Loan Application Checklist *211*
Residential Loan Applicaiton *213*
FHA/VA Loan Application *215*

Reverse of the FHA or VA Loan Application *217*
FHA Appraisal (Conditional Commitment) *218*
Uniform Residential Appraisal Report *219*
FHA Conditional Commitment *221*
Types of Self-Employed Borrowers *223*
Underwriting Analysis of the Self-Employed Borrower *224*
U.S. Individual Income Tax Return 1040 *226*
Schedule A: Itemized Deductions *228*
Schedule E: Supplemental Income and Loss *230*
Depreciation and Amortization 4562 *232*
Home Equity Line of Credit Checklist *234*
Refinance Worksheet *235*
Construction Loan Checklist *237*
Estimated Construction Financing Worksheet *238*
Description of Materials *239*
Maximum FHA Loan Amount Worksheet *243*
Construction Cost Breakdown *244*
HUD 1 Settlement Statement *245*
Schedule of Real Estate Owned *247*

Glossary *249*

Index *267*

Preface

If you have decided it's time to buy your first home, if you're thinking about refinancing the home you own, or if you've been considering using the equity in your home to invest, you'll probably be approaching a lender about a mortgage loan to complete this transaction. You already know that there are tax advantages to property ownership, and you already know the need to invest for future income, but what you need to know is how to get through the dreaded loan application and approval process without undue stress. The loan process can be a horror story for the novice, and it can be no better the second time around. We've all heard the horror stories.

Remember John in purchasing who "got the shaft" when he bought his first home, or Aunt Rose who was "ripped off" by the mortgage company, or your neighbor's sister Madeleine whose lender delayed the transaction "on purpose, just to get more money out of me." You are a logical, educated person and you know that there are two sides to every story, even the horror stories, but most homeowners only hear the side of the unhappy homeowner, not the side of the lender.

Yes, there are two sides to each "problem" transaction. Your goal is to avoid the problems by learning the mortgage loan application process and using that knowledge to control the transaction to your advantage. This book can give you the tools to evaluate the process as it applies to your individual case (yes, you too will be a case!). You need to avoid the irritation as much as possible by knowing the step-by-step process of the transaction. The key to this is the "you" part! You have the most at stake, and so you must take the time and effort to arm yourself with the knowledge to follow the transaction to its conclusion. Real estate brokers or agents, attorneys, loan officers, and title or escrow officers will assist you, but ultimately, you must make it happen by insisting that the persons responsible for each step do their jobs. Therefore, you must know what the other parties to this transaction actually do and how their jobs are affecting your goal.

I, too, have heard the horror stories; as a matter of fact, I've probably been accused of causing horror stories. I've been the loan officer, the loan processor, the loan closer, the underwriter, the branch manager, and finally, the homebuyer, and I've seen the most uncomplicated transactions develop into "horror" stories. I now conduct seminars on lending for people both in the lending business and out. The common complaint I hear from the participants is that the offending person did not know the correct process, whether it was the loan originator (the loan officer), the loan processor, or the real estate representative, or anyone in between.

On the next pages you may find more information about the mortgage process than you ever wanted to know. Believe me, you will be prepared to avoid problems if you read this entire book and use the checklists and worksheets provided.

It would be much easier to find your dream home, sign on the dotted line, and let everyone do their own jobs and blame everyone else if the transaction does not close, but I'm the kind of person who wants to know where and why my money is spent, and I want to know that I'm getting full value for my money. I want you to know where and why your money is spent and that you are getting full value for your money. By knowing the finance process, you can then control the financing of a home. The first home can be the stepping stone to future investments if you learn before and during this transaction. If you already have been through this once, you should benefit from the errors made the first time and brush up on the new guidelines. The fact that you once qualified for a mortgage loan is no guarantee that you will again. The rules have changed and are constantly changing. Right now the rules are becoming tighter, and though you may be refinancing your current home or buying a second home, you still must be able to qualify all over again with the new guidelines. The fact that you have an excellent mortgage credit history is an important step in the right direction, but there are many more steps.

The type of financing you used for that first home purchase or are now choosing may have an effect on the second and third home you wish to finance. You must know the features of your loan: its assumability, any prepayment penalties, and other variables that could affect your future investments.

To prepare yourself for the loan application, you'll need to know the questions to ask and what information to bring to the lender. The second most frequent complaint from participants in my seminars is that the lender kept asking for more and more information throughout the transaction. Obviously, there will be some unexpected requirements that no lender or applicant can fully prepare for, but most loan officers will agree that a "well prepared" borrower supplies all the information necessary to complete the transaction on time and usually without frustration.

The guidelines contained in this book do vary somewhat from region to region, and I've included the variables wherever necessary. Naturally, the mortgage-lending guidelines of each lender may vary, but most lending institutions follow "prudent" lending practices common to all lenders of mortgage money. Unfortunately, those guidelines are also subject to interpretation by the individual underwriter who has the final decision about the approval of your loan. More and more lenders are now introducing underwriting committees to enlist the opinion of several underwriters on difficult cases, thus reducing the possibility of poorly underwritten loans.

If you disagree with the decision of the lender, I have described steps you can take to dispute the case. The government agencies who insure or guaranty loans are quick to point out that consistency between agencies is their goal, and they have come a long way in that pursuit. Still, they have not achieved complete consistency yet, and the rules still vary according to the type of loan program you have chosen.

Finally, in the mortgage business the rules or guidelines, as well as the interest rates and fees, do change. For example, in 1988 the Federal Housing Administration issued to lenders more than thirty-nine mortgagee letters with updated or changed information, including some specific changes that will probably affect your new FHA-insured loan and some more technical information about the paperwork involved in the lender's preparation of the loan file. Each local field or regional office may then issue their own interpretation of the mortgagee letters in the form of circular letters to lenders in their region. The Veterans Administration issues changes to their guaranteed loan program in the form of bulletins by regional office to lenders interpreting the national VA guidelines as they change. The Federal National Mortgage Association (FNMA or FannieMae) and the Federal Home Loan Mortgage Corporation (FHLMC or FreddieMac), the major purchasers of conventional loans and the agencies who set the conventional guidelines for all mortgage investors, issue bulletins and manual changes outlining their own sets of rules that apply to the loans that they will purchase. I think you get the point: a lender's biggest problem is keeping up with the changes for all the programs offered to make sure that the program offered you is the best for your needs and conforms to prudent lending practices.

I hope that the information contained in this book will give you the tools to decide what loan is best for you and what steps you can take to avoid problems. Do not forget that you, the homebuyer, have almost total control over this transaction. Exercise that control!

Section I

Chapter

Prepare for this Major Transaction

IF YOU'VE NOW DECIDED THAT IT'S TIME to purchase your first home or a move-up home, then you most likely have decided to apply for the biggest loan of you life. This chapter is written for the average wage earner or self-employed worker who needs a loan to buy or refinance a home, whether it's a first home, a move-up home, or an investment property. If you own a home and want specific information on refinancing, home equity, or other types of financing you may need, you will find more information in chapters devoted to those topics. However, you may want to read this chapter first to avoid some of the problems you went through with your first transaction or to discover what changes have occurred and avoid any new problems that could come up. You may also want to know what limitations you can run across on a second home loan. As you've probably read recently, guidelines for qualifying for a home loan will be much stricter, and the type of loan you chose for your first several purchases may not now be available to you or may not be the best choice.

If you have cash to purchase a home, consult an accountant to determine if your tax situation makes that the best way for you to use your money. If you have equity in another home or have a large cash down payment, you also might want to consult your tax advisor to determine how that money can best be spent, given the current tax advantages. However, if you are like most of us, you'll need to apply for a mortgage loan through a local lender for most of the purchase price. This chapter is devoted to teaching the average homebuyer or homeowner the "tech talk" used in the business and the type of loans to be considered for a first purchase and for all future purchases, refinances and investments.

In order to understand why this transaction is so complicated and so valuable to your lender, and to protect your own interests and avoid being overwhelmed by the terminology used by your loan officer, you should know the basics of mortgage lending. You'll be bombarded with "tech talk" during your loan interview (especially if things don't go well, if the loan officer is pressured, or, most especially, if the rates change for the worse!). Also, the "Rise and Fall of the Savings and Loan Industry" is a regular topic on the nightly news lately, and knowing the basics of mortgage lending may help you understand this important national problem a little better. Some of the savings and loans (or thrifts as the news reporters insist on calling them) and other financial organizations that may be having problems have a limited number of loans secured by residential properties. This type of loan is considered the most secure loan type since the loans are secured by customers' "homes" rather than investment properties. Commercial loans secured by investment properties in areas where business is declining have been a big part of the S and L problem. Finally, even the most profitable loans secured by residences are risky when the property is in an area declining because of business problems. Understanding the mortgage market may help you understand some of these problems in the business world and why they may affect your mortgage transaction.

I'll be using the term *mortgage loan*, though some states use a mortgage instrument and some use a deed of trust, security deed, or trust deed along with a promissory note. The combination of a promissory note (the promise to pay) and a mortgage/deed of trust (describing the security, or property) is considered a mortgage loan for our purposes. The legal aspect of the transaction should be left to the legal professionals you pay to assist you in this transaction.

A mortgage loan—your mortgage loan—is a commodity. It can be traded on the secondary market because it has value. The promise to pay (the promissory note) is secured by real property (the mortgage, trust deed or deed of trust). The *secondary market* is merely the marketplace for investors of mortgage loans. The term "investor" will be used often in this book as it relates to two different persons: the investor who buys and sells mortgage loans and the borrower who owns properties for investment purposes.

The promissory note combined with the mortgage instrument meets the requirements of a *negotiable instrument*, a banking term for checks, stocks, bonds, trade bills and other trade or negotiated instruments of value. Because it's traded, its value may vary according to the market. The value of your mortgage loan is the unpaid principal, the interest you will pay over the remainder of the term, and the discount fees or points you pay up front or at the closing in a lump sum. Additional value may be placed on the collection of your monthly payments. An investor can own your loan and receive the monthly payments you make, but pay another investor to collect the payments, pay the taxes and insurance, and maintain all the other routine tasks to protect the security. This is called *servicing* the loan. Finally, your loan is secured by real property, which has a value that can vary over the term of the loan. If your investment in this property (your down payment) is minimal, the lender may obtain *mortgage insurance* (MI) at your expense to protect against future losses or reduce the risk to the lender. (This has nothing to do with fire, flood, or life insurance, as I will explain in more detail later.) The larger the down payment, the less risk to the lender and the less need for the added protection of mortgage insurance.

Mortgage loans, usually in groups of similar loans, are freely assignable to investors (other lenders who may only buy and sell closed loans for profit) on the secondary market. Mortgage loans may also be used as collateral for mortgage-backed securities, commonly called *pools*. The Government National Mortgage Association (GNMA or GinneMae) is a major purchaser of the FHA or VA loans that your lender originates. Therefore, GNMA may also set some guidelines for purchasing certain types of loans.

The fact that your loan may be sold by your lender should not affect your choice of a lender or loan program. All loans may be sold at some point, depending on market conditions, but you're protected by laws governing this practice. You must be notified of the sale, and you'll be provided in advance with information on your future payment methods. New, more strict legislation is anticipated that will require a lender to notify you fifteen days prior to the sale and to give you the information about where and when to make your next payment. This new legislation will also ensure that you are not penalized with a late fee for up to sixty days after the lender sells your loan. Though selling your mortgage loan may be profitable for your lender, retaining the servicing may be equally profitable if the investor will allow the lender to keep a portion of the monthly payment for that service. The servicing can be accomplished better by computers and a centralized, specialized staff able to handle huge volumes of loans.

During the course of your loan transaction, some or all of these terms will be thrown into a conversation by the loan officer or processor. Your processor may say, "we need more information (they will ask for everything but your shorts size!) so your loan can be put in a pool, sold to FNMA or FHLMC, sold on the secondary market," or whatever. "Tech-talk" is commonly used to mask the real reason for the request—usually, the lender simply forgot to ask for the information up front, or didn't know what was needed. Since their goal, like yours, is to close this transaction quickly, I would suggest that you comply as quickly as possible.

Because your loan is a valuable commodity capable of being traded on the market, walking into your local bank or savings and loan association may not be the only or best choice. There is a lot of competition among lenders, and it's to your advantage to know what to shop for. You should be able to compare rates, points, and services of all the lenders available, or you should know enough to evaluate the choices offered by your realtor.

Types of Loans

For this discussion of mortgage loans, I have chosen the three types of loans that are most available, and least costly to you, the buyer, and that generally fit the needs of most homebuyers. Homeowners who are preparing to buy more properties or move up to more expensive homes will benefit from this material, as well as the persons who are approaching this process for the first time, since some of these programs are offered for owner-occupied and nonowner-occupied properties, second home purchases, and refinances.

FHA Insured Loans

I'll concentrate in this book most heavily on the Title II FHA loan, which is insured under Section 203(B) and Section 234(C) of the National Housing Act. These two programs or sections of the Act include the purchase or refinance of owner-occupied single family dwellings, two-to-four family dwellings, and condominiums in approved projects. If you're purchasing or refinancing an investment property, the FHA loan may no longer be available to you, but the move-up homeowner and those who wish to refinance their owner-occupied property still are eligible with some limitations.

The FHA programs and guidelines are the most misunderstood because of their complicated procedures and forms. This program is my personal favorite because it allows the most flexibility for the underwriter and it fits best for most first-time homebuyers. These loans offer the most challenge to underwriters, but unfortunately cause the most headaches for borrowers because of the time involved and the paperwork needed. Don't let this deter you from selecting this loan—any lender worth their salt should offer and know how to process this type of loan promptly!

VA Guaranteed Loans

I'll include the requirements for qualifying for a VA guaranteed loan and describe how this program differs from FHA loans. Your parents may call this a GI loan and many real estate agents still call this the no-down loan. It is both, though the rules have changed very recently and the VA loan is less attractive now. Still, it may be a good option for you if you are a qualified veteran.

Conventional Loans

Finally, I've lumped all the loans that are not insured by the FHA or guaranteed by the VA into one category: *conventional loans*. A conventional loan can be sold to FNMA, FHLMC, or to any other conventional loan investor, with servicing either retained by your lender or sold to another third party. (Remember, servicing is collecting your payments monthly after the close—a very valuable part of this transaction to the lender.) Historically, FNMA and FHLMC have set the guidelines for all conventional financing because they have been the major purchasers of these loans. A lender may also *portfolio* a loan, or keep all originated loans for the duration of the loan. However, in case market conditions ever require the sale of some of their portfolio loans, lenders would be wise to underwrite all loans to comply with accepted guidelines in order to have marketable loans.

Prequalify Yourself Before You Shop

Before you shop for a home, shop for a mortgage loan. Sounds like putting the cart before the horse! Yes, it is, in a way, but it may save you time and money. You don't want to spend time looking at a home you can't get financing for. All the previously mentioned loan programs can be secured for most single family properties, duplexes, and three-to-four unit properties; however, the most important variable for most homebuyers is the down payment. The FHA, for instance, limits the loan amount to 90 percent of the value of the property on a home built within the last year without FHA inspections during construction. Should you choose this type of home (a new home in a new subdivision not approved by the FHA), you may need a larger down payment than for another home. The point is: if your available cash is limited and you need the benefit of the low–down-payment FHA loan, it would be pointless to look at a home without asking about the availability of FHA loans in that particular subdivision. Know the mortgage loan that best suits your income and down payment requirements before you shop for a home or consider refinancing the one you now own.

When you first approach a lender regarding a loan, you will be referred to the lender's representative, called the loan officer, loan interviewer, or any number of other names. If your inquiry is by phone, the loan officer may set up an appointment to discuss your lending needs, depending on whether you've owned a home before or not. When you call in to inquire about loan rates and services, tell the loan officer just where you are in your transaction—you have started looking, you have found a home, or you are just inquiring prior to starting anything. You may want to set up an appointment to prequalify with a lender before shopping. I would highly recommend this for a first-time homebuyer especially. You may want to do your own prequalifying with the help of the worksheets provided in this book, either before you contact a lender or instead of contacting a lender. There is no charge for prequalifying with a lender and your lender will take the time to prepare you in many ways. However, if you have doubts about your qualifications, use the worksheets first.

Your interview with the loan officer will be confidential and should determine your ability and qualifications to obtain a mortgage loan. This shouldn't be an interrogation! If it becomes too complicated, too technical, or is going too fast for you, tell your loan officer to back up and repeat or explain some things. Remember this is your transaction and you have total control over most of the process. The loan officer will consider the type of property you want to buy, the types of loans available in your area for that type of property, your income (both for adequacy and type), your expenses beyond the housing expense, your down payment requirements, and the number of properties you now own to determine the best loan for you. She'll also compare rates, points, term (thirty years versus fifteen years), adjustable rate loans versus fixed rate loans, and other types of loans currently available. Finally, she'll compare your income to your current expenses plus various new house payments to arrive at acceptable ratios and residual income requirements for each program. This type of prequalifying may also be done by your realtor prior to the loan interview to determine which lender will be best suited to your needs. Unfortunately, one formula does not fit all the programs we discussed earlier, so I will outline the differences in the qualifiying procedures for each of the three types of loans we are considering: FHA, VA, and conventional.

Insuring and guaranteeing agencies are trying to establish consistency between the lending programs with regard to ratios and residual income. Success is a long way off, though several attempts have been made recently to simplify the guidelines.

You should find out before you shop for a home what house payment you can afford and what you'll be comfortable with. The numbers may click, but if you are denying yourself all the luxuries in order to pay for the home of your dreams, the benefits of homeownership will fade very quickly! You don't want to go through a bad case of "payment shock," a term used by lenders to describe the pressure of making large house payments during the first critical months. You may have been accumulating monthly savings for the down payment for awhile with this goal of buying a home in mind, giving up many luxuries, but do you want to do without luxuries for the next ten years? If your goal is to refinance in order to use the equity to pay off bills or buy something major, carefully consider how larger payments will affect your household budget. Think hard about how this house payment plus your other expenses will affect your daily lives.

Qualifying Guidelines

The numbers to work with are on the worksheets in the appendix. Run off a few copies (at work, right?) and play with the figures to see what best suits your needs before you start house hunting or before you contact your lender to do some heavy-duty shopping. When you have a better idea of what loan you can afford, you'll know your price range for a home and can limit your shopping to those areas. This should save a lot of time and grief. House shopping in unaffordable areas is fun if you're not seriously expecting to buy, but if you're now ready to buy that first home or sell your existing home and move up, house hunting in the wrong area can be frustrating.

You may have read that your housing expense should be a certain percentage of your income, some say 25 percent of your gross income, some say more like 28 percent. This is a good starting point but too vague to use for all the programs available. You may neglect to consider more attractive programs for your needs by using one set of guidelines. Everyone should use the worksheets for the FHA program and the conventional program to compare, and the VA program worksheet only if you are an eligible veteran. Take one extra step before you go any further: check with a local lender to find out what the maximum FHA loan is in your area for the type of home you want, (single family or two-to-four units) and compare to the average sales price in the area you want to live in. Take the average sales price in your chosen area, subtract approximately 5 percent for a down payment and compare to the maximum FHA loan. If the loan you need is over the maximum FHA loan you will have to pay the difference in cash at the closing. A rule of thumb: if you have very little for a down payment, are a first-time homebuyer, or are expecting to buy in a low to moderately priced area, use the FHA worksheet first.

Finally, before using the worksheets, you need to understand the term *housing expense*. The housing expense is the amount it costs monthly to live in the home. It is a total of the principal and the interest on the loan, the amount of property taxes due yearly divided by twelve months, the amount of the fire/flood or hazard insurance policy yearly divided by twelve months and the amount of a yearly mortgage insurance premium divided by twelve months. The impound account is the accumulation of monthly taxes and insurance collected by the lender to pay your yearly taxes and insurance (fire, flood, or mortgage). You include these monthly fees in your housing expense whether your lender collects them monthly from you and deposits them in an impound account or you pay it yourself yearly, quarterly, or however. You will be expected to use this total monthly housing expense in your qualifying ratios and residuals, and it will be the key to whether you qualify for a loan. Your *loan-to-value ratio* (LTV) will be an important part of all the programs and will be mentioned throughout this book. The value part of the ratio is the lesser of the sales price or appraised value of the home. If you buy a home for $92,000 and it appraises at $91,000, your loan will be based on $91,000. An 80 percent LTV would be $91,000 times 80 percent, which equals $72,800; meaning you would have to put a down payment of $19,200 on this transaction. When prequalifying, use the anticipated sales price as the value—just assume that the appraised value will be the same. You may pay more than the appraised value, but for most programs you will have to pay the difference in cash from your own funds and probably will have to sign a statement that you are aware that you are paying more than the value.

Let's recap:

1. Everyone should use the Conventional Worksheet. The loan amount you use to qualify will depend on the money you have available for a down payment. Start with as little as 5 percent down, and then calculate with 10 percent, 15 percent—up to 20 percent down, if you have it. You will need to calculate an additional monthly fee for mortgage

insurance if you have a down payment of less than 20 percent along with your principal and interest, taxes and insurance.
2. To use the FHA worksheet, first call a local lender or your local FHA (HUD) office (listed under Federal or United States in your phone book, usually under Department of Housing and Urban Development) and ask what the loan limits (maximum loans available) are for a single-family dwelling, or duplex, etc., whatever you are considering. Get out the old newspaper under real estate and check the area you want to live in for sales prices. Second, use the maximum loan worksheet in the appendix to determine the loan amount from the FHA worksheet. If the resulting loan amount is more than your area's maximum FHA and you don't have the additional cash available (the amount between the sales price and the maximum loan) go back to the Conventional Worksheet.
3. Use the VA worksheet only if you are a qualified veteran (read the section on VA loans in Chapter Four to see if you qualify before you use the worksheet).

You may end up with two or more worksheets or you may end up using only one worksheet, the conventional, in high cost areas. Remember, FHA allows smaller down payments, so check that worksheet just to make sure you are not eliminating an excellent program. FHA may soon change their loan limits so don't rely on relatives or nonexperts. Call the lender or FHA, or if you have already chosen a realtor to represent you, ask your realtor to do the checking for you. Remember, your realtor has to be experienced in lending as well as selling homes.

These are the beginning guidelines, a place to start before you take your time to shop for a home. Play with the numbers—higher and lower sales prices, with some bills paid, larger and smaller down payments, etc.. Your choice of a program will start with the down payment you have. I've included factors to figure principal and interest. Call your insurance agent to get a ballpark figure for the fire insurance. Just explain that you are shopping and need the average yearly fire insurance premium for the area you're going to be living in. If you are considering a condominium, call the homeowner's association for the monthly fees (look it up in the phone book, usually under the name of the condominium development) or ask your realtor to do this for you since this fee will be considered when you try to qualify. For the property tax calculation call your county assessor's office. They will give you the formula for calculating the taxes based on the value of the home you're considering. Example: They may say the tax rate is $1.85 per $100.00 of assessed valuation (use the sales price for now, whether or not the land has been reassessed recently) and the rate is applied to 35 percent of the assessed valuation. Ask what the rate is applied to (could be anywhere from 24 percent to 100 percent of the assessed valuation, depending on the state). Calculate as follows: 35 percent of the sales price ($72,000.00) is $25,200.00. Divide by 100, then multiply by $1.85 to get $466.20. Divide that by 12 for $38.00 per month—a calculation close enough for prequalifying purposes

For fire insurance or homeowner's association dues, you may be given a yearly figure—divide by twelve for the qualifying figure to add to your monthly housing expense. Remember these figures may not be accurate to the penny but they're close enough for shopping. You may already know of some special assessments in the area you choose; if not, ask your tax assessor when calling about property taxes or ask your realtor. Add those special fees to your monthly housing expense as a monthly figure; your lender will when you apply.

Your next step will be to use the information to shop for a mortgage loan. You know what you can afford and you should be able to see what you'll actually qualify for. I know you'll be tempted to go out and shop for a home, but it would be more practical to contact a lender with your prequalifying worksheet in hand and make sure your chosen program and payments coincide with the lender's requirements. It's probably time to choose a realtor if you're going to be using the services of a real estate office. Your realtor will probably recommend a lender to contact to prequalify and may prepare a sampling of the homes available in the area you've chosen. If you don't choose your own realtor and use the realtor that represents the seller, you may not be adequately represented. In most cases, the listing (selling) agent is representing and getting paid by the seller, not you. It's your choice, but you may consider buying a home directly from the seller (For Sale By Owner) taking advantage of the lower price usually offered.

The Loan Package

After you've used the worksheets and have become more comfortable with a sales price, payment, and program, you should next be aware of the loan process and the documentation that will be required of you. Remember, if you leave the entire process up to others without first preparing yourself, expect to be at their mercy. Some preparation on your part may save a very important transaction from becoming a nightmare.

Let's say, at this point, that you've prequalified yourselves, visited with a lender who agrees with your figures and qualifications, have shopped and found the home you want to buy, and are starting the loan process. Your contract of purchase may be called many names: the offer and acceptance, the purchase contract, the agreement to purchase and sell, the receipt and option contract, the deposit receipt and contract, or whatever titled contract is commonly used in your area. It will detail the transaction, the terms and the agreed-upon sales price, including the limitations on the time for closing and the conditions for closing. With a copy of your contract in hand, you're ready to apply for a mortgage loan. If you have prequalified, your lender has probably taken most of the information necessary for the application and only needs to fill in the blanks and have you sign the forms to start the process. From your initial loan application the lender will prepare a loan package that consists of:

1. The Appraisal Package: Written proof that the security (the property) for this loan has enough value to support the lender's risk.

2. The Credit Package: Written proof that the borrower has sufficient, consistent income to support the mortgage debt and all other continuing expenses, that the borrower has established an acceptable credit history, and that the borrower has accumulated enough assets to complete the transaction, with enough remaining to buffer against future unexpected expenses.

The Appraisal Package

The appraisal package is mostly out of your hands. You can't help with this part of the loan package except to check regularly with your loan officer that the appraisal is being done and to request a copy of the appraisal for your information. Most lenders reading this are now shuddering because they prefer not to release this information; however, you should persist. The person who pays for this report is the person who should expect a copy of it. If the seller is paying this fee, obviously you may not be entitled to this report. This is a very controversial topic and most lenders will release a copy of the appraisal to all parties involved if requested. Ask for a copy and most particularly ask if there are any repairs indicated to be completed prior to the close of this transaction. Most lenders are very cooperative and will at least give you a written summary of the appraisal report. You'll need to know about the completion of the repairs and how this will affect the closing. This is a potential delay in your transaction if not completed on time and you should make sure that your realtor or the seller is aware of this and actually does something about it! Check several times during the transaction to make sure that the repairs are completed by either driving by the property for outside repairs or by asking those involved to check for you. Do not assume that repairs will be done on time without help from you.

The Credit Package

Unlike the appraisal package, the credit package is almost totally up to you. The key is the "written proof." Unlike a smaller consumer loan, which relies on telephone verifications of income and expenses, every statement of income and expense on a mortgage loan transaction must be supported by "written proof." Be prepared to bring all your financial records to the loan interview as written proof. Let me explain why.

Rarely do FHA, VA, FNMA, FHLMC, or any of the agencies who purchase mortgage loans make a decision about your loan. FHA insures loans, VA guarantees loans, and FNMA and FHLMC purchase loans, but they don't normally approve or deny loan applications. They do issue guidelines that they expect lenders to follow when approving loans that they insure and purchase, but the decision to approve or reject is now almost totally in the hands of the lender. This is a relatively new feature for some lenders of FHA and VA loans. Both agencies are available to assist with advice and updated information on the guidelines, but the ultimate decision is made by the lender's staff of underwriters or a loan committee. Underwriting decisions made by lenders may lead to defaults on loans by unqualified borrowers and a high default rate can lead to a lender's demise. Those agencies who insure, guaranty, or purchase loans will simply refuse to do business with a lender who produces low-quality, high-default-rate loans. High default rates can reflect on an underwriter's reputation too, and the best way for the underwriter to avoid possible defaults is to determine that the borrower will be able to meet the obligations of the home and all other debts. This assumption on how the borrower can handle what will happen in the future must be based on past performances, thus the need for written proof.

Just to keep the lenders on their toes, each lender must also maintain a quality control department, which randomly reviews closed loan files. The quality control departments reprocess a sampling of completed loan files to determine that the files contain accurate information and to determine that the underwriter based the decision to approve the loan on adequate documentation. Their results must be reported to FHA, VA, FNMA and FHLMC, and to other licensing entities along with the lender's own internal audit procedures. Making a mortgage loan decision based on a "gut feeling" is long gone! Underwriters must answer for their decisions, and though they still rely on instinct, they must support their decisions with logical, documented proof in order to continue underwriting.

How to Calculate Your Income

This is the most important ingredient of the application process, so let me share some methods of income calculation that underwriters use. Persons who are self-employed should refer to Chapter Five for separate calculations.

If you're a wage earner, like most of us, we need to add up all the income you receive to qualify you and your family for this home. You and your spouse probably receive *base* wages, or the income you receive regularly—monthly, semimonthly, biweekly, weekly, or daily—that we can use. Most working people have some additional income added onto their paychecks not-so-regularly that we can also use. We can add to that base income an average figure of all secondary income such as overtime, bonuses, commissions or shift differential to arrive at your total income. Let me emphasize the term *average*. If you receive income over and above your base income regularly, expect to provide proof that you've received it regularly for some time, usually at least two years. How do you prove it? By showing the lender your paystubs (that show year-to-date earnings) and the W-2s you use to file your federal and state income tax returns. If you don't keep them from year to year, start now to put all your income receipts away for this purpose or get a copy of your tax returns from your tax preparer if you've not kept one. If you receive secondary income prepare to prove it to use it to qualify for this loan.

Let's start with base income. If you earn an hourly wage, multiply that hourly wage by the number of hours you work per week like so: $8.00 per hour times forty hours per week equals $320.00. Multiply by fifty-two weeks to get $16,640.00. $16,640.00 divided by twelve months equals $1,386.67 per month.

If your paycheck is for a regular work week and is paid weekly, we will multiply the weekly amount by fifty-two weeks and divide by twelve to arrive at your useable income.

If you work regularly over forty hours a week and get paid overtime, we take from your paycheck stub or voucher (under the year-to-date section) the total amount, deduct your base earnings, and divide by the appropriate period. Your paycheck stub ending 15 June, which shows total year-to-date income of $18,400 (with a base salary of $1,250 semimonthly), will be averaged over five and a half months or eleven pay periods (January through May plus one half month). $1,250 times eleven paychecks equals $13,750 base income. Your total income of $18,400 less the base of $13,750 equals $4,650 overtime divided by five and a half months equals an average overtime earning of $845 a month. If you get paid semimonthly (twice a month usually on the fifteenth and thirtieth or last of the month) you receive twenty-four paychecks a year. Your semimonthly paycheck times two equals your monthly income for qualifying. However, make sure it is semimonthly not biweekly, because there is a difference. Biweekly means every two weeks, or twenty-six times a year. Your base pay times twenty-six divided by twelve may be quite different.

Exhibit 1

Paid Semimonthly	Paid Biweekly
$850.00 x 24 paychecks	$850.00 x 26 paychecks
= $20,400.00	= $22,100.00
Divided by 12	Divided by 12
= $1700.00 monthly	= $1841.67 monthly

A difference of $141.67 per month (or a small car payment!)

What Are Your Continuing Expenses?

FHA and conventional loan programs have two sets of ratios used for qualifying purposes: VA uses one ratio and residual income. The top ratio is used for comparing your income to your housing expense and the bottom ratio for comparing your income to your housing expense plus all other expenses. The gross income is divided by the appropriate expenses to determine the top and bottom ratios. VA still uses net income, or your income after taxes, both federal and state and social security and retirement deductions, for the residual guideline.

The top ratio will include the housing expense, or the principal, interest, the monthly payment for property taxes, fire insurance, flood insurance, mortgage insurance, homeowner's association dues, and any special assessments to be paid in connection with the upkeep of the property and improvements. For the VA loan, the cost of maintaining the home (maintainance fee from a special chart for your area) and the expense for utilities (also from a chart for your area) is included in the residual guideline.

The bottom ratio calculation differs greatly between the programs. The FHA suggests that debts of a continual nature (more than six months) must be included. Child care expenses, excessive commuting expenses (usually over a sixty mile commute is considered excessive), child support, and alimony payments, as well as required union dues or employment expenses not paid by the employer, must be considered if they are continuing expenses—especially if they will continue for the first five years of the loan.

VA requires that the same debts be included as FHA, with short-term debts (less than six months) considered only if they severely affect the first few critical months. Social security (FICA on your paycheck) must also be included in the bottom ratio, as well as any state income tax deducted.

Conventional loan guidelines require that debts that mature within the first ten months may be excluded from the total debts, except those that may have a major impact on the borrower's income. Child care, union dues, social security, and income taxes are not included, but child support and alimony must be included. Most lenders include excessive commuting expenses also.

Revolving charge accounts or open-end lines of credit cause the most confusion. FHA and VA differ on this issue in different regions. Most FHA offices suggest that no monthly payment on these accounts be included in the bottom ratio unless there is an outstanding balance as reported on the credit report. Some lenders include a minimum payment of ten to fifteen dollars a month or 0.5 percent of the outstanding balance for each credit line. VA feels that open-end type accounts of several years duration must be considered as a long-term obligation and be included in the bottom ratio. Conventional investors don't require that these types of accounts be included, but most lenders include minimum balances, especially if there is a history of credit abuse. This is a widely discussed issue among underwriters with no clear answer yet, though each lender has their own approach to this subject. For you, the homebuyer, better to be safe than sorry—include a minimum of fifteen dollars a month in your total debt for each active charge account even if there is no balance currently.

Ratios and Residuals

The prequalifying worksheet is used as a guideline. Underwriters must be flexible and take everything into consideration. The agencies that write the guidelines stress that an underwriter needs to look at the overall picture rather than making a decision based on the "numbers." If you've completed the worksheet and the ratios are high or the residuals are low, don't hesitate to contact your lender for advice. There are some other programs available, and you may have missed some compensating factor that can offset the excessive ratios.

The FHA is currently using 29%/41% ratios with gross income for qualifying. They also suggest that each region establish a residual guideline to be set according to the income level for the area. For instance, in some areas a residual income figure for a single person with no dependents would be four hundred dollars a month. That means that after you have calculated the ratios, you should determine that you have four hundred dollars a month left over (residual) after paying all your bills, including housing expenses. The residual figure used in each area is based on the cost of living and increases by the members of the family to occupy the property.

The VA also uses a residual figure by region and a total ratio or bottom ratio of 41 percent. Any loan approved over the 41 percent limit or that has 20 percent less residual than required in that region must have a second approving opinion, the signature of the underwriter's superior, and all the reasons well documented.

Conventional guidelines use ratios of 28%/36% or 25%/33% depending on the loan-to-value (LTV) and the lender's own requirements. Gross income is used and a loan with more than a 20 percent down payment (that is less than 80 percent LTV) may exceed those ratio guidelines if there are compensating factors. On the other hand, an LTV ratio of 95 percent (or a 5 percent down payment) would normally require strict 25%/33% ratios.

All of the three programs allow for compensating factors to override excessive ratios/residuals. Following are a few compensating factors that you should be aware of and that you may mention to your loan officer if you have any doubts about qualifying.

1. You have a large cash investment in the property (a larger than necessary down payment reduces the lender's risk).
2. You have been paying a housing expense in excess of or the same as the new payment but have no credit problems and have accumulated assets while doing so.
3. You have no credit history but you have paid rents and utilities in a timely manner and have supplied letters from landlords and utilities to prove it. If you're renting, start now to ask your landlord for a letter of recommendation every time you move and save those letters.
4. You are requesting a shorter term loan (usually fifteen years), which results in a higher monthly payment but which will increase your equity faster.
5. Your family has access to public transportation and uses it regularly to commute, thus eliminating the expense of an auto (assuming that the public transportation expense is less). On the other hand, if you are moving to an area that will require a longer commute, that expense may have to be included.
6. Your family receives income that is due but not yet received and that can be proven. Letters from employers explaining increases, stability, advancements, or potential increases are very helpful. Employment contracts that state specific increases are great compensating factors.

7. You receive an auto allowance or reimbursements for expenses. Though not always considered as income, these may be excellent compensating factors when documented by tax returns. If this is a major portion of your income, check with your lender before using it to prequalify. This is only a partial list of the potential compensating factors. The obvious tax benefits of homeownership, good credit, and adequate income are "givens" in a quality loan package; we are looking for reasons over and above these to add to the marginal loan.

Calculating Your Loan Amount

In order to use the prequalifying worksheet effectively you'll need some more information about FHA and VA loans.

FHA guidelines will require more work to calculate the maximum loan amount available and the FHA Maximum Loan Worksheet in the appendix should help you arrive at your own loan amount based on a given sales price. Remember, the FHA sets maximum loans for each area, from high cost areas in which the limits are up to $124,875, for a single family home to less costly areas with limits much lower.

Maximum Loans Per 1990 Housing Legislation

One Family	$124,875
Two Family	$140,000
Three Family	$170,200
Four Family	$197,950
Condominium	$124,850

In 1990, the HUD Appropriations Act allowed for increased limits temporarily, so call your local FHA/HUD office or a lender who offers FHA loans for the current maximum loan in your area. You'll notice on the worksheet that the loan amount is affected by the closing costs you pay. If you've negotiated with the seller to pay some of your closing costs, you must take that into consideration because you may only use the closing costs you actually pay. The closing costs may be added to the lesser of the sales price or the estimate of value (appraisal) to arrive at the maximum loan. In the maximum loan worksheet used to prequalify you, I've included 1.5 percent for closing costs instead of including actual closing costs since the amount used in this must be only the costs allowed by the FHA. Your lender can advise you better what you can include in the calculation. The closing costs vary by region according to custom. If the seller pays more than 6 percent of the maximum loan amount in closing costs your maximum loan will be reduced by anything over the 6 percent. You'll then need to increase your down payment, so remember this when negotiating your contract. If you've made arrangements for your seller to pay any of your normal closing costs, or if you're not sure which closing costs are yours, ask your lender. It gets complicated, which is why many lenders shy away from FHA loans. Just beware of this type of FHA requirement and mention it to your lender if it applies to your transaction to avoid potential delays. This could mean a difference of several hundred dollars in the cash you need to close.

VA guaranteed loans require very few calculations. If you or your spouse are a veteran you can take advantage of the no-down-payment loan with full eligibility and your loan amount will be the lesser of the sales price or the VA appraised value (called the Certificate of Reasonable Value or CRV). Add on the VA funding fee, 1.875 percent of the loan amount, if you choose to finance it, and calculate the monthly principal and interest payment from that. If you choose to pay the VA funding fee in cash, add that fee to your closing costs. The VA funding fee is charged by the VA and varies with the amount of the down payment. See page 69 for the different VA funding fees required.

Exhibit 2: VA Funding Fee Example

Sales Price	$80,000
Appraisal	$79,000
Maximum loan is the lesser, or	$79,000
Plus the VA funding fee of 1.875 percent	$1,481
Total loan for qualifying	$80,481

The VA recently has adopted a policy similar to the FHA for seller's concessions. If a seller or builder adds anything of value that the buyer would normally pay for, the value of that concession cannot exceed 4 percent of the established value of the property. The VA feels that this may entice unqualified veterans into mortgage loans that they can't afford.

Conventional loans are available with as little as a 5 percent down payment but the ratios must be 25 percent for the top ratio and 33 percent for the bottom ratio, applicants must have an excellent credit history and adequate, stable income. The mortgage insurance required for loans of over 90 percent LTV is more costly because of the increased risk, so your monthly payments will be higher. The danger for homebuyers is that when problems occur, the owner who cannot continue with the mortgage payments may have to spend 7 to 10 percent to sell the home, and with only 5 percent invested, the homeowner is already in trouble. Also, the homeowner is stuck with those payments until the equity in the home is great enough to cover selling costs, and at today's rates, it can take seven years to amortize the remainder due to break even. I've always advocated using the maximum loan available, except when the resulting monthly payment is out of reach. Your tax advisor can be consulted to determine which would be best for you. With the worksheets provided, you can compare the monthly payments several ways to arrive at a payment you can afford.

Chapter

How Much Will Be Enough?

ONE KEY INGREDIENT IN THE LOAN PROCESS is the amount of fees or closing costs you'll pay on top of the down payment. I know you've heard the "horror" stories told by homebuyers that feel that they've been "ripped off" right at the close of the transaction with unexpected costs. Those unexpected costs shouldn't *be* unexpected if you're prepared. First, you're required by law to receive within three days of a loan application a statement of the prepaid finance charges. Unfortunately, these laws don't require disclosure of all the costs you'll have to pay. You must take the extra step, if your lender doesn't, to have all the fees explained to you. Almost all lenders now do this as a part of the loan interview to avoid misunderstandings at the closing. There are fees that will vary at closing. I've included a listing of the fees commonly charged and the purpose of the charge. Naturally, these fees vary by region and loan program, and just to make it more complicated, they also vary in their limitations on who may pay what. Some fees are allowable borrower fees and some are not, depending on the program you have chosen. The limitations are identified in the Types of Closing Costs list in the appendix. These fees may be called a variety of names, and I've tried to include most of the common ones. As soon as you receive your good faith estimate of closing costs, go over each fee and compare them to this list. If you have any doubts about a fee, call your lender for an explanation of each and every fee. Ask what the fee is for and who receives it.

Closing Costs — Normal vs. Abnormal

Closing costs may vary by amount and by name but they all add up to money out of your pocket. It is customary in some states to use the services of an attorney in all real estate transactions. You may want the added protection (and fees) of an attorney, or you may use a title company or escrow agent to research the title, survey the property, close, and record the transaction. Ask what your attorney is providing for her fee and what the title or escrow company is providing to make sure there isn't an overlap of services. For instance, forms prepared by a title company are reviewed by an attorney in some states. Why not pay once to have the attorney both prepare and review the forms? Ask what services are provided by each!

FHA allows the borrower to pay closing costs that are customary for all transactions in your area. These fees are identified by your local FHA office and your lender should help you determine who can pay what. VA sets the allowable closing costs that a veteran may pay nationwide, although the local VA office may set additional limits. Ask your lender if you're not sure what fees must be paid by the seller. FNMA, FHLMC, and most conventional lenders will allow any distribution of the closing costs between the seller and buyer; however, property tax and insurance pro-rations (impounds) must be paid by the borrowers. If your lender requires an impound account, only the borrower may pay these fees.

All three programs have limitations on the amount of the borrower's closing costs that a seller may pay without affecting the maximum loan amount available. They consider a large contribution by the seller a *seller's concession*, which may artificially inflate the sales price. These limitations are discussed further in Chapter Four. You must consider this when negotiating the purchase of your house since a contribution by the seller may mean a larger down payment requirement from you. You must also consider this when adding up the total money you'll need to close this transaction. I've seen many a transaction grind to a halt just before the close of escrow because of an undisclosed seller's contribution, discovered by the lender and altering the maximum loan available to the borrower. These delays caused everyone time and money, but could've been avoided by an informed borrower or realtor.

FHA will allow some of the closing costs to be added to the lesser of the appraised value or the sales price to calculate the maximum loan amount available. The amount of the closing costs is determined by region (based on the value). They must be paid by the borrower to be included in the loan amount (within a variance of one hundred dollars). Unplanned buydowns (usually discount points) paid by the seller, which would normally be considered a seller's concession, may be allowed but only in a volatile market situation.

Types of Closing Costs
Impounds, Prepaids, or Escrows

Impound, or prepaids, are usually not considered actual closing costs since they're not one-time fees but are part of the on-going housing expense. When you receive your good faith estimate at the beginning of this transaction, prepaids are not usually included. These costs are due monthly or quarterly to maintain the home: property taxes, fire/hazard insurance, homeowner's association dues, or any other special assessments. I include them here because you will have to pay for the first several months in advance at the closing. Below are some of the guidelines associated with the collection of these costs.

Property Taxes and Special Assessments

For FHA and VA loans, the funds for county/city/municipal property taxes are collected monthly and paid to the taxing entity annually, semiannually, or quarterly. The collection of taxes by the lender assures that taxes will not become delinquent, which could create a lien against the property prior to the first lien, putting the lender in a second position. A few lenders still allow a waiver of the impounds on conventional loans with a loan to value ratio of 80 percent or less.

At the closing several months of taxes and any other special assessments will be collected, sometimes up to 14 months, depending on the month your loan closes. For instance, if your yearly property taxes are $660 or $55 a month, you may be expected to advance or pay in to the impound account as much as $770 ($55 x 14 months) at the closing. This can be a major portion of your cash required for closing, so you should check with your loan officer about the amount the lender will require. This monthly amount should be added to your payment for prequalifying purposes on the worksheet at the end of this book. Ask your realtor, call your lender, or call the County Tax Assessor's office for the yearly property tax figure of the property you have chosen.

Fire Insurance and Flood Insurance

For FHA and VA loans and for most conventional loans with a LTV of over 80 percent, an impound or escrow account will be established for the payment of a yearly fire insurance policy (in all cases) and flood insurance (where applicable). You will be expected to furnish a homeowner's policy that is in effect to cover the lender for any loss from fire, etc., and you'll pay for the first year's premium at the closing. In addition, two extra months may be collected to add to the next ten months of monthly payments, in order to have enough for the renewal premium to be paid. Check with your loan officer at the loan interview, as lender requirements vary and this can be a substantial sum to consider at the closing. If he estimates fourteen months of insurance, he means the first year's premium plus the two months for next year.

Your insurance agent must also be notified in time to shop for the best rates for you and to prepare the insurance policy for the closing.

Shop for an insurance agent just as you would any other service. Start with your current auto insurance agent but shop at several others. Make sure you choose an insurance agent who'll take the time to know your needs. There are many savings you can take advantage of if you ask. Every area is different, but most areas offer discounts for deadbolt locks, fire protection equipment, low crime areas, etc. Ask what allowances your company has and if you don't get the answer you like, call around to other companies to compare. Consider the convenience of the insurance company—make sure it's open hours that suit your needs in case you need to drop off paperwork or premiums in the future. Ask your agent about higher deductibles. Your savings yearly with a one thousand dollar deductible policy may make that the best policy for you over a long period of time. Compare the yearly fees on higher and lower deductibles for your area and determine your risk with and without high deductibles.

Private Mortgage Insurance

Private companies will reduce the risk to the lender for a fees, this is commonly called *mortgage insurance* (MI). This is not to be confused with *life mortgage insurance* (or the hazard/fire insurance mentioned above). Mortgage insurance protects only the lender from loss should you default on your mortgage loan during the first critical years. Life mortgage insurance can be obtained from your agent separately and provides protection for your family should you or your spouse die.

You'll pay a mortgage insurance premium for an FHA loan, whether you pay it in cash or finance it, and for conventional loans over 80 percent LTV. Mortgage loans 80% or less of the property value (the lesser of the sales price or appraised value) are considered less risky since you have contributed more of your own money to the transaction. The fee for this insurance is paid much like the fire insurance: one year prepaid at the closing plus two extra months to be added to the ten months collected throughout the year monthly for the new premium at the end of the year. This monthly figure will be paid along with your house payment to the lender and will need to be included in your qualifying ratios on the worksheet. Your renewal premium will be calculated at the closing. Each year your monthly payments will be reduced because your shrinking principal means less risk for the lender.

Your lender may allow you to finance the mortgage insurance premium under certain circumstances, just like the FHA Mortgage Insurance Premium. Check with your lender on this fee but remember that financing it will increase your loan and also your monthly payments. If it is available for your type of loan, compare your monthly payments both ways to determine which is best for you. Use the conventional loan prequalifying worksheet to calculate your MI and add it to your monthly payments. Actually, your premium will be reduced each year because of the reduced risk, but this initial calculation will be close enough for prequalifying.

Prepaid or Per Day Interest (Per Diem)

This fee is one of the most misunderstood and miscalculated fees to be paid at the closing. You need to understand the way it affects your total closing fees to avoid a shock. Interest on your mortgage loan principal is collected daily from the date of closing (including the day of closing) until the first of the next month. Why? Because the mortgage payments are in arrears, unlike rents, which are in advance. Normally, if you are renting on July 1, your rent is paying for the use of your apartment from July 1 thru July 31. If you are making a mortgage payment on July 1, the payment is for the use of the money from June 1st thru June 30—in arrears instead of in advance.

If you close escrow on June 15, you will owe the lender for the use of the principal from June 15 thru June 30 including the fifteenth, for a total of sixteen days. Then on the first payment date, August 1, you will pay for July 1 thru July 31 and so on. The first time you buy a home financed, you may have an extra month when no house payment or rent is due. It only happens with your first home, so enjoy it! Every home after that is prorated so you pay for one home up to the closing and the new one after closing, usually a like amount so you will not notice any savings. Since the closing may depend on your seller's occupancy requirements, I would suggest allowing a complete month of prepaid interest in your closing costs estimate, and then you may be pleasantly suprised if it's less!

FHA Mortgage Insurance Premium (MIP)

If you've chosen the FHA mortgage program (203b) to buy or refinance a one to four unit property, the fee to FHA for their mortgage insurance may be financed or may be paid in cash at the closing, depending on the amount of cash you have available. For example, a loan of $95,000 for thirty years would have a mortgage insurance premium of $3,610 due to the FHA. You'll get part of this back (refer to the worksheet in the appendix for refund calculations) when you sell if the loan is paid off. For most homebuyers, the purpose of choosing the FHA loan is to take advantage of the lower down payment requirements, and financing the MIP is the only option. If you choose to finance the premium, then $3,610 would be added on to the loan amount resulting in a loan of $98,610 which will naturally increase the monthly payment accordingly. (You may go over the maximum loan amount in your FHA area if the excess is caused by the added mortgage insurance premium.) If you choose to finance it, use the chart on the Factor Sheet in the appendix and add the monthly figure to the FHA prequalifying worksheet. If you choose to pay the MIP in cash, use the chart and add the figure to the closing costs on the Closing Costs Worksheet. (Are you with me, so far?)

One exception to the one-time MIP payment (there's always an exception to government policies to make it more difficult!) applies to the 234(c) condo program. FHA still requires that mortgage insurance be paid monthly (rather than in cash or financed in the loan) for loans insured for purchasing or refinancing *condominiums* in an approved project. Don't confuse a condominium with other multifamily dwellings such as townhouses, zero-lot-line projects, patio homes or others. For simplification, a condominium project under the FHA 234(c) program, includes units that consist of air space only, surrounded by walls, ceilings, floors, utility services, etc. that are owned by the condominum homeowner's association. A Planned United Development (PUD), townhouse, or other row-type unit usually includes ownership of the walls, roof, and land under the unit, together with an interest in the common areas. FHA requires that the mortgage insurance fee be collected monthly for condos, and you will need to use this monthly fee for prequalifying purposes on the FHA prequalifying worksheet.

Closing Costs That You Can Control

Attorney's Fees

Should you hire an attorney to assist you in this transaction, your fee should be set as a flat fee and should be negotiated at the time you hire your attorney. Ask your realtor if this is required in your area and if so to suggest a real estate attorney. I would go beyond this advice and contact several others to compare prices. Seeking legal advice is always wise, but if you can use the services of a title or escrow company and if your interests will be protected, you may not need to add the costs of an attorney to the other fees. You may want your attorney to prepare the closing papers and your lender to prepare the security papers (promissory note and trust deed). Or, you may use a title/escrow fee for all of the transaction, whatever is customary in your area. If you have doubts about your transaction, by all means, protect yourself by hiring an attorney. However, if this is a fairly simple purchase transaction, your realtor and your title and escrow company will protect your interests adequately.

Flood Insurance

Check with your lender about the flood insurance requirements of your area. If your property is located in a flood zone starting with the letter A, you may be required to purchase a special flood insurance policy. The policy will be issued by your local insurance agent through the Federal Emergency Management Agency regional office and the fee will be set according to the risk in your area. Your insurance agent will contact that office and order a policy, and the premium will be added to your homeowner's policy. Be sure you ask your lender after the appraisal is done if flood insurance will be required (it will be indicated on the appraisal) so you can advise the insurance agents to include this cost in their premium estimates when shopping for a homeowner's policy. You need to compare fire and flood both with several agents.

Inspection Fees

This fee is over and above the appraisal and reinspection fees required by the lender and is strictly up to you and the seller. There are many home inspection companys now who will do a structural inspection of your home prior to purchase to reveal any defects you should be aware of. Ask your realtor about the disclosure laws in your state and how they protect you. Many states now require disclosure by the seller of any major defects in the property. This means that after you have moved in and discover a major problem (roof, plumbing, etc.) that the seller didn't disclose to you, you can require that the seller reimburse you for repair of these items. The laws differ by state and you may avoid the added expense of a home inspection fee by discussing this with your realtor or attorney. The home inspection is a good idea if you are suspicious of roof, plumbing, soil, drainage, or foundation problems, but once the report is done, you'll have to renegotiate with the seller for items you want repaired. Discuss this with the seller and the realtor to negotiate the inspection fee or the need for an additional inspection expense. If everyone involved agrees to have the inspection done, as with many other fees, shop around to find the best price. Read the inspection report, if you can get past all the disclaimers, and compare it to what you have actually observed at the property.

You may notice that I'm somewhat skeptical about the need for an additional inspection. Your appraiser will inspect the property to determine it's value and any repairs necessary, your pest inspector (a structural pest inspection is required by most lenders in many areas) will inspect the structure for pests or moisture, and between the two of them, any major defects should be revealed. If you read both of these reports, do a detailed inspection with your realtor, and check on the disclosure laws in your state that govern this transaction, you should be adequately protected. It's your money though, and you may feel more secure with the transaction with this additional inspection.

While I am on the subject of inspections, let me caution you about your inspection of the property with your realtor. I am a lender and am not about to second-guess the role of the realtor in this transaction. Let me just caution homebuyers to do a thorough inspection of the property yourself and ask *lots* of questions. Ask your realtor to give you a copy of the listing (the information sheet used to include the property on the Multiple Listing Service in your area) and a copy of any inspections that have been done prior to your inquiry. Ask the seller or the seller's realtor about the condition of the roof, foundation, stability of soil and drainage if on a slope, types of zoning in the area, distances to schools, shopping, churches, parks, and the limitations (sometimes called CC&R's or conditions, covenants, and restrictions) on the use of the property both by the local entities and state laws. Your escrow/title company will supply you with a copy of the CC&R's at the close of escrow but you should review them now if you want to make any additions or remove any parts of the building soon. If you've asked about everything up front and have a problem later, you may have recourse against those who didn't disclose potential problems. Remember, protect yourself first and don't be hurried in this major decision. Inspect the property at several different times of day to determine traffic, noise pollution, day and nighttime lighting, and any other factors that could change during the course of a weekday or a weekend.

Consider what you don't like about where you live now or have lived in the past and look for those same drawbacks in your new home. If you garden, want to use your home for business, or have any special needs for expansion or use of the property, check now with your realtor to make sure you choose the property that will suit your future needs as well.

Title Company or Escrow Company Fees

Using an attorney versus using title company is controlled by local or state custom. Check with your lender, realtor, or title company for the requirements in your area. You may be able to use the services of a third party, an escrow company who will order a preliminary title report (called a prelim.) or a title commitment, and a survey of the property if not included in the prelim, handle the distribution of money, purchase a title policy from a title company for you, the seller, and the lender (sometimes the escrow and title company are one and the same or affiliated), assist in signing of the documents, explain some of the fees, and record the necessary legal documents to finalize this transaction. You'll be charged fees for this service so, again, shop around! The realtor, the seller, neighbors, co-workers, and the lender will all have an opinion about the best escrow company or title company to use so ask their opinions first. There is usually an escrow fee and a title fee, separate ones for each service. In most areas, all of the companies charge the same escrow and title fees so use the company that has been recommended with the best service and the one that is most convenient to all the parties. Compare prices on your transaction by calling several escrow companies. Have the sales price, loan amount, lender's name, and property location handy since they will use this for quoting prices, and tell them you are comparing escrow and title fees only, not lender fees. Ask them to add on any delivery, notary, recording, document, or survey fees you'll have to pay to be sure you are being quoted all the fees charged.

Discount Points and Loan Orgination Fees

The discount fee, or discount points, deserves special attention because it is a major bargaining tool with the FHA and VA loans. It's often a costly fee and should be included as part of the contract so that all fees are disclosed to both the borrower and the seller.

Question: When is a discount not a discount? Answer: When it is money *out* of your pocket instead of in your pocket! This is basically the confusion regarding discount points.

First, the discount points are collected with the closing costs and are calculated on the mortgage loan amount. Each discount point is 1 percent of the loan amount (in the case of the financed mortgage insurance premium, the discount point will be based on the total loan with the premium). The discount points fee is a one-time fee paid at the closing that is added to the value of the loan throughout its term. The loan origination fee is 1 percent of the base loan amount without any financed MIP and is a one-time processing fee assessed by the lender and paid to the lender. The discount points and the loan origination fee will generally be disclosed separately on the good faith estimate of closing costs at your loan application or in the final disclosure papers at the closing of government insured or guaranteed loans. On conventional loans, the loan origination fee is a flat fee collected up front in one lump sum, usually 1 percent to 2.5 percent of the base loan amount.

To understand the purpose behind discount points we'll need to go back to the original intent of the government programs, the FHA and the VA housing program. (Very short history lesson on lending.) After the Depression, the housing market had all but collapsed, and banks or building and loans (remember George's problems in "It's a Wonderful Life?") were at the mercy of the depositors with an unstable supply of money to lend. The Housing Act of 1932 created: 1. The Federal Reserve System to regulate the flow of funds on the secondary market; 2. FNMA to keep the circulation of funds in the secondary market; and 3. FHA (now part of the Department of Housing and Urban Development) to offer low-interest, federally insured loans with a minimal down payment. (No quiz will be given on this!) These more attractive government loans would "corner the mortgage market" if offered in the same marketplace as conventional loans. In order for government and conventional loans to maintain equal value for trading purposes, a one-time discount fee or "point" was collected and, spread over the life of the loan, to offset the lower interest rate. Thus, the more discount points charged, the lower your interest rate, and vice versa. The term for the value of the loan (interest collected on the principal *and* the discount points) is called *yield*, an important commodity when considering the salability or negotiability of your loan on the secondary market. A loan of $72,000 with discount points of four (4% of the loan of $72,000 = $2,880) would be sold for $69,120 (discounted) to another investor on the secondary market who would actually collect a total of $72,000 (plus interest) upon full repayment of your loan. Discount points on FHA loans may be paid by the borrower or the seller, however the contract is negotiated. If the amount of points is excessive, it will be considered a seller's concession and is subject to limitations. Discount points on VA loans must be paid by the seller on a purchase transaction, but may be paid by the veteran on a refinance.

The loan origination fee is set by the lender and is charged to cover the cost of processing the loan package. This fee is a one-time charge and is retained by the lender or the branch office to offset office expenses. It is generally set as 1 percent of the loan amount on an FHA or VA loan, and 1 percent to 3 percent on a conventional loan. If you're paying the loan origination fee on a conventional loan, shop around. Generally, the higher the loan amount (jumbo loans), the higher the loan origination fee. For loans in more risky areas or for nonowner occupied properties, the loan origination fee may be much higher. You may be able to negotiate this fee with the loan officer since this fee may determine the amount of her commission. It's worth a try, and during high interest rate times when business is hard to come by, you may be successful in saving yourself ¼ percent ($225 on a $90,000 loan) or more at the closing. Remind your loan officer that this modest savings may encourage you to recommend her services to many of your relatives, co-workers, etc.

Finally, when comparing any of the above fees make sure you compare the service provided as well. Ask your neighbors, relatives, co-workers, and realtor which company they would recommend for each service and why. If they say that they have seen lots of advertisements for the company, ask if they know anyone who has used their services. Effective advertising is fine for buying shoes, but for this major transaction you want to hire the services of proven professionals who will provide good service for a fair price.

Chapter

Shopping for a Mortgage Loan

Choosing a Realtor

How you approach mortgage loan shopping will depend on your choice of representation. If you choose to use the services of a real estate agent in your search for a home, the realtor will probably have some suggestions about the best lender for your needs. This may be the best way for you to go, if you've better things to do with your time than shopping for a mortgage loan— like earning a living to pay for the house. Naturally, before showing you properties the realtor will narrow down the choices to homes you can afford and homes that fit your needs. Unfortunately, they will probably also narrow the choices of homes to only those with sellers who are willing to pay a fee or commission for the service. This eliminates the for-sale-by-owner properties, which may be a bargain. On the other hand, they will provide many services which you won't have to worry about, though you still should keep on top of this transaction to protect your own interests. The realtor should prequalify you for a mortgage loan before recommending you to any lender. The sales commission for the services will probably be split between the listing agent (who represents the seller) and your agent. Make it clear up front and in writing that they should represent you exclusively, though they will still be acting as a subagent of the listing agent in this transaction. Normally, the commission is paid by the seller. If you don't choose a real estate agent of your own and choose a home with a realtor involved, the agent will be representing the seller—*not you.* Since the full fee is due someone, the listing agent then gets the whole fee; therefore, it would be only logical to have an agent represent you and share the fee to protect your interests. Choose a real estate agent who has been recommended to you and who has a proven track record. All agents are required to treat buyers fairly and honestly and fully disclose all that they know about the property and the transaction, and almost all do. Everyone has a "friend" in the real estate business; just remember this is a business. You need a business person to represent you in this most important transaction, and that may be someone who is more than a "friend." Check around with many real estate offices and listen to the advice of other homebuyers rather than relying on advertising to choose a realtor. Realtors use the amount of their closed transactions as a guide to their value as an agent, but that should not necessarily be your measure. A few large transactions can boost a realtor's rating but satisfied clients are a much better gauge of their ability to help you.

You may feel comfortable with the realtor's choice of a lender, especially if you know that the realtor has used this lender regularly. My theory in life, though, is to "protect myself," and it has brought me through pretty well so far. Often that means doing it myself—from the luggage that was supposed to change planes in San Francisco, which I found by checking the no-claim section just in case, to double-checking the "talking machine" (you know that sweet voice that can't read prices at the grocery check-out counter) when it hits a "high" note occasionally. I protect my own interest; I double-check everything that I can. Ask around about the real estate agent you've chosen, about the lender chosen for you, about the insurance company that's best, about the schools in the area (if not for your children, then for resale value), ask local elected officials about zoning changes in your area, and most importantly, ask for copies of all contracts you sign. *Protect yourself.* When you are a week or two into this transaction, if you don't hear from the realtor and the loan processor or loan officer, start calling at least weekly to make sure all is going well. (I'm sure I will hear about this from the lending community!) Your calls should be returned or accepted with a thorough answer about the status of your loan from anyone involved in this transaction, not just your realtor. If they can't give you a phone response, either insist on a letter or a Fax regarding the status or drop in to their office for an update regularly. An "everything is going fine" statement is not very reassuring to me. I want to hear what, specifically, is being done and how close the loan package is to being complete, not platitudes. Don't be afraid to "step on toes," "rock the boat," or whatever phrase you may use for getting the job done! Many times I've heard the realtors or loan officers complain about a persistent borrower or seller who "bothers" them with questions constantly. Having been on most ends of the transaction, I can assure you that it is part of their job to keep you informed, just as it's your job to make sure things go smoothly. If you meet with rudeness, lack of information, or downright incorrect information, don't hesitate to contact the manager of the lender's office or the home office, the manager or owner of the real estate office, or anyone of authority who can help you with your problem. Always be courteous and calm, but expect answers from those who have control over this transaction.

For Sale By Owner

If you've chosen to purchase a home without the benefit of a realtor and have some business background , there's no reason why you shouldn't succeed in this transaction. Your shopping may take longer and you may want to hire an attorney to review the legal documents or prepare a contract, but in the end you'll have saved yourselves a considerable sum. Get all the literature on the subject available; there are some excellent how-to books out now on the subject of buying a home. Start looking for the for-sale-by-owner signs. Weigh the savings in the real estate commission, usually around 6 percent of the sales price, with the risk involved in the transaction—and go for it! I've always been a do-it-yourself person and am aware that certain things can go wrong, but then things go wrong even with an agent. I strongly recommend that, in this case, you hire an attorney to review the contract or to write the contract for you and the seller. This should be a flat fee arrangement between you and the attorney in advance. If you choose to negotiate the contract yourself and require only the legal review by the attorney, make sure that the fee reflects what part you're doing yourself. Compare the fees of several attorneys for just the services you require. You'll find a purchase contract at your local office supply store, the title and escrow company and your attorney will assist you in the remainder of the paperwork, and, if you have ready and willing sellers to do their part, you shouldn't have any more problems than you would with representation. Expect to give a check to the seller for a good faith deposit when signing the contract to purchase. This check should go directly to the title or escrow company or to the attorney to hold for the closing and this amount will be credited towards your closing costs and down payment. A check for $500 to $1000 is normal for a deposit on this transaction. You should make sure that this deposit is refundable if you are unable to complete the transaction due to circumstances out of your control. If you're looking on your own for a lender and want to know where to start, I have included a brief opinion on the types of lenders. Please understand that my opinion is from the perspective of a lender. I have worked for all the types I mention and I know that each type of lender is capable of giving you good service and a good price—if you make sure that they do!

Types of Lenders
Your Local Banker
Most banks offer all the loan programs: FHA, VA, and conventional financing. In addition, they may offer their own brands of loans, which they can portfolio. They are governed by federal regulations and audited, so their guidelines will be similar to all other lenders, but they may offer the option of some nonconforming features. This may be your first stop, if you want to start with your own bank, but it shouldn't be your only stop. Compare rates, points, and all the programs and expect the loan officers to be able to prequalify you and compare the different programs. Contact your branch to direct you to the lending division or department or to a real estate loan officer. Generally, banks have centralized their real estate lending into one department. Call and talk to a loan officer for information and to set up an appointment to discuss your needs. If you don't get the attention you deserve at your bank, go to another. Your accounts are not generally going to get you any special rates, and you might want to bank with an institution that can supply all your needs: checking, savings, *and loans.*

Your Local Savings Bank
(Alias Savings and Loan Association)
Savings and loan associations, or savings banks as many are now called, are still the major source of residential mortgage lending money, regardless of the problems some are having in some areas. They began originally to fill that need and they still do. Usually savings banks have the full range of programs, including some nonconforming financing with some higher loan amounts in case you need them. Lenders may call these jumbo loans, and you're most apt to find this type of loan at a bank or savings bank since they have the option of portfolioing loans. Savings banks usually have centralized real estate departments, so call to find out where and who to talk to. Shop around to compare the service and rates. Again, if the loan officer doesn't impress you as knowledgeable after you have gained some

knowledge yourself, move on to one that does. If you're a customer of a savings bank, start there but don't limit yourself. They all want your business. I would advise that you stick with larger, well-known and well-advertised savings banks who actively advertise mortgage loans because they may be more competititve.

The Local Mortgage Banker vs. the Not-So-Local Mortgage Banker

This category refers to the actual mortgage company or banker as opposed to the mortgage broker described below. The mortgage banker processes and closes loans in their own name and sells them to larger investors. The mortgage broker generally acts as a middleman between large investors or larger lenders and customers and does not actually close their own loans. A mortgage banker has all the same programs, but since they can't portfolio as many loans as a bank or savings bank, they may be limited on jumbo or nonconforming loans. They do offer highly competitive rates and they specialize in mortgage loans, so what they may lack in programs, they may make up for in service. Mortgage bankers, brokers, savings banks, and banks all sell their loans to investors as part of the business, so this should not be a factor in your choice. The buying and selling of loans is so sophisticated now that the borrower is rarely inconvenienced by this practice. This also increases competition and allows for many more places for you to shop. I would choose a mortgage banker who advertises local processing and closing. There are some mortgage companies who have branch origination offices but actually prepare the file at the headquarters, many times in another state. Ask your mortgage banker if he has local processing, underwriting, and funding. If the answer is no you may want to move on to a company that can control the closing of your loan locally. If you are in a small suburban area or rural area, this may be common and quite successful. Today with the use of the FAX and computer processing, your local mortgage banker may do a great job. Again, check with your friends, neighbors, etc., to see who has used which mortgage banker in your town.

The Mortgage Broker and Other Lending Sources

More popular than ever is the mortgage broker. If you are shopping, give one a try. Mortgage brokers shop for a mortgage for you. The fees charged by mortgage brokers used to be higher, allowing for their commission, but that is not necessarily the case anymore. Banks and savings banks accept loans from licensed mortgage brokers commonly now, and they pay them the commisssion you would have paid the bank. They have the option of shopping for your loan right up to the closing too, in case you are in a volatile market. They can better negotiate the fees and points to your advantage since they have better control over each loan. The drawback may be in the closing. Since most mortgage brokers close the loans through another lender (mortgage banker, bank, or savings bank), they may not have total control. Ask what process your mortgage broker uses. Do they process, approve, and close in their own office, or must they rely on the lender to do any portion of this? Your broker may not want to admit to any delay caused by this, but you are protecting your interests first and should find out in advance. Any hesitancy on her part might be reason to look further. You want a quick, professional transaction by an experienced mortgage broker with control over the closing.

Your local credit union may offer first mortgage loans, but usually their programs are limited. My surveys of lenders have shown that credit unions are usually quite competitive on consumer loans (personal property, auto, RV's, etc.), but have limited funds for mortgage loans. Shop there too, though you may have to be a member to participate.

Private lenders are out there too. For hard-to-place loans, many times mortgage brokers can put you in touch with private money, sometimes called hard money lenders. You may pay a higher price, either in the interest rate or in the fees at closing, but, if you have problems with credit or undocumented income, this type of lender might be fine. Private lenders are not always more expensive, and you might find this source suits your needs. Expect to put a larger down payment on these types of transactions, but for nonconforming loans you should expect to make some concessions. One piece of advice in this case: If you don't use the services of a real estate professional in this transaction, contact any attorney who specializes in real estate transactions to review the legal documents prior to signing, even if the private lender is a relative or friend. You'll be protecting both your money and your friendship!

The Role of the Lender

Let's follow the loan process according to the players in this transaction. Knowing the names of the persons who handle your file will help you communicate better should problems arise and will let those persons know that you are watching them! Call and talk regularly to the loan officer, loan processor, or anyone you choose to make sure that your loan is being completed in a timely manner. Contact by the loan applicant prompts a response and a review of the file, which brings the file to someone's attention.

The Loan Officer

The loan officer you initially contact will usually be in control of this transaction or, at the very least, responsible for it. They receive all or part of their commission from these transactions, and the goal is to build up a client base by giving good service. A loan officer hopes that the satisfied customers will tell their friends and relatives and that you will consider them for your second home, a refinance, or an equity loan later. Set up a time and place for the loan application, usually in her office so you won't be distracted. Loan interviews conducted in the client's office, home, or elsewhere usually end up incomplete due to distractions by the phone or children and family in the home. You can avoid follow-up contact with your loan officer by giving her your undivided time for this one important interview. Also, if there's a co-borrower involved (Mom and Dad or whomever), set up separate interviews because even the closest relationship may be strained by revealing personal financial information. The loan officer will complete the application from the information you provide or will ask you to complete the forms. If she completes the forms, read them before signing. Have the program thoroughly explained, and ask for copies of any of the forms you want to read later. Your primary questions should be: what is the down payment, what are the closing costs, what is the monthly payment and when can you expect an approval on your loan request. She should be prepared to answer all of those questions at the initial loan interview though she will hedge on the loan closing date since there are so many factors that she can't control. If you ask informed questions at the interview, you'll put her on notice that you're are going to be expecting good service from everyone involved.

She'll ask that you sign some blank forms, verification of income, deposit, and a verification of your other mortgage loan, if applicable, which will be completed and mailed to the employers, banks etc. These are the only forms that may not be completed prior to your signature. This is normal procedure and allows the lender to complete the forms and mail them out after you leave. However, you may complete the applicant's portion if you choose. "Do not sign blank forms" is good advice, and the only exceptions should be those verifications mentioned above. Otherwise, ask that the forms be completed and ask for copies of the completed forms. Generally, she'll expect you to write a check for the application fee to start the process and to order the appraisal and credit report. This should be the only fee required at the interview, since the loan officer gets her commission at the closing, and most other fees are paid at the closing. If this transaction isn't completed, regardless of the cause, the fee for the appraisal and credit report will be kept by the lender if the appraisal and credit report are already completed. Check with your lender about the remainder of the application fee and ask at the application interview what portion is refundable.

In Chapter Five I'll help to prepare you for the loan application by telling you what documentation you should bring to the interview.

The Loan Processor

The completed loan application will be given to a loan processor or several loan processors, who will order the appraisal from either an independent appraiser or a staff appraiser, depending on the size of the lender you've chosen. The appraiser will contact the seller or the seller's agent for access to the property. You'll have very little to do with this part of the documentation. The loan processor will order a credit report—you have authorized her to do so on some of the up-front forms—and the credit agency will check your open loans, several repository agencies (large companies who accumulate credit data like TRW), your employment, and the legal records in any county in which you've lived for the past two years. Your credit and legal records will cover the past seven years, so be prepared to explain anything that may show up. More on your credit and how it affects your application in Chapter Five.

The loan processor also mails direct written requests for verification of employment, deposits, and previous mortgage loans and sets the file up for logging/inventory purposes. At the loan interview, upon loan application, or within three days of loan application, the loan processor will prepare a Good Faith Estimate of Settlement Charges and a Regulation Z statement, both showing the cost of your loan and the fees you'll be required to pay at the closing. The loan officer will give you or mail to you a booklet titled "Settlement Costs and You," which will help to explain the fees, and, if you've applied for an adjustable rate mortgage (ARM), included will be a copy of the booklet "The Consumer's Handbook on Adjustable Rate Mortgages." Loan processors are required to send these upon loan application, so call if you haven't received them within five days or so. Both the booklets and the forms contain some valuable information that will help you understand the fees charged. Be sure to contact your loan officer or processor with any questions about the fees now. Don't wait until the closing. The most frequently asked question is regarding the APR, or the annual percentage rate, disclosed on the form. The APR reflects the cost of the mortgage as a yearly rate, based upon the anticipated term of the mortgage. The APR typically will be higher than the interest rate on a mortgage loan because it includes, in addition to the interest rate cost, the loan origination fees, commitment fees, prepaid interest and other credit costs. Follow the instructions with your good faith estimate and the other forms and return the signed forms to the lender as soon as possible. Call your lender (the forms should be signed by the preparer) and question any fees that differ from the fees quoted at the interview.

Most lenders now require a face-to-face interview with the loan applicant at the time of the application or, at the very least, at the final application to eliminate the possibility of fraudulent cases or "strawbuyers," buyers who qualify for a loan with no intention of living on the property or making the payments for an unqualified buyer. Many lenders require identification now on all loans, though the FHA began this requirement several years ago. Expect to bring your driver's license or other picture ID and a copy of your social security card or other evidence that you have a social security number.

The Underwriter and the Closer

When the written verifications of employment, bank accounts, and other mortgage loans return, when the credit report is complete, and when the appraisal is received, the file is ready for the final loan application using the verified information. Your signature on this final loan application will be required now or at the closing, depending on the lender's procedures. This final application along with all the documentation accumulated regarding your file is the loan package and will go to the underwriter for review and an approving signature. It then goes to the closing department for preparation of the legal documents, the promissory note, the mortgage or trust deed securing the property, and more disclosures and statements for your signature. These papers are usually forwarded to the closing agent, the title or escrow company, or your attorney; although occasionally the lender will handle the closing within their office. Expect a complete explanation about the fees from whomever handles the closing—that is their job! The title company or attorney will disburse the funds (from the lender), less fees due to the insurance company for the premiums due, and to the county for property taxes due. They will record the mortgage or deed of trust and issue to both the lender and the borrower an appropriate title insurance policy protecting and insuring the title (very important so insist on one for yourself as well as the lender). Again, be sure all these procedures are explained to you, especially if this is your first escrow or closing—that's what the professionals get paid to do! Expect to provide a certified check or cashier's check for the amount of the down payment and closing costs less the amount you have given the title company or escrow as a deposit on this transaction. Rarely do title companies, escrow companies, or attorneys accept personal checks for this transaction. Ask how much you should bring to close and what type of check is required. You should expect to receive a copy of all the documents that you have signed at the closing, not several days later. Of course if you ask to close on the last day of the month, typically the busiest day of the month for title and escrow offices, be prepared to accomodate the closing or escrow officer.

After the Closing: Servicing Your Loan

Your payment book or the billing statement to use for making payments will follow in a few weeks after the closing from your lender, and you may receive along with it an amortization schedule, or a list of all your 360 or 180 payments (thirty year or fifteen year) with a breakdown of the principal and interest applied to the loan during the term and the balance due after each payment. Some lenders will supply you with an amortization schedule for a fee if you're curious. At the end of each year you'll receive a statement of the interest paid during that year for tax purposes, plus an accounting of the principal and impound disbursements for taxes, fire and flood insurance, etc. Some companies include the interest and principal information with the billings in advance—keep these records for income tax purposes.

If you have chosen an adjustable rate loan you'll be contacted forty-five days prior to any adjustment of the interest rate and will be advised of the new rate and the method of calculating the new rate (based on what index). Be aware if you have an adjustable rate loan that may be converted to a fixed rate loan during a certain time period. More on the adjustable rate caps and conversion options in Chapter Seven.

Processing procedures vary by lender, and yours may be handled somewhat differently than what I have described, but you now know the basic steps of a mortgage loan transaction and can monitor your own file by using the phrases mentioned above. Certain files are picked randomly for audit by a quality control department, either the lender's or a government agency's, so you may be contacted after the closing with follow-up questions. Make sure you check with your lender that this is the case before completing any information about your file or giving any information over the phone. Also, your name may end up on a mailing list and you'll be bombarded with requests to convert your loan to many alternative payment plans. Check with your original loan officer before taking advantage of anything that sounds suspicious or too good to be true.

Chapter

Types of Loans Available

I'VE CHOSEN, AGAIN, THE THREE TYPICAL LOANS used for financing single family purchase and refinance transactions for this discussion. This chapter will provide more detailed explanations of the guidelines common to all three types: FHA (HUD), VA, and conventional. Manuals and handbooks are provided to lenders with thousands of pages of "the rules." Those rules that may affect your case or that differ from program to program are included in this section.

Loans Insured by the FHA

The Federal Housing Administration (FHA) is part of the Department of Housing and Urban Development (HUD) and insures loans under Section 203 (b) and Section 234 (c) and many other sections of the National Housing Act. Some common FHA section numbers and programs available under Title II of the National Housing Act are:

#203 (b)   Purchase or refinance of one-to-four Family dwellings.

#203 (i)   Purchase or refinance of rural area dwellings, farm housing of 2 1/2 acres or more.

#203 (k)   Rehabilitation or improvement of one-to-four family dwellings.

#220   Urban renewal of One-to-eleven family structures—purchase or rehabilitation.

#221 (d) 2   Purchase or rehabilitation of low-cost housing, one-to-four family.

#234 (c)   Purchase or refinance of condominiums.

#235   Homeownership assistance for lower income families.

#245 (a)   Graduated payment mortgage, five plans available.

#255   Home equity conversion or reverse equity mortgage.

The Direct Endorsement program(commonly called the D.E. program) introduced in the early 1980s, allows lenders to use their own staff/HUD trained D.E. underwriters to approve FHA loans. Ask if your lender is D.E. approved; if not, I don't consider them a full-service lender. The use of the D.E. underwriter may save everyone time and, more importantly, tells me that the lender has taken the time and effort to train the staff to handle FHA loans. Below are some of the basic guidelines of the FHA program.

FHA Maximum Mortgage Amounts

1. Single-family home: from $67,500 to $124,875, depending on home prices in the area.
2. Two-family home: from $76,000 to $140,600
3. Three-family home: from $92,000 to $170,200
4. Four-family home: from $107,000 to $197,950
5. Condominums: from $67,500 to $124,850

Maximum loans vary by region or area according to special Congressional appropriations effective late 1990. No minimums for loans are allowed, but proposals have been made to allow higher fees for smaller loans.

Check with your lender prior to shopping for a home about the limits in your area of all the types of loans available. FHA now has two calculations to determine the maximum loan available for your new loan. Use column one or two depending on the value of the home you are buying or refinancing.

Purchase Owner-Occupied Maximum Loan to Value Ratio (LTV)

$50,000.00 or less in value   OVER $50,000 in value
(Value meaning the lesser of the sales price or appraised value)

FIRST CALCULATION:
1. 97% of the value   1. 97% of the first $25,000
   (plus closing costs)   95% of the remainder
                                (plus closing costs)

SECOND CALCULATION:
2. 98.75% of the value   2. 97.75% of the value

The maximum loan is the lesser of the two calculations, see below for an example of the maximum loan on a $90,000 value

FIRST CALCULATION:
   $90,000 lesser of sales price or appraised value
   + 1,350 closing costs (1.5% estimate)
   $91,350
   − 25,000 x 97% = $24,250
   $66,350 x 95% = 63,032
Loan amount $87,282 or $87,250 rounded

SECOND CALCULATION:
   $90,000 lesser of sales price or appraised value
      x 97.75% no closing costs added
   $87,975 loan amount

Your loan amount will be the lesser of the two or $87,250.

Refinance Owner-Occupied

85% of value with cash back allowed, 97/95% without cash back.

Strict limitations as to what liens and closing costs may be included in the new loan amount exist on these refinances. Also, some refinances don't require a new appraisal; see Chapter Eight for more details on FHA streamline refinances and other refinance transactions available to investors.

Mortgage Insurance Premium (MIP)

Effective early 1991 FHA requires a one-time mortgage insurance payment at the close of escrow to be paid in cash or financed along with the loan (estimate 3.8 percent of the base loan amount) plus an annual premium (estimate 0.50 percent divided by twelve months) collected monthly on most FHA loans. Check with your lender about the current method of collecting and paying your mortgage insurance as several changes have been made in the past several years.

The mortgage insurance on the FHA loan may be paid in cash at the close of escrow from the buyer's funds or may be financed by the lender along with your base loan amount. To calculate the MIP use the factors below.

One-Time and Annual Mortgage Insurance Premium Factor Table:

Fiscal year	Premium Amt.	LTV	Annual Premium
1991	3.8% of loan	89.99 & under	0.5% for 5 yrs.
thur	3.8% of loan	90.00–95.00	0.5% for 8 yrs.
1992	3.8% of loan	95.01 & over	0.5% for 10 yrs.

Most homebuyers finance the mortgage insurance premium for lack of money, just remember that you would be receiving the unused portion of the one-time mortgage premium at the repayment of the loan, should you sell. If you have the type of old FHA loan that's assumable you must consider this as part of the sale price. More on assumption policies of FHA loans later in this chapter.

Would that mortgage insurance premium paid up front with the closing costs be used better towards the larger down payment? Would it be used better earning interest? Your individual circumstances will determine this. Don't hesitate to contact your tax advisor for more information about the effect on your finances.

Prepayment Penalty

There is currently no allowance for a prepayment penalty on the FHA 203B and 234C loan programs.

Assumability

Your new FHA loan is no longer "fully assumable." In the appendix is a chart on the assumablility of the FHA loans over the last 5 years—the years since assumability has become an issue. Effective 15 December 1989, your new FHA loan is assumable only to a credit-worthy person who will occupy the property. Quite a change! This reduces the attractiveness of an FHA loan, although I can understand the new rules, given the abuses of the program. The FHA programs 203B and 234C were never intended to be used by investors, and for years the limitations were minimal.

Multiple FHA Loans

If you have an FHA loan, and sell the property allowing an assumption without approval from the lender and then wish to be considered for another FHA loan, you'll have to prove that the loan is paid down to the 75 percent loan-to-value ratio or that the assumptor is an owner-occupant. The FHA limits the number of owner-occupied originated loans that you may have. The FHA may allow another FHA loan if the applicants sign a statement that, in the event of a default, the lender may seek a deficiency judgement for the benefit of the FHA.

Property Requirements

Properties may be detached, semidetached, row, or end-row dwellings on a single lot. They must be free from hazards that affect the safety and health of the occupants or the soundness of the dwelling. There must be a continuing supply of safe, potable water, sanitary facilities, adequate heating, domestic hot water, electricity, and adequate living space. The primary use of the property must be residential (not commercial) and vehicular access to the property must be provided under all weather conditions. These requirements are purposefully vague. What may be safe in New Mexico may be hazardous in New York. Basically, the FHA considers the market area and other dwellings of equal value when evaluating a property.

After safety and health standards are met, the FHA considers the remainder of the qualities adjustments to value, rather than a positive or negative factor. As explained earlier, the value is the lesser of the sales price or the FHA estimate of value. If the property you choose is in poor shape, it's less valuable and the property may appraise lower than the sales price. This would require you to make a larger down payment because the loan amount is calculated on the lesser of the sales price or the appraised value.

Other limitations apply to the type and age of the dwelling. Below are just a few of the limitations, the most common types that cause problems for first-time homebuyers. If you're looking at a nonconforming piece of property, be prepared to invest more money in the property. You may not feel that a nonconforming feature of a house is a problem but future purchasers may, reducing the potential resale value should the lender have to resell the home because of a default.

Mobile Homes on Land

Regional restrictions apply to the conversion of a mobile or modular dwelling on to real property (land). All local codes must be met and the mobile home must be converted both structurally and legally to taxable real property. These loans are eligible for the 203(b) program. Title I of the National Housing Act does allow for mobile home financing, but only permanentized mobile homes are eligible for Title II loans.

Home Built Within 12 Months of Your Application

If the building plans for the construction of a new home (finished in the twelve months before your application) were not approved by the FHA or the VA prior to the start of construction, or the finished home will *not* be covered by an acceptable ten year home warranty program, then the loan-to-value ratio may not exceed 90 percent. That means that you must put at least a 10 percent down payment on this type of transaction. After the one year period, the maximum financing is available if the appraisal doesn't indicate any deficiencies. There is quite a difference between "building an FHA house" and "building a house with FHA inspections." Many builders will say that their homes are FHA quality but you won't be able to take advantage of an FHA insured loan unless the builder purchases a ten year warranty from an FHA approved warranty program.

For a new home to be approved for FHA financing, the FHA must approve the plans and specifications prior to the beginning of construction, and a series of inspections must be performed on the home and the subdivision during construction. Some new rules apply to a subdivision approved by the VA but not the FHA. A VA project could be converted to FHA approval in the past; however, that is no longer the case and a series of approvals must be issued by the FHA on the project too. To find out if a new subdivision or recently constructed home has FHA approval, ask your lender, ask the builder, or call the local FHA (HUD) office and ask for the Valuation Department.

Condominiums

The FHA will accept loans in approved condominium projects with limitations on the number of nonowner-occupied units in the project. A condominium project must be occupied a minimum of 50-70 percent by owner-occupants (depending on regional requirements) to be eligible for FHA financing. Your local FHA office keeps a current listing of the approved projects which it provides to all approved FHA lenders. If you're considering a particular project and want FHA financing, check with your lender first to see if the project is established and approved.

Credit Requirements

Your lender will order a residential mortgage credit report from an acceptable credit agency for your new FHA loan package. The report will include a two year history of your employment and residences, all inquiries of your credit history from other sources within the last ninety days, all legal information available for the last seven years, and a payment history on all closed or open loans. These reports are strictly confidential and information can't be shared with a third party. You can get a copy of your report by calling your lender or you can order a copy from the credit agency. If you have some questionable items on your report, you'll automatically be sent a copy of the report to allow you to respond or correct the information. Your response will become a part of the credit report if you want, for anyone else who inquires.

The underwriter will look for a general pattern of credit behavior. An isolated case of slow or late payments need only be explained in writing from you. Situations beyond your control that aren't likely to occur again are the most acceptable. Your explanation should include the facts. Don't attempt to create a reason or use an excessively detailed reason; just write a brief note explaining what happened.

Bankruptcy

Filing for protection under the bankruptcy laws and being *discharged* are important terms for lending purposes. Filing is starting the bankruptcy procedure, with the discharge being the final court approval. The date of discharge is the important date to use when discussing this part of your credit history.

If you've had a bankruptcy discharged more than two years ago, you'll be asked to write an explanation of the circumstances causing the bankruptcy. The credit accounts you've established since that time must be current with no late notices reported. If your discharge of bankruptcy was less than two years ago, you should've re-established acceptable credit over the last year with no negative credit history or you must be able to prove that you've arranged your finances to eliminate the need for credit purchases. A discharge of bankruptcy over one year ago but less than two is acceptable only if there are good reasons *beyond your control* that caused the bankruptcy. Medical bills without insurance, a business failure that you had no control over, or other circumstances that you couldn't avoid may be acceptable reasons for filing bankruptcy. You'll be required to bring in a copy of the Discharge of Bankruptcy and the Schedule of Liabilities, which should support your reasons. If medical bills are the reason, then the schedule should indicate doctor or hospital bills in the liability section. Bankruptcies caused by a prior divorce should be supported by a recorded divorce decree on the legal section of your credit report. The two most common types of bankruptcy (though your attorney should be consulted for more detailed information on all legal matters) are Chapter 7, your complete release from responsibility for all listed liabilities and Chapter 13, wage earners bankruptcy, an attempt to reorganize your bills and continue to repay debts under a court appointed trustee plan. You're more apt to be eligible for an FHA or VA loan with the second choice, Chapter 13, since they may allow a new mortgage loan when your debts are close to being repaid in full and your payment history is acceptable and court approved. If you've been involved in a bankruptcy, before shopping for a home or spending any money, get the advice of your lender on your approach to a new loan.

Collections

An account that appears on the credit report as having been assigned to a collection agency must be paid in full if there's an amount owing and must be explained fully. Any paid collections that appear on your report during the last several years must be explained as well. A pattern of allowing credit accounts to remain unpaid is considered unacceptable credit. Collections accounts outstanding are viewed as potential liens against your property or your future earnings and must be paid prior to loan application rather than as a condition of approval. As a rule, collection accounts are viewed negatively. Every attempt should be made to avoid or, at the least, to correct the problem before it becomes a collection matter if you intend to apply for a mortgage loan. All factors are considered so it is not likely that your loan would be denied because of a negative credit history alone.

Late Notices

Credit accounts which have had more than one thirty-day notice within the last year are viewed negatively. It's likely that one or two accounts may have been paid late over the last several years but more than a few late notices (thirty days) or any sixty and ninety days notices are important to avoid. If the late payments are on another mortgage debt within the last twelve months, I would strongly suggest putting some time between the last late payment and the application for a new mortgage loan. There are always extenuating circumstances, but obviously your credit history is very important in determining your ability and responsibility to repay the new debt. Although "lost in the mail" may be a logical explanation, I wouldn't allow my credit to deteriorate during the two years prior to a loan application.

Inconsistent Information

Any time your employment, residency, or open account information differs from the application, you may be expected to explain in writing the reason. Auditing and quality control departments look for inconsistencies that could suggest fraudulent cases, so be very careful to give complete and accurate information on the application to avoid these "red flags" and, more importantly, to avoid delays in the process. On the lender side, more delays are caused by incomplete or inaccurate information provided by the borrower than any other reason. Don't sugarcoat or hide problems with credit, tell it all up front and let the lender figure out how to deal with it. Your loan officer wants you to be approved for this loan almost as much as you do.

Stability and Adequacy

The FHA requires that the underwriter analyze your source of income for stability and consistency. They want to see a probability of continued employment for the first five years of the loan. The only way to predict future income stability is to rely on a past history of employment. If you have been employed with the same employer for two years, no problem. If you have changed jobs but have stayed in the same field, still no problem. If you have changed jobs and fields, you may have to be in the new field for at least a year to qualify for "job stability." No one expects you to stay in a dead-end job just to buy a home, but consider that the underwriter can only prove future job stability with past job stability. FHA loans differ from VA and conventional with a five year guideline. The FHA does consider all verifiable income: overtime, bonuses, commissions, self-employment, interest income. More details about proving this income are given in Chapter Five. Income that is not reported to the IRS is not acceptable and neither is projected income, though future raises are a good compensating factor.

Negotiated Discount Points

Discount points charged by the lender on an FHA loan may be negotiated between the buyer and the seller with certain limitations. If you are paying the discount points, discuss with your lender the benefits of paying more points for a lower interest rate. There is one potential problem with discount points you need to avoid: If your lock-in, protecting the interest and points, expires prior to the closing but after the loan is approved you may have to have your loan re-approved if the points change or if the interest rate changes more than 1 percent. If you have negotiated a lock-in with your lender, whether or not you are paying the discount points, be aware of when it expires, especially in a volatile market. Keep a copy of it and remind your loan officer throughout the transaction so no one will allow the lock-in to expire.

If your seller has agreed to pay the discount points, they may not exceed 6 percent of the maximum loan amount with MIP included. Seller buydowns include payment for discount points, interest buydowns, and any other normal buyer's costs paid by the seller. Trips, carpet allowances and similar gifts as inducements to purchase are considered seller's concessions. A seller buydown of interest is allowed up to 2 percent of the first year's interest (subject to the 6 percent limitation for all of the seller's contributions). You may be qualified at the lower buydown rate and the funds put up by the seller must be held by an authorized escrow agent for repayment monthly until used.

Loans Guaranteed by the Veterans Administration
Eligibility

You are eligible for VA financing if your active military service falls within any of the following categories:

1. Wartime Service:
   World War II from 9-16-40 to 7-25-47
   Korean Conflict from 6-27-50 to 1-31-55
   Vietnam Era from 8-6-64 to 5-7-75
   You must have served at least ninety days of active duty and you must have been honorably discharged.
2. Peacetime Service:
   7-26-47 to 6-26-50
   2-1-55 to 8-4-64
   5-8-75 to 9-7-80 if enlisted or
   5-8-75 to 10-16-81 if an officer

You must have served for at least 181 days of continuous active duty and have been honorably discharged. Service after 7 September 1980 (enlisted) or 16 October 1981 (officer) must have completed twenty-four continuous months of active duty. Active duty service personnel must have served on continuous active status for at least 181 days, regardless of when your service began. Unmarried surviving spouses of eligible persons who died from service-connected injuries or a spouse of a service person listed as missing-in-action have certain types of eligibility. The Veterans Administration will send you several pamphlets with more information on your rights with just a phone call to your local office. They are there to serve the veteran and should be contacted with any questions.

The VA does not actually guarantee the entire loan amount. They do guarantee the "risk" portion, similar to FHA and conventional programs. The rules for your entitlement (or the amount of guaranty) change frequently so you should contact your local lender to see what the current rules are. Effective December 1989 the VA entitlement is calculated as follows:

The maximum amount of entitlement is currently the lesser of $46,000 or 25 percent of the loan when the loan amount exceeds $144,000. In addition, the following provisions apply:

1. For loans of $45,000 or less, 50 percent of the loan is guaranteed.
2. For loans of more than $45,000 and not more than $56,250, $22,500 of the loan is guaranteed.
3. For loans of more than $56,250 and not more than $144,000 the lesser of $36,000 or 40 percent of the loan is guaranted.
4. For loans of more than $144,000 made for the purchase or construction of a home or farm residence or to purchase a residential unit in a condominium, the lesser of $46,000 or 25 percent of the loan is guaranteed.

The average loan falls within the range of number 3. A loan of $80,000, for instance, would be guaranteed for 40 percent of the loan or $32,000. The risk portion (or $48,000) is the part that the lender has to worry about. In effect, the lender has only a 60 percent risk on this loan. Even though the veteran may not make any down payment on this loan, the lender can be assured that should the lender default, the risk is minimal, assuming that the lender verified all entitlement and eligibility and made a prudent underwriting decision.

There are many other regulations for veterans who have used their VA loan entitlement more than once but who may have remaining entitlement. These will have to be computed by your lender since the entitlement has increased over the past ten years and you may be eligible for a VA loan even though you have used one in the past. In addition, if you've had VA entitlement in the past and wish to have restoration of entitlement, you should contact a lender who will send the necessary paperwork to prove this to the VA office to get you started on your next VA loan.

The key to the VA loan is the Certificate of Eligibility issued to all veterans after 1955 with their discharge papers. This form must be included in the file and must be an "unconditional" certificate so your lender can approve your file in-house or as an automactic VA loan rather than taking the time to send the loan package to the local VA office for approval. If you're an eligible veteran, I'd suggest you deal only with a lender who has automatic VA loan approval authority. The VA encourages lenders to become approved, and you'll save yourself a great deal of time and many headaches dealing with the lender directly. In my opinion, if your lender is not VA automatic approved, they're not a full service lender.

If you don't have a Certificate of Eligibility, you can get one quite easily from your local VA office by submitting a request for one (VA #1880) along with your DD214 (your discharge papers) to the local VA office. Remember you may use your VA entitlement over and over or you may use your remaining entitlement if you've allowed someone to assume your old VA loan. You'll be issued a Certificate of Eligibility showing your remaining entitlement for the next home, especially if the entitlement has been increased. You may refinance your home if the interest rates fall using a new VA loan but you'll be limited to 90 percent of the value if you receive cash back. This is called a rate reduction refinance (RRR). You'll have to pay reasonable discount points and the closing costs but you may get a loan up to the value of the property or the payoff of the existing loan plus closing costs. You must have an existing lien to refinance your home regardless of the value. There are a few exceptions to the 90 percent limitation on a refinance. You may receive 100% refinancing if:

1. You refinance a construction loan.
2. You refinance an installment land sale contract.
3. You refinance an existing loan you assumed provided that the new VA loan is at an interest rate lower than that of the loan being refinanced.

The maximum term for a VA loan is thirty years, and the interest rate you pay, unlike FHA loans, is regulated by the VA regardless of the discount points paid by the seller or builder. Check with your local lender about the current rate and points. The loan doesn't have a prepayment penalty and the interest rate is fixed for the term of the loan; however, the loan-to-value ratio of 100 percent is the best feature of the VA loan.

Owner-occupancy is required on all purchase transactions. A no-cash-back refinance on nonveteran occupied property is allowed if the veteran previously occupied the residence. The veteran who is on active duty elsewhere temporarily is eligible if his family occupies the property.

Loan Guaranty Funding Fee

Like the mortgage insurance premium on an FHA loan, the VA funding fee may be financed or paid in cash at the closing. The VA funding fee is temporarily increased as follows until 1 October 1991:

1. The basic funding fee is 1.875 percent with less than a 5 percent down payment.
2. 1.375 percent funding fee for purchase or construction loans with a down payment of at least 5 percent but less than 10 percent of the purchase price.
3. 1.125 percent funding fee for purchase or construction loans with a down payment of 10 percent or more of the purchase price.
4. .5 percent funding fee for assumptions.
5. 1.875 percent funding fee on refinances.

The funding fee is a percentage of the loan amount.

Exhibit 4: VA Funding Fee Example

Value (lesser of the sales price or appraised value)

$80,000
x 1.875% (with no down payment)
─────────
$1,500

Loan amount $80,000 plus VA funding fee $1,500 equals
Loan $81,500 (the only time the loan amount can exceed the value)

The VA funding fee is a one-time fee sent to VA with no refund upon repayment of the loan. Closing costs may be paid by the seller or the buyer according to local custom determined by the regional VA office, and discount points on a purchase must be paid by the seller except on a refinance. The funding fee may be waived for a veteran who receives certain types of service-related disability benefits. Your lender will have you sign a form that is used to determine if your fee may be waived and to verify that you don't owe any money to VA or to any federal agency for previously defaulted loans or educational benefits.

Assumability

Loans made before 1 March 1988 are fully assumable. If a release of liability was not granted by the VA at the assumption the veteran is liable for the original VA loan. If the VA suffers no loss because of a default of an assumptor, you'll never be notified. However, if the VA suffers a loss of money on a default, they'll attempt to notify you for repayment of the loss. If they're unable to contact you the loss doesn't go away! Your next credit report will probably reveal this loss and you'll have to make amends with the VA. You, the veteran, are at risk on any default or loss incurred by the VA upon foreclosure of anyone who assumes your VA loan unless you obtain a release of liability from the VA. There are new collection procedures adopted by the VA, and you will now be notified on each new VA loan what your responsibilities are and what collection attempts will be made. A veteran or nonveteran who assumes your loan now will be required to qualify for the loan with the regional office and pay the .5 percent funding fee (assumption fee). That's the bad part. The good part is that the veteran will receive a release of liability if the assumptor is proven to be creditworthy and his or her VA eligibility will be reinstated. Veterans who have used their VA loans prior to 1 March 1988 may have their entitlement limited by any VA loans assumed by others.

Property Requirements

The VA guarantees single family and two-to-four-family properties as long as the veteran occupies one of the units. For two-to-four-family properties, the rents received from the other units may be used to qualify the veteran only if he has a history of being a successful landlord in the past. The VA issues a Certificate of Reasonable Value (CRV) completed by a staff VA appraiser. The appraisal method has changed recently, but the end result, the CRV, remains the same. Only the procedure for preparing the CRV has changed, and it should now take less time to complete the loan application process.

The VA has many of the same minimum property standards as the FHA. They require that plans for new construction be approved by the VA prior to the start of construction or they'll convert an FHA appraisal to a CRV upon request, with limitations.

The VA has the same health and safety requirements as the FHA, (see page 59 for those requirements) and the VA property requirements vary by region. Both the FHA and the VA do not issue actual appraisals, they issue estimates of value based on comparable home sales in the area. If your VA estimate of value (CRV) is lower than the sales price, you may still use the VA loan but you must pay the difference between the value and the sales price in cash from your own funds.

Credit Analysis

The lender will order the same residential mortgage credit report for the VA loan package as for the FHA loan. The report will include two years history of employment and residences, legal searches for the most recent seven years, ratings on all open

FHA procedure. A pattern of late payments won't be acceptable, but isolated late payments can be explained by the veteran. One full year of acceptable credit is required, with some exceptions. The VA accepts the absence of a credit history for veterans recently discharged or for veterans who show enough assets.

Bankruptcy

As mentioned in the FHA credit section on page 62, *filing* for protection under the bankruptcy laws is different than being *discharged*. Filing is the start of the process; the discharge is the court approval. For lending purposes the date of the discharge is important.

A bankruptcy discharged over two to three years ago need only be explained in writing by the veteran. Bankruptcies over five years ago should not be considered by the underwriter. Some lenders are more conservative and you should expect to explain all derogatory credit. A Chapter 13 wage earner's bankruptcy may be acceptable when repaid or even when in the payout period if at least three-fourths of the debt has been repaid satisfactorily and the court approves the new credit.

Collections

Paid collections must be adequately explained. A history of collections will adversely affect the credit history portion of your file. Collections paid in exchange for loan approval are unacceptable. If you feel strongly that a bill shouldn't have been referred to a collection agency, pay the bill and contact legal counsel or seek restitution in small claims court *after* the mortgage loan closes. Collections can be future liens against property and earnings so I'd suggest that you not let a disagreement in the purchase of a small item affect your qualifying for a mortgage loan.

Residual Income

The VA uses a two-tier system of loan approval: a residual income requirement outlined below and a 41 percent ratio. Residuals and ratios are not the only determining factors in the approval process. A VA automatic underwriter (the lender's employee) may approve the loan with a ratio in excess of 41 percent, if she can justify the reasons for approval in writing and enlist a second opinion from her supervisor. The following table of residuals was in effect 1 January 1990, but may be changed according to cost-of-living figures released every few years:

Exhibit 5: Residual Income by Region

For Loan Amounts of $70,000 and Above

Family Size	Northeast	Midwest	South	West
1	$401	$393	$393	$437
2	673	658	658	733
3	810	792	792	882
4	913	893	893	995
5	946	925	925	1031

For Loan Amounts of $69,999 and Below

Family Size	Northeast	Midwest	South	West
1	343	340	340	379
2	583	570	570	635
3	702	687	687	765
4	791	773	773	861
5	821	803	803	894

Note: For families with more than five members, add seventy dollars for each additional member up to a family of seven.

Income Stability

The VA requires that all income be verified and included if it's likely that it will be received in the foreseeable future. Lenders have used the two year history as a guideline to prove continuous income. All of your employers within the past two years will receive a verfication of employment form from the lender, which they must return for your file. Certain types of military pay are subject to review periodically and usually are not considered. Income from service in the reserves may be used if a past history exists. Service records and letters from commanding officers will help to prove continuous income.

Conventional Loans

Since this category includes loans sold to FNMA, FHLMC and other investors, the guidelines may vary greatly by lender. I've found the biggest differences occur because of the loose interpretation of the guidelines. Manuals distributed by FNMA and FHLMC contain some general information with specifics on qualifying ratios and loan-to-value ratios. A low loan-to-value ratio will be approached more leniently than other loans.

There aren't actual limits for conventional loans; it's up to the investor. Many lenders deal in jumbo loans, loans over the following limits, but FNMA and FHLMC do set limits on the loans they'll purchase:

Exhibit 6: FNMA and FHLMC Maximum Loans

	Continental U.S.	Alaska and Hawaii
One Units	$191,250	$286,875
Two Units	244,650	366,975
Three Units	285,650	443,475
Four Units	367,500	558,250

Generally, all conventional loans conform to similar underwriting guidelines. The maximum loan is determined by the type of loan and the occupancy. Below is a summary of the current loans available, but like all guidelines, changes are occuring constantly—be sure to check with your lender for specific changes.

Maximum Number of Properties Financed

FNMA recently changed the rules on the number of mortgages a borrower may have, and most conventional lenders have conformed to these rules. If you're purchasing an owner occupied property no limitations exist on the number of properties you may own that have mortgages. If you're buying a second home or aren't going to occupy the property, you may own only four properties that are currently being financed, including your principal residence, for the loan to be eligible to be sold on the secondary market. Some lenders don't sell on this market, so you might ask your loan officer; it's only relevant if you don't intend to occupy the property and you own other properties.

Loan-to-Value Ratios

The loan-to-value limits set by FNMA and FHLMC are used as guidelines for most conventional loans. *Value* for the purpose of determining the loan-to-value ratio, or LTV, is defined as the lower of the sales price or the appraised value of the property. For refinancing property purchased over a year prior to application, the loan-to-value is based upon the appraised value. On property purchased less than one year ago (or where the borrower has held title to a lien-free property less than one year), the LTV ratio should be based upon the lesser of the current appraised value or the original value. Secondary financing or a seller carryback is allowed if the total loan-to-value does not exceed 90 percent and the first does not exceed 75 percent LTV.

Exhibit 7: FNMA Maximum Loan-to-Value Ratios

Category	One Family Fixed Rate (%)	One Family ARM (%)	Two Family Fixed Rate (%)	Two Family ARM (%)	Three-Four Family Fixed Rate (%)	Three-Four Family ARM (%)
Owner-occupied purchase	95	90	90	90	80	80
Nonowner-occupied purchase	70	–	70	–	70	–
Owner-occupied refinance with cash-out	75	75	75	75	75	75
Owner-occupied refinance with no cash out	90	90	90	90	80	80
Second home purchase	80	80	–	–	–	–
Second home refinance with no cash out	70	70	–	–	–	–
Nonowner-occupied refinance with no cash out	70	–	70	–	70	–
Nonpermanent resident alien	75	75	75	75	75	75

Exhibit 8: FHLMC Maximum Loan-to-Value Ratios

	One-Unit Property (%)	ARM	Two-Unit Property (%)	Three-to-Four-Unit Property (%)
Owner-occupied	95	90	80	80
FXD	–		–	–
Owner-occupied refinance with cash out	75		75	75
Owner-occupied refinance with no cash out	90		80	80
Second home purchase	80			
Second home refinance with no cash out	70			

Sales Concessions, or Contributions by the Seller

Contributions by the seller include additional monies paid to reduce the interest rate of the loan, as well as payments by the seller of any other fees that would normally be paid by the buyer. FNMA and FHLMC require that any other incentive contributions, such as furniture, decorator allowances, or other "giveaways" always be deducted in full from the value before calculating the loan-to-value ratio. Contributions from the borrower's relatives or employers are not considered in the limits. If the employer contributes an advance against future earnings, the obligation must be considered as a debt when qualifying.

Exhibit 9: Seller Contribution Limits
(in percent of the value of the home)

	FNMA			FHLMC	
	75% or less LTV	75%-90% LTV	90% or more LTV	Less than 90% LTV	More than 90% LTV
Owner-occupied and second homes	9%	6%	3%	6%	3%

Private Mortgage Insurance

Most lenders require that loans with a loan-to-value ratio in excess of 80 percent be insured by a private mortgage insurance company (MI). There are many such companies, such as Mortgage Guaranty Insurance Corporation or MGIC, commonly called MAGIC. As a matter of fact, loans over 80 percent LTV were commonly called MAGIC loans when the program was first announced. Many other private mortgage companies exist, but your lender may be limited to the companies approved by FNMA or FHLMC, if they sell their loans on the secondary market. Though you may not have much say in the choice of a company, you should expect your loan officer to shop for the best rates within their list of approved companies. You'll pay for one year's mortgage insurance policy at the closing and will pay the lender for the next year's premium monthly with your taxes and fire insurance. The protection required varies by investor, with rates for the first year ranging from 1 percent of the loan amount to 0.25 percent of the loan amount and renewal rates of 0.5 percent to 0.25 percent of the loan amount depending on the loan-to-value, on the term (thirty year or fifteen year), on the rate (fixed or nonfixed, with or without negative amortization), on the coverage required in your area, and finally, on the payment of the premium, either paid in cash at closing or financed along with the loan. If you're purchasing an owner-occupied property with a loan-to-value ratio of 90 percent or less, you may finance the premium, up to 95 percent LTV, and the fees are slightly higher due to the increased risk. Your lender may choose a mortgage insurance company who specializes in your area or your type of home so be prepared to ask what coverage is required before you prequalify yourself. The monthly premium, if not financed, or the increased loan amount due to the addition of the mortgage insurance premium will result in a larger monthly payment, which needs to be considered when determining the amount of down payment you make. Below is an example of a calculation using current rates.

(Remember this insurance protects the lender from a loss should you default on your loan and has nothing to do with fire or hazard insurance, which protects *you* from damage to the home, or with mortgage life insurance, which protects your family in case of your death by paying off the mortgage.)

Exhibit 10: Example of Mortgage Insurance Premium

$72,000 loan amount with a LTV of 90 percent
Fixed rate loan with thirty-year term
First year's premium paid up-front with closing costs:
    $72,000 x 0.55% = $396
Renewal premium:
    $72,000 x 0.35% = $252 divided by 12 = $21 monthly
    (Until the loan is paid to 80 percent LTV)

Property Requirements

Conventional investors buy loans secured by one-to-four family residences, second homes, or condominiums in approved projects. There are no limitations on loan limits for new construction or homes under construction as with the FHA and the VA. The appraisal is done by an independent appraiser or a staff appraiser who is responsible for preparing an appraisal that meets the lender's guidelines. Fortunately, guidelines for conventional investors are more consistent than with FHA and VA. The investor relies on the underwriter to review and accept the appraisal and to approve the property as well as the borrower. Loans may be secured by properties in urban, suburban or rural areas that are residential in nature. Investors don't normally purchase loans secured by agricultural-type properties (generally over 5 acres or income-producing land, farm land), undeveloped lands (raw land) or lands with commercial zoning or use. All properties must be readily accessible by roads that meet local standards and are maintained year-round by a public entity or by agreement of the landowners through a private road maintainence agreement recorded and executed by all parties. Areas that are less than 25 percent developed are not eligible for maximum financing (90 to 95 percent LTV). Properties must meet local health and safety codes and improvements must constitute a legally permissible use of the land.

Credit Requirements

Conventional investors rely on the same residential mortgage credit report and evaluate credit using much the same criteria as FHA and VA. A written explanation of all slow payment is required, undisclosed debts must be explained, collections must be paid and explained, the report must contain a two year history of employment and residency, and legal records must be checked for the past seven years. Recent (within the last one to two years) discharges of bankruptcy are only acceptable with excellent re-established credit and a logical reason. For loans in excess of 90 percent LTV, the borrower must not have any credit card payments sixty days or more past due and no more than two payments thirty days past due over the past twelve months. Installment debts (autos, furniture accounts with fixed payments) should have no payments sixty days or more past due and no more than one payment thirty days past due over the past twelve months. The borrower who has a previous mortgage loan should have no payments past due at all over the past twelve months. Credit requirements are somewhat more lenient for loans of 90 percent LTV or less, but all negative credit must be well explained.

Income Stability

Employment verifications are required, though any acceptable source of income verification may be used as long as it indicates past and current earnings for the last two years and a year-to-date figure. Many lenders will accept current paystubs, within thirty days of the loan application, and two years W-2's as verification. All types of income including wages must be proven to be continuous for the past two years with a probability of continuation for the next three years. Overtime, bonuses, and commission earnings will be averaged and any lapses of employment of over one month must be explained. Tax returns should be included when secondary income exceeds 25 percent of the total income. Changes of jobs or occupation within the past two years will affect the impression of job stability, and self-employment income must be continuous and adequate for two full years. Tax returns for the past two years and a current financial statement (within ninety days) will be required. For lower LTV's, self-employed income over one year but less than two is acceptable, as long as the occupation prior to self-employment makes sense: a computer salesman who opens a computer store or supply center for example. Since the loan limits are higher than on the government programs, different types of self-employed, commissioned earnings are common and acceptable with most conventional lenders. The larger the down payment, the easier you will find qualifying for these types of loans.

Buyer and Seller Fees

Closing costs may be paid by the seller or the buyer, subject to the limitations previously mentioned in this chapter. Prepaids or impounds for taxes, fire, and mortgage insurance must be paid by the buyer, as well as the down payment within the limitations for loan-to-value ratios. A gift letter from a relative for all but 5 percent of the down payment is allowed for all LTV's 80 percent or over.

Reduced Documentation, Timesaver and Timesaver Plus

Many lenders have programs that allow for reduced or no documentation, depending on the LTV. For most lenders the qualifications vary, but generally there are two programs allowed by FNMA and FHLMC. Alternative documentation programs (*timesaver*) simply mean that instead of actual mailed verifications of employment and deposit you may provide your lender with paystubs and W-2's for employment verification as long as your employment is verified on the credit report and three months of bank statements to prove your assets available for closing.

Timesaver plus (sometimes called *no income, no qualifier*) program by FNMA is popular now, but is restricted to owner-occupied properties with an LTV of 70 percent or less. Income is verified by the credit agency and appears on the residential credit report and three months of bank statements prove your assets.

Secondary income is more difficult to prove and the underwriter has the option of requiring either additional documentation to prove it, such as tax returns, financial statements, etc., or a statement from the borrower, depending on the type of income. With a down payment of 30 percent, guidelines are sometimes very flexible!

These types of programs are great for those who have more money for a down payment and want a speedy loan. Check with your lender about their individual requirements—this type of loan may be for you.

These guidelines and requirements for all three of the typical loan programs change regularly, and for each guideline there is generally an exception allowed somewhere by some lender. So ask your lender how their program might fit your particular needs. For instance, ask what the minimum down payment is for a particular type of property, type of income, type of asset to use for a down payment, etc. If you've had credit problems, order a credit report through your lender before you even shop to see just what the problem is. Work with your lender and know the questions to ask to avoid suprises when you're well into the transaction. Your loan officer should be able to answer most of your questions or should be willing and able to find the answers for you. This book covers the basics that every loan officer should know, allowing for the variations of particular lender requirements.

Assumability

Most conventional lenders who sell their loans on the secondary market allow for loans to be assumed by qualified borrowers only on adjustable rate loans (ARMS), and then only if the borrower pays an assumption fee and is qualified with a complete credit package. Fixed rate conventional loans are generally not assumable, and many lenders have provisions for acceleration of the loan should a nonauthorized transfer of ownership occur. Of course, portfolio loans, jumbo loans and other loans not traded can have provisions limited only by local laws. Check with your lender on your conventional loan assumability.

Prepayment Penalty

Prepayment penalties are not common for conventional loans originated within the past several years, but they do exist for some conventional lenders, especially for jumbo loans or loans on commercial or non-conforming properties. For this feature on an unusual type of loan, you'll have to check with your lender up front. Generally, loans sold to FNMA or FHLMC don't contain a prepayment penalty clause.

Chapter

The Loan Interview and Application

How to Prepare, What to Expect

If you have prequalified yourself, have chosen a lender, have chosen a home in your price range, and have chosen a program that fits your needs, you're ready to meet with your loan officer to apply for the loan. This is really a preapplication or interview, and you should expect privacy, information, and assurances (preferably in writing) about the features of the loan you have chosen. You're already well informed if you've read the previous sections and used the worksheets to answer your own questions about prequalifying and about the programs that best fit your needs. In the appendix I've included a checklist of what to bring and what to ask. This is going to be a brief interview to complete the application and to let the loan officer know what you want. Bring the checklist with you to the interview. Your goal is to prepare for the interview so you can avoid follow-up requests for information and delays in processing. This is the number one complaint today of loan applicants. In so many cases, homeowners felt that they were harassed needlessly for more and more information. They were asked to bring in or required to copy, call, or follow up with additional forms they should have known to bring with them. If your loan officer doesn't mention an item or request some information that you think you may need, ask about it or bring it anyway. Ask to meet in a conference room or in the loan officer's office if it is other than a cubbyhole with partitions. You want the complete attention of the loan officer and you want the interview to be quick and thorough. You shouldn't be expected to reveal your most personal financial information within earshot of the entire office. You should not be interrupted by phone calls or messages, and you should take notes on everything that the loan officer says to protect yourself later. Notes well taken can settle discrepancies in fees and costs later. I once took an application while the borrowers taped the interview—talk about strain!

Commitments for a lock-in of the interest rate or points must be in writing and the expiration date should be logical. Allow yourself at least an hour for the loan inteview, including questions and explanations. This is the major purchase of your life; it should not be hurried or incomplete. Remember, you only want to have to see the loan officer once, no matter how nice they are.

Bring with you all the documents mentioned on the checklist that apply to your transaction and ask the loan officer if you need any others. Don't offer any information over and above financial questions asked and don't embellish on any of the answers. There are many protected areas; your marital status (except where it affects your ability to repay the debt, such as child support due, etc.), your age, sex, religion, receipt of public assistance, and child bearing information can and will not be considered on your loan application. Your loan officer will avoid any of those topics. Don't bring relatives or friends with you except those directly involved in the transaction. You'll be sharing with them more financial information than you had intended, or you won't give a complete application and follow-up information will be necessary.

One section of the loan application requests personal information (race, sex, etc.), the same information that your loan officer cannot ask. The federal government *can* ask for this information, for "government monitoring purposes" only. You may answer the questions regarding your ethnic background or you may initial that you prefer not to share that information.

Expect to receive a copy of everything you've signed, and don't sign any blank forms, with the exception of the verifications of deposit and employment, which will be completed later and mailed. Remember, this interview will provide preliminary information that will be verified, so estimate your income and assets as closely as possible.

The Loan Application Forms

Included in the appendix are sample forms used in the typical interview. Complete the form for you and your spouse prior to going to the interview and you may save everyone a lot of time. Ask the loan officer to accept this generic form for the application. If you're buying the home with someone that you have shared a home with before, have shared credit accounts, and have shared bank accounts, you may use one application for both of you. If you keep separate finances, use two separate forms for each person. If relatives will co-borrow to help you qualify, ask them to complete separate applications. The forms that most lenders use for your loan package are the same, though they may be personalized with logos or letterheads. The basic forms used that you need to be concerned with are:

1. An all-purpose residential loan application form #1003 used for the interview on all loans, FHA, VA, and conventional, and also used as the final application for conventional loans.
2. The FHA/VA final loan application, which contains some finely printed legal information about your rights and obligations. Read the fine print before you go for your loan interview and ask your loan officer about any part you

don't understand. The areas of interest are highlighted in the appendix after each form.
3. The FHA appraisal (conditional commitment). You'll receive a copy of this form from your lender and, again, you should read the fine print ahead of time.
4. The uniform residential appraisal report (URAR), the all-purpose appraisal report used for FHA, VA, and conventional appraisals. If you have paid for the report you may request a copy; however, the lender may not release a copy to you and is not required to do so.

What to Bring and Say — What Not to Bring and Say

You'll be expected to identify yourself, especially on an FHA loan but many prudent lenders require identification on all loans. Bring your driver's license (the original to copy), your social security card (the original to copy) or two pieces of identification that show your picture and your social security number. The Department of Motor Vehicles in most states issues identification cards just for this purpose. Employment badges with your picture, school ID or other ID will be helpful. Your W-2's and paystubs will help verify your social security number. Do not bring mounds of paperwork, do not bring your "beeper," do not bring your relatives, children, pets, boyfriend/girlfriend (unless they are involved financially), realtor, or anyone else who will distract you from the main purpose of this loan interview. Try not to offer stories or advice off the subject and discourage your loan interviewer from doing the same.

The Residential Mortgage Loan Application Checklist

I've included a checklist in the appendix to assist you in preparing for the loan application. This is your opportunity to ask questions, so you should read all the items to determine what you should ask and what you should bring with you to the interview, according to your particular situation. Allow ample time for this application, it's very important to do it right the first time to avoid follow-up questions by the loan officer or loan processor.

You should review the list regarding what to ask about your particular loan type and some of the variables that you may need to consider. Although your loan officer should compare a fixed rate loan to an ARM loan for you just to give you an idea of the benefits of both, often times you need to ask, particularly during a low-interest rate market. You should ask about all the different options from the list anyway to see if you're getting the best loan for you—that's what shopping is all about. I'm afraid that most loan officers rely on the same common products because they're more familiar with the guidelines. Let your loan officer know that you want the best available and ask that he do the research necessary to find that for you. Just asking the questions on the checklist will put him on notice that you've done your homework and he'll respond with more information and programs to compare. This is going to take time, but after all you have to pay on this loan for thirty years (actually the average length of a mortgage loan is more like three to five years because we're such a mobile society). I may be prejudiced on this subject but I feel that most mortgage brokers take the time and effort to learn their products and will shop better for you because they have access to many lenders and many programs. They also are not distracted by the requirements of the employees of large lenders and can devote more time and service to your file. Consider the services of a mortgage broker if there are some available in your area. We use an insurance broker for our insurance needs, a real estate broker for our housing needs, and we may in the future use a loan or mortgage broker for all our financing needs.

The Property Appraisal (Or, It's Worth What?!!)

The conventional appraisal (URAR), the FHA estimate of value (Conditional Commitment), and the VA certificate of value (CRV) will be received and reviewed, or underwritten, by the underwriter during the approval process. You don't have much control over this process. If there are some repairs indicated, you may have to negotiate with the seller to complete the repairs according to any dollar limit written into the original contract. Ask for a copy of the repairs indicated, if any, so you can check that they're completed to your satisfaction when you do the final walk-thru of the property. Remember, we're stressing that you have control over this transaction. Expect items to be repaired prior to closing.

All three loan programs rely most on the comparable sales data approach, or market approach, to arrive at the value, though they also use the cost approach for new and previously owned single family property. In addition, they will include the income approach to the estimate of value for nonowner-occupied properties or for properties that are located in primarily rental areas. With a market approach, the appraiser chooses three or more other sales in the same or a similar (comparable) area, typically sales that used other types of financing or cash sales, and sales that occured within the last six months. The appraiser adjusts the value of the comparables by adding or subtracting amenities. If a similar home has several hundred square feet more living area, a per foot adjustment may be subtracted from its sales price, assuming that it sold for more because it was a bit larger; now it compares more closely with the sales price of the subject property. A larger patio, another bedroom, more kitchen equipment, larger lot size, better landscaping; these all require adjustments to value. All three comparables, after they are adjusted, will be considered when arriving at the final value of the subject property.

The appraisal will also indicate all the factors that give value to the home: the adequacy of utilities, public transportation, schools, shopping, and other neighborhood factors that could increase or decrease the value of your home. The appraiser will note any indication of changes in the use of the property; a change from residential to multifamily, for instance, may be a negative factor if this property ever needs to be resold as a single family residence. Any functional obsolescence will be noted; some people make improvements or build additions to their own individual needs without regard to the resale value. A dining room add-on without immediate access to the kitchen or a bedroom addition with access through another room rather than a hallway would be less desirable to future buyers, and the value may be decreased accordingly. A common problem in subdivisions is the conversion of a garage, detached or attached, to a family room, den, etc., without local permits and without proper insulation, fire doors, or other local code requirements. Your appraiser may note the problem, and if local codes are violated by this addition, corrections may have to be made by the seller, escpecially on an FHA or VA loan.

Finally, the appraiser will note any repairs other than cosmetic (lawns, minor fence problems) that need to be completed for the final value. Your survey, ordered along with the title commitment at the opening of escrow, or the plat map, included with your preliminary title report, should also disclose any violations in the use of the property. A garage built within a set-back line needs to be noted so you're aware of the violation and can expect the seller to correct the situation. (Set-back lines are restrictions on building right up to a fence or lot line. If you have to go on your neighbor's land to paint the side of your garage, you've built too close!) You'll get a copy of the survey and title commitment in some states or the preliminary title report with the same information in other states. Read the information to determine how it might affect you and your transaction. Ask questions of your title or cscrow officer if you don't understand some item on the reports, and expect a complete answer *prior* to signing anything.

If the appraised value is lower than the sales price, you may have a problem. Since the loan amount is based on the lesser of the sales price or the appraised value, you may have to increase the down payment. Your only recourse in the case of a low appraised value is to work with your realtor to obtain some additional comparable sales in the area which, when adjusted, will help to reflect a higher value. Work with your loan officer and realtor to present this new information to the appraiser. Most will look at their appraisal again or, at the least, will review the new information and give you a reconsideration of value, hopefully higher than before. If the appraised value means money out of your pocket, you should be involved in it and not simply take the word of the lender. Your sellers certainly have an interest in this appraisal, and you may enlist their help to encourage the lender to look again at the appraised value. Your underwriter may have the authority to increase or decrease the value indicated on the appraisal with enough documentation to support the decision. Make sure that you ask your loan officer, realtor, or seller to provide that information to the underwriter. Your realtor has the best access to sales information in the neighborhood and I would put her to work on it immediately. This might also work to your advantage in some cases, you may approach the seller with an adjustment in the sales price if your contract has a clause that you won't pay over the appraised value. The point is, this is *your* transaction and you have to be on top of it at all times.

Creditworthiness (Or It's in the Mail!)

The analysis of the residential credit report will start with a comparison to your original application, especially the information on employment history and residences. Any differences must be explained. Your credit report takes three to five days to prepare unless you've moved from another area or county. Legal searches must be conducted in all the counties that you've resided in for the last two years and may add a few days to the process. During this process *don't* change your credit status if it can be avoided. Hold off on major purchases (don't buy that living room furniture yet!), paying major bills, trading your car in or applying for new credit. If you do buy something major or pay off some large bill, get and keep a copy of the receipt or any paperwork involved. Your credit reporting agency may not be able to verify the transaction while the paperwork is being processed and this could cause a delay. Cancelled checks sometimes take weeks to get from the bank, and written proof may be required for the file. If you qualify for a loan based on a paid auto loan, then you'll have to provide written proof that it's paid. Simply mailing a check to the lender doesn't prove anything. You can see the problem; just remember not to make any major credit changes during the mortgage transaction. You can go crazy with credit after the closing!

Credit Problems

Avoiding credit problems is easier said than done. I know, I've been there; almost everyone has! The only advice I can offer is that you should attempt to prepare for this major purchase by keeping your payments current, particularly for the year prior to the loan application. You've probably had to concentrate on saving money for this purchase—give your credit the same concentration. Don't neglect to make each and every payment on time and make every attempt to resolve credit disputes *before* they result in collection procedures. Most frustrating are the credit problems that aren't even yours and that will haunt you now. We paid for an unjustified veterinary bill caused by a neighbor's dog to keep our credit rating because we didn't have much else going for us but credit! We also ate peanut butter sandwiches and gave up all the luxuries for what seemed like an eternity. It was a small price to pay for the security and satisfaction of owning our own small piece of this earth!

As I stated before, lack of credit is not necessarily a problem. If you've paid rent (other than to relatives) or utilities on time, proof that you've met these obligations in a timely manner can be credit. Start now to keep all receipts for everything. Save those cancelled checks, keep your bank statements, paystubs, and all your tax returns for every year.

Credit Reporting and Your Rights

The Fair Credit Reporting Act of 1971 establishes your right to know what's in your credit file and to challenge whatever information you believe to be inaccurate. Any negative information can remain in your report for up to seven years, and bankruptcies are reported for ten years. Negative information about you that is wrong needs to be corrected no matter how minor it seems. You should request a copy of your credit report and respond to the information with documentation and an explanation of the circumstances. Keeping cancelled checks can be a pain but they just might be your proof that a bill was paid on time throughout the term of the loan. At the least, keep those bank statements; they are also good proof that you have received income or paid bills on time. Follow up to make sure that your credit report is correct and any incorrect information has been removed. Your credit history is almost as important as your income in the loan analysis and should be preserved for future purchases.

Types of Acceptable Income
Wage Earners

Your income will be verified by a form (a Verification of Employment or VOE) sent to your current employer requesting income totals for the last two years and asking when you started, what you do, and what are the chances you will be around awhile (likelihood of continuance). This form is sent directly to your employer or all of your employers for the last two years, and your loan officer will ask that you bring your most recent paystubs and your W-2's for the last two years. The form for verification may not be hand-carried by you or your realtor, so you cannot help with this process. If you've changed jobs recently, your current income can be used as long as there is a history of like employment in the same or a similar field. You may have to wait until your probationary period is over to expect the lender to consider this new job as permanent. Problems arise when your income, though sufficient to repay this debt, is from sources other than normal, verifiable wages. Below are some common types of income and the documentation you may need to prove it.

Overtime

Two years history is required for overtime and the employer must check the appropriate boxes on the Verification of Employment stating that it is expected to continue. You'll need two years W-2's, year-to-date paystubs, including paystubs for last year to separate base wages from overtime, and this type of income must be logical for your type of employment. Overtime from a new job will not be counted since the history doesn't exist. All overtime will be averaged over the period of verification.

Second Job

The job history is critical to the use of income from a second job. If you start a new second job to qualify for the loan, the income won't be counted as you have no history of being able to handle two jobs. A two year history is required, along with a verification of employment, paystubs and W-2's.

Bonuses and Commission Income

Both of these types of income require two full years history, though job changes with the same or an increased amount of commission is common and acceptable in the same field. Bonus income is normally received by employees who have been with the company for more than one year and may only be used when common for your field of employment. Your bonus and commissions will be averaged for a two year period. You must supply paystubs and W-2's, and the Verification of Employment received by the lender from your employer must indicate that your bonuses or commissions are expected to continue.

If you claim expenses related to commission income on your tax returns (meals, travel, dues, publications, etc.), be prepared to provide a copy of your last two years tax returns as well as a profit and loss statement for the period from your last tax return showing current income and expenses from this type of income. Your net income will then be used for qualifying. This type of income is in a gray area; you are not quite self-employed but you have more employee expenses than other wage earners. If you haven't claimed any expenses over the normal commute and entertainment expenses associated with your job, just write up a statement to that effect and include it instead of a profit and loss statement as an additional certification. You may be asked to do this later, so include it now.

Tips and Gratuities

Persons employed in the service industry may use all the tips that are reported on their tax returns. Two years of tax returns will be required and the tips will be averaged. W-2's, paystubs and tax returns for the last two years will be required to prove tip income.

Interest and Dividends

This income is relatively easy to prove and perfectly acceptable. A verification of deposit form will be sent to the depository (bank) or the broker who handles your portfolio to verify that the assets still exist, proving the continuance of the interest or dividends. Nontaxable interest or dividends may be included if indicated on the tax return. A history of receipt for at least one year is required. If you haven't reported this type of income yet on a tax return, bring in the statements you have received indicating the interest and dividends earned. This will prove the assets as well as the income. Make sure you are not using these same assets (CD's, stocks, bonds) for the close of this transaction, since the income can't be included if the asset is gone.

Note Receivable Income

If you sold something (property, a business) and received a note payable to you monthly, the income may be included if proven on the last two year's tax returns, and if there are three years of monthly payments remaining or five years for the FHA. You must prove that the payments have been made for the last year, and you must include a copy of the note and security instrument or agreement in your file.

Real Estate Income

If you receive rents from other real estate, your lender will ask you to complete a *Schedule of Real Estate Owned* (a copy is included in the appendix) showing the mortgages on these properties, the payments for these mortgages as well as the other expenses (taxes, insurance, maintainence, rental costs, etc.), and the income received for each property. The mortgages against your properties will be verified and a credit history obtained using a verification of mortgage loan form sent to the individual lenders. The net income will be added to your total income or the net loss will be included in your qualifying ratios. The lender starts with the monthly rent for all your properties less a vacancy factor (7-15 percent on FHA loans, depending on the area, and 25 percent for conventional) and deducts the mortgage payment, property taxes, insurance, and the other costs of maintaining the property. If you own more than eight to ten investment properties, your lender may rely on your tax return analysis (see Self Employed Tax Analysis in the appendix) for net rental income, and you may be required to provide two years tax returns to support your income from rentals. The lender may send several verification of mortgage loan forms as a sampling of your credit or may rely on the credit information provided on your credit report. If you've bought and sold properties during the last two years, include a statement showing the dates and properties to help clarify the returns. Also, your capital gains or losses may be included in your income if you have regularly bought and sold assets (property or equipment) for the past two to three years. The capital gains claimed on your tax returns and averaged over three years may increase your allowable income and help to qualify you for this new transaction. Like all other income, you have to prove it to use it! There are limitations to the number of FHA, VA and conventional loans and properties you may own, so be prepared to provide tax returns as proof of the number of your properties.

Child Support and Alimony

The same income criteria applies to child support as all other types of income. You must have received it for the last two years and it must continue for three more years, five years for the FHA. The divorce decree showing property settlement and obligations will prove that the child support is owing, but now comes the hard part. It's not always easy to *prove* the income. You may have to get copies of the cancelled checks from the payer, hopefully a cooperative ex-spouse, or you may have bank statements that clearly show the check deposited each month. If the income to be used is 25 percent of your total income, some conventional underwriters require that the payer submit a letter of intent as further proof. Be sure to bring the entire divorce papers to eliminate any questions.

Alimony is acceptable with the same guidelines as child support, though it is somewhat easier to prove. Your tax returns will show the amount you have received and reported to the IRS. The divorce papers, proof that the payments have been received, and a letter of intent from the payer if the income is more than 25 percent of your total income will probably be required. Unlike child support, alimony is rarely considered more than a compensating factor since its continuance is dependent on a payer without the incentive of providing for children. If it's been received for two full years and you can document that it will continue for three more years for conventional and VA guidelines, and five years for FHA, include it.

VA Benefits

Only VA benefits other than educational can be included. The two year history applies to this type of income as well, unless the veteran was recently retired or disabled. This must be documented with a copy of the letter or distribution form issued by the VA. The remaining years of this income must be clearly stated by the VA and it must continue for three years for conventional and VA guidelines and five years for FHA. The VA can help you prove this income. Also, disability income from the VA will exempt you from paying the VA funding fee charged on VA loans. Normal service retirement income does not count for this exemption.

Unemployment or Public Assistance Income

Both of these types of income are acceptable to the FHA as long as this income is proven to be continuous for five years. The VA considers unemployment as a compensating factor more than as allowable income. Conventional guidelines do not specifically address this income, and it's very difficult to allow as on-going for qualifying purposes unless it can be proven to be continuous in nature. Both of these types of income are temporary by nature and should not be included as a major source of income for qualifying purposes.

Unemployment income may be used in trade-type employment (carpenters, construction workers in regions where weather is a factor) or seasonal employees who have a history of unemployment. It must be logical for the type of employment, tax returns must prove this type of income, and it must be averaged over a two year history. I am reminded of the person who groomed ski slopes in the winter, fought fires in the summer and collected unemployment for the few weeks in between.

Public assistance may be considered as income when it will continue. If it's received due to a permanent disability, for instance, and proof is provided, it may well be included. Aid to Dependent Children depends on the age and number of children and also on the other income of the recipient. Using this as the basis for the repayment of a thirty year mortgage loan debt is difficult but allowable. You will need to provide proof from the payer (city, county, state) that the amount is continuous for three to five years.

Trust Income

A letter from the trustee of the estate or the attorney that handles the trust must be included to determine the amount of the distribution to the applicant and the frequency of the payments. If this is over 25 percent of your income, tax returns will be required. A two year history is necessary except for a newly formed trust. Three years of remaining income from the trust is required for conventional and VA loans, with five years for FHA.

Retirement Income

Let me begin this section by stating that lenders *don't* consider the age of the applicant in the approval process, only the continuous nature of the income. Applicants who will retire within three to five years may be requested to provide information regarding the amount of retirement income they'll be receiving. For a wage earner, a copy of the retirement plan that applies to the applicant should do. For those who will rely on interest and dividend income, the same proof regarding asset verification will be required along with tax returns showing the income from that source. Using retirement income is not a problem as long as there is enough to continue the mortgage payments. The problem arises when the applicants qualify on full income, which may be reduced considerably upon retirement. One compensating factor may be that normal work-related expenses will be reduced (commuting, clothing, insurance, etc.), offsetting the reduced income. Most retirement income is indicated on your tax returns, both taxable and nontaxable.

Social Security and Military Retirement Income

Retirement benefits from social security can be proven with a copy of the award certificate, the original notice of retirement benefits. Copies of the last six months of bank statements showing the deposit or copies of the actual benefit checks will prove current income. Military retirement income can be proven with a similar award letter, and most recipients receive a yearly statement of income for tax purposes. Bank statements or automatic deposit notifications will prove the current amount you receive, since the amount may have increased over the years. Some of these types of income are based on dependent or educational benefits and are not necessarily continuous. The same three year and five year limits apply for it to be considered continuous income.

Part-Time or Seasonal Employment

Applicants who regularly work additional jobs may include the total income averaged over their two year history. W-2's and paystubs will be required, and it must be logical that they can continue to do this type of work in addition or instead of their regular employment. A good example of this type of acceptable income is the teacher who works summers or who coaches sports seasonally and often relies very heavily on these other sources of income.

Income from Boarders and Relatives Residing in the Home

This is generally an unacceptable source of income to be used for qualifying.

Self-Employed Borrowers

FHA, VA, and Conventional guidelines require two full years of proven self-employment income. Two years of complete tax returns, both federal and state, will be required. Complete means all the schedules and attachments must be included. Less than two years but more than one year may be acceptable if the applicant's previous employment was in the same field as the new business. This is not always acceptable and certainly applies best to very low loan-to-value transactions or applications for borrowers with additional sources of income. Anyone who owns 25 percent or more of a business may be considered self-employed. The underwriter will start with the adjusted gross income on the front of the 1040 and add-back or subtract any adjustments to the income to arrive at the net (useable) income. The complete form used by most underwriters to adjust income contains at least thirty-five to forty potential adjustments to income. I have included a sample worksheet that you can use to calculate your own net income when prequalifying yourself. Lenders and investors differ on the actual calculations, but by using this worksheet you'll be better prepared and your lender will be more likely to include all of your self-employed income.

Problems in qualifying for a mortgage loan most often occur when wage earners have a small business that they use as a "tax write-off," to offset some of their wage income. The tax advantages of owning a small business are great at tax time but the same "paper loss" used to offset income must be used in the analysis of your self-employment and may reduce your qualifying income. If it has a negative impact on your income, it can't be overlooked. If you have questions about the acceptability of your type of income, take your last two years of tax returns to your loan officer before going too much further, to make sure shopping now is wise. You may need to be in business a while longer to qualify for a new loan. If you are refinancing, more weight will be given to the pay history of your current debts with the new business income. If you're using the new home as your business headquarters, expect your lender to question whether the local codes allow this type of business activity in this residential area. After all, if your repayment of the mortgage debt depends on this business, you may have to prove you can operate it from your new home.

There are several different types of self-employed borrowers. In the appendix I have included the common types and the tax forms used to analyze the income. The lines used to calculate income change, but the forms have stayed the same for many years. When supplying tax returns, be sure to include all schedules, attachments, and W-2's if applicable. (Be careful not to copy your W-2's over the front page of the return, the 1040.) You'll be asked to sign the returns (the copies provided), certifying the accuracy. Some lenders also require that you sign a form #4506, a Request for a Copy of Returns. The reasoning behind this is simple. As a protection against future audit or quality control inquiries or in the case of a default, the lender may double-check that the returns you provided were the same as the ones you sent to the IRS.

In addition to tax returns, the lender will order a business credit report, which may cost you a little more in up-front application fees, fifty to one hundred dollars more in most areas. The report will check state corporation and licensing records to determine that there is a business in existence, as well as check the ownership, legal records, and the credit rating of the business. Finally, if the most recent tax information is more than ninety days old, a financial statement will be required, prepared by an accountant for most large businesses. This must include a profit and loss statement (or income statement) and a balance sheet, giving the lender a good picture of the current financial status of your business for the current year. This is especially important if you regularly depend on extensions for your tax filing. Both the copies of the tax returns and the financial statements must be signed by the borrowers, certifying their accuracy. For a small business that is not your major source of income and that does not warrant the use of a CPA, borrower-prepared financial statements may be acceptable. However, if the lender sees that tax returns were prepared by a CPA, it is only logical that financial statements also be prepared by the same CPA or tax accountant.

Take the completed underwriter's self-employed worksheet provided in the Appendix with you to the loan interview as notice to the loan officer that you are prepared for the questions regarding income. If you have reviewed the types of self-employment form and you've completed the self-employed analysis worksheet, you may eliminate a great deal of time and stress.

Assets Verification (or, It's 11 p.m., Do You Know Where Your Assets Are?)

Verifying the assets available to close this transaction may seem quite simple. A verification of deposit form is sent to all your banks or depositories, and the total of all the funds indicated on the verifications is your available assets. Unfortunately, assets have a habit of moving around and we have to wait until they "land" somewhere to be verified. The check you gave the seller for the good faith deposit, for instance, can be included in your total cash available, but was it cashed before the verification of deposit was completed by the bank or is it being held? Also, assets can be moved around and can appear to have "landed" in *several* banks. Most lenders require some cash investment from the borrower, which must be money you have saved or earned. To avoid any questions about the source of your funds, don't transfer your funds or open new accounts just before applying for a mortgage loan. That will help to avoid delays in verifying your money. Hold off on major purchases and avoid transferring or buying or selling securities during this process. Money that is borrowed for the down payment and closing costs is generally a red flag to a lender. There are some exceptions to this rule. If you borrow against existing assets, such as stocks, CDs, or other properties you own that are not being used for qualifying purposes, and if the loan repayment is considered in your ratios, these funds will be allowed. You still must have a minimum cash investment, so check with your lender about their guidelines.

Secondary Financing

Secondary financing is allowed in some cases (for example, a seller carry-back of part of the purchase price, a second mortgage instead of cash), but the total of the first and the second cannot exceed the loan-to-value ratio or maximum loan for your program. For the FHA that means that the new loan plus the secondary financing cannot exceed the maximum loan amount you figured on the FHA worksheet in the appendix. The secondary financing must have regular set payments (monthly, quarterly) and no balloon payments before ten years, it must allow for prepayment without penalty, and the monthly payment must be included in the qualifying ratios. The VA allows secondary financing if: 1. it is carried by the seller, 2. the combination of the two loans don't exceed the appraised value, 3. the second loan fully amortizes (no balloon payments), and 4. the interest rate doesn't exceed the VA interest rate. Conventional guidelines allow secondary financing with much the same rules. Check with your lender about their own particular requirements if your seller has agreed to accept part of the sales price as a note or secondary financing.

Gifts

A gift from a relative as part of the down payment is allowed by FHA and conventional guidelines, but with limits. The FHA allows a gift from a close relative or close friend who doesn't have a financial interest in the transaction. The gift must be donated without repayment expected. A gift letter is required that states the name, address, and phone number of the donor; states that repayment is not expected; states the amount; states the relationship; and is dated and signed by the donor. The money must be deposited in the applicant's account and verified. Conventional requirements for the gift letter are similar but the borrowers must use 5 percent of their own money unless the total loan-to-value is 80 percent or less. In all cases, the money must be received by the applicant and the transfer must be documented. VA does not require a cash down payment in most transactions, but does require that the veteran have cash assets to cover closing costs or to cover the difference between the appraised value and the loan amount. Remember, if the value of the property (the CRV) is less than the sales price, you may only borrow the value amount and you must pay a down payment from your own cash.

Borrowed Funds

Signature loans, unsecured lines of credit, credit cards, or any other unsecured loans used for the purpose of acquiring cash are generally not acceptable sources for the down payment. The theory is that you have very little investment in the property and are more likely to have problems repaying the debt since you borrowed the money for the down payment and for the purchase. You may simply be too far in debt to be expected to continue all the payments. There are exceptions to these guidelines with some lenders, so check first before you take out another loan just before your mortgage loan application.

Time Deposits

IRA's and time deposits (CD's) are acceptable assets to be used as long as any penalties for early withdrawal are considered, and as long as the funds are held in the borrower's name. Bring in bank statements, the actual certificates of deposit, or the bank books that indicate the balances of these accounts. You may be requested to explain new accounts (six months or less) to eliminate the possibility of borrowed funds. Also, if your account shows a new balance in excess of the average balance for the past three months, the lender may question the appearance of large assets not normal for your income situation. There may be a perfectly good explanation, so provide proof of large increases in your assets at the loan interview to avoid questions later in the process.

Stocks and Bonds

Using your stock/bond portfolio for the down payment and closing costs is a perfectly acceptable source of funds. The lender will verify the portfolio, require that the sale of the stocks and bonds be documented by the broker, and require that the funds be deposited in your bank or put on deposit with escrow. A receipt for the deposit of the funds will be required. You don't have to liquidate your stocks or bonds prior to the close, but it'll probably be a closing condition. Evidence of the value of the portfolio is only required for loan approval if you're not using any for this transaction. One potential problem arises when you claim interest or dividend income for qualifying and you're selling the *source* of that income. You'll need to prove that you have remaining assets to make up for that loss of interest or dividends, if it's being used as more than a compensating factor.

Sale of Previous Home

If this isn't your first home and you're selling a property to buy the subject property, you'll need to supply a copy of the sales contract, a verification of the mortgage loans on the property to prove credit history, a statement from you or your escrow or title company estimating the net proceeds from this sale, and a copy of the final closing statement (HUD-l). All but the HUD-l will be required for approval if the closing of both transactions will be simultaneous; however, you'll need to supply the HUD-l at the close of this transaction. Make sure that your title or escrow company knows that there are *two* transactions from the beginning to avoid any delays at the end. Normally the lender will require a HUD-1 on both transactions prior to releasing funds. To coordinate both closings, your escrow officer will make the necessary arrangements with the title or escrow company used in the other transaction.

Co-borrowers and Co-signers

FHA guidelines allow for the use of a co-borrower as long as the co-borrower signs the legal documents and will not benefit financially from it. The co-borrower's income may be used for the housing expense ratio. Co-borrowers don't have to occupy the property, but the use of a co-borrower must be logical for the transaction. All of the co-borrower's income and expenses will be considered to verify that, if needed, he or she is financially capable of helping with your payments in the future.

VA does allow for co-borrowers using their net income after all of their expenses and debts are deducted. However, for co-borrowers that are not eligible veterans, the amount of guaranty is limited to the veteran's portion of ownership—definitely not an attractive VA loan for most lenders.

Conventional guidelines require that the co-borrower occupy the property if the loan-to-value ratio is greater than 90 percent though the co-borrower need not be a relative or have a close personal relationship.

If the purpose of using a co-borrower is to help you qualify, expect the same documentation requirements for the co-borrower's income, credit and assets. Prepare your co-borrower for this too; they need to know their responsibilites should something happen to you. Allow for more money up front to cover extra credit reports, and prepare your co-borrower for this, too. Advise your lender at the outset so a separate loan interview can be scheduled. Ask what additional requirements your lender has for co-borrowers or co-signers. The use of a co-borrower is particularly helpful for the first-time homebuyer. Prequalify yourself without a co-borrower first to see if you need one, but if you do, don't hesitate to ask. You may be required to be able to make a certain percentage of the payment without assistance, and the nonoccupant co-borrower will be expected to sign all legal documents too. Your lender may also require that the co-borrower reside in the same state as the property for collection purposes, so consult with your loan officer before asking someone in your family to co-borrow.

Chapter 6

Loan Approval and the Closing

YOUR LOAN FILE NOW WEIGHS TWENTY-TWO POUNDS, you've been asked to provide everything but the size of your shorts, and you were prepared for it all! The file is now ready for the dreaded underwriter to approve. Your loan should be approved with no conditions due to your advance preparation and your ability to follow the transaction and avoid problems before they happened. Theoretically, that should be the way it happens, but even the best prepared cases do have setbacks. Generally, any delays now are caused by closing dates. It's difficult for everyone to coordinate the date for a closing, so work closely with your loan officer. After approval, there are a few steps you'll need to take to close the transaction. First, tell your realtor, if you are represented by one, of the loan approval, and, second, make sure that the seller's agent has their people ready to close. Everyone must be available to sign the final papers at the closing agent's office, though not necessarily at the same time. It always seems to me that the sellers plan extended vacations right after selling a house, thinking their job is done and wanting to get away before the move! Many people buy and move during the summer months and very few will give up their yearly vacations. I don't blame them. Let's hope this won't be the case for you. You and the seller should settle as soon as possible on a closing date so prorated taxes, interest, etc., can be calculated and moving vans ordered.

If Your Application Is Rejected

Well, let's not get ahead of ourselves. Most loan applications as well planned as yours get approved, but, unfortunately, not all do. Let me stress that the goal of the underwriter is to approve as many loans as possible. The underwriters may be licensed by government agencies but they are paid by the lender. When the lender doesn't close loans or when the lender has a high foreclosure rate, the underwriter is often the first to be blamed. The point is that most underwriters reject loans only as a last resort. They may request more documents (which is annoying) but they do not reject applications unless they have exhausted all possibilities. The FHA *wants* the D.E. underwriter to approve marginal cases, especially for first-time homebuyers. The VA functions for the benefit of the veteran and wants the underwriter to reject a VA loan *only* if it's clear that this loan is beyond the veteran's reach. Conventional lenders are more conservative, but they also handle larger loans that require more income and often require more careful underwriting.

If your loan is absolutely rejected, you still have some recourse. First, you need to find out why! You must be given a written disposition of loan application identifying why you don't qualify. Next, you need to discuss the case and your alternatives with your lender now while the case is still fresh in everyone's mind. You should set up an appointment *now* with your loan officer. Don't sulk or rant and rave about it for a week or two and chance losing your home. Don't expect your realtor to be able to help too much with this part of the transaction, although he needs to know that you really do want this home and that you are willing to cooperate fully in advising the sellers of the delay and writing extentions to the contract. At this point discretion on the part of the realtor and the lender is important, your financial information is not to be shared with anyone other than your lender.

Your top priority is to make sure that your loan application contained all the information you provided. For instance, if lack of income was the reason for your loan being denied, make sure that the tax returns or whatever documentation *you* provided was also included in the file to the underwriter.

Usually the lender takes great care to get a second opinion from another underwriter or two. Then the lender will suggest other options: paying off bills, using a co-borrower, putting more money down, or allowing some time between past credit problems. You should request in writing a reconsideration of your loan application based on some new or additional facts you can add to the file. If your second request is denied you probably have exhausted your chances with this lender. You have the option of contacting another lender since FHA and VA cases can be assigned to other lenders. However, with an FHA case, the denial will be reported to the FHA and the next underwriter will know why the first denied the loan. Your best option on an FHA loan is to request that the case be reviewed by the local FHA office to see if they will override the lender's decision and issue insurance on the case. The FHA may commit to the insurance for the loan, and even though the lender is responsible for the payments, usually they will be glad to have an approved, insured FHA loan on the books. The FHA would probably prefer not to be involved in a rejected application, but it is certainly worth a try. If your VA loan is rejected you may request a reconsideration. If that fails, you may ask that the case be submitted directly to the VA for approval. You are not bypassing the lender, only allowing the FHA or the VA to approve the loan, taking the responsibility for the case from the lender. For a conventional loan, the case may or may not be assignable, depending on the lender. You may go to another lender but you will probably have to start all over with a new appraisal and new fees up front. Most conventional lenders will assign a loan to a new lender if the other lender has a different program, but they are not obligated to do so. If you simply do not qualify because of lack of income or lack of adequate assets, the lender may be doing you a favor. You just might be getting in over your head, and no lender wants to set you or themselves up for a default. You may want more of a home than you can realistically afford; listen to the lender for now and reapply when you have more income, more assets, or have established a better credit history.

After the Approval

When your loan is approved you'll probably receive a call from the loan officer. I remember the exact place and time I got my call; it's a nice feeling, especially the first time. You should celebrate: Now you are really in debt!

If your loan is approved subject to specific items that are required to be completed after the approval but before closing, you'll need to know what the conditions are and who is expected to comply with the conditions. Repairing the property, paying off accounts, selling previous homes, selling stocks or bonds, or providing additional paystubs or bank statements are examples of closing conditions. Usually termite inspections, roof inspections or reinspections by the appraiser are closing conditions and will be ordered by the seller or the seller's realtor. Most sellers would rather not spend the money on inspections until the borrower is qualified for the new loan. After your loan officer calls you with an approval, she will usually follow up with a letter of approval which includes the conditions of closing. Ask her over the phone if there are any closing conditions so you won't be suprised at closing and also so you can remind the seller's realtor or yours that items need to be completed in order to close on time. Follow up on this one, since any delay on the part of another person can cost *you* money. I've often seen needless expenses for overnight couriers and trips to deliver documents that could have been avoided had everyone done their job on time.

Next, you should arrange for your fire and flood insurance with your agent, gather your money in the form of a cashier's check (usually no personal checks are accepted for the closing) and set up a time with your closing agent to sign the final legal documents for recording. Remember, read the fine print of all the loan papers and expect an explanation of all the fees you're paying from the closing agent or the lender. Bring a copy of the estimated closing statement you received at the beginning to compare to the final fees. Expect to receive a copy of everything you sign to read later or file away.

If the property must be reinspected for completed repairs, wait until the repairs are done before you do the final walk-thru. Reread the sales contract before the walk-thru to refresh your memory about what repairs were to be completed in the house, and don't sign the final closing papers unless you're happy with the results. Once money changes hands, the incentive to complete repairs is gone! Make sure that the seller has kept the property in good condition since you last saw it and do several inspections if necessary to be sure you see everything. I know this may not make the sellers or their agent particularly happy, but you should protect yourself.

The Closing

At the closing you will receive a HUD-1 settlement statement detailing the disbursement of all the funds. A copy of the HUD-1 is included in the appendix as a sample of what you may look for particularly on the form. Ask about any fees you don't understand.

Your lender will require that you pay for an Alta title insurance policy both for the lender and for you. This is important to protect your legal right to the property. Title insurance also insures the lender that the mortgage is valid and enforceable. It insures against unfiled mechanics liens, leases unrecorded, easements or encroachments that affect your use of the property, and other questions of survey that could hamper your legal access to the property. You will pay for this as a part of your closing costs and the seller will pay for his own policy. You should find this among your closing papers; if not, tell the attorney or the escrow company that you want a title policy.

One of the variables on the closing statement is the interest you pay per day at closing on the principal balance of your loan. The way the interest is calculated was explained more fully in Chapter Two. If you wish to save money at the closing you may want to close at the end of the month. You'll pay less up front but you'll be moving your first payment date closer, so consider both options. As an example, a loan that closes on the fifteenth of the month will require sixteen days prepaid interest in a thirty day month with the first payment due in forty-five days. A loan closed on the thirtieth will require one day prepaid interest but the first payment will be due in thirty days. Choose your poison! Pay now or pay later.

Servicing Your Loan

Expect to bring home copies of all your closing documents; your closing agent should automatically give them to you. If not, ask for them. About ten to fifteen days after the closing, you'll receive a coupon book, a billing, or a statement with an explanation of where and when your payments are to be made (usually accompanied by a welcome letter). You may also receive a letter stating that your loan has been sold to an investor; it will include more instructions. If you have problems with the new servicing company, contact your loan officer. He will know who to contact to correct the problem and will be able to intervene. Your repeat business is important to him; he will be happy to provide service after the closing too.

For those who have chosen an adjustable rate mortgage (ARM), your servicing company will notify you well in advance of any adjustments to your payment (usually increases) so you can prepare for the new monthly payment. Each time your payments adjust they will send you an explanation of the change in the index and how it affects your payment. If you've chosen the ARM program with a conversion option to a fixed rate within a certain period of time, usually you'll be notified of the conversion period on the closing papers only. So remember to mark your calendar and check with your lender during that time to see if the fixed rate is attractive enough to convert. There is usually a conversion fee involved, also disclosed on the closing papers, so weigh all the factors. More on ARMs and conversion features in the next chapter. The assumability feature of your loan may also be affected upon conversion, so check on that too.

If you have a conventional loan over 80 percent loan-to-value, you will probably be paying a mortgage insurance premium monthly, as well as a one-year premium at the closing. There are some companies who self-insure their loans, but you will pay higher fees up front or higher interest rates to compensate. Remember down the line to consider having the mortgage insurance removed by proving to the lender that the value of your property versus the loan amount is now 80 percent or less. A new appraisal establishing the value should accomplish that, though you'll have to pay for it.

At the end of the year, most borrowers receive a statement of the activity on their loan describing the application of the payments, interest, principal, taxes, and insurance (if applicable). Throughout the year you may receive a copy of the insurance billing or the property tax billing for your records. Check to see if it's your copy or the original; it should be clearly marked. Notify your servicing company if you are not sure. They need to pay the taxes and insurance if you have an impound or escrow account established. FHA and VA guidelines require this account and most lenders require impound accounts on loans over the 80 percent loan-to-value ratio. Send them a copy of the billings you receive if you have any doubts. Whenever corresponding with your servicer write your account number on every single piece of paper to help them get the information to your file. Use their toll-free number if you have any questions that need immediate attention. Order an amortization schedule if you are curious about the term and application of your payments, but don't look at the last page to see how much you actually will pay if the loan runs its full fifteen or thirty year term! It is very depressing. Fortunately, you are in good company. The average homeowner changes residences about every three to five years so it is unlikely you'll ever pay that total.

Now that wasn't so bad, was it? Whether it was your first home purchase, a refinance, or the purchase of rental or second properties, your level of involvement in the transaction should have been the same. If you've bought before you know how important it is to watch every step of the transaction. Now you may consider buying more properties for investment purposes. I'm not a tax advisor, so consult your tax preparer or accountant before you invest. Real estate is still a wonderful investment and most of the tax advantages of homeownership have survived the new tax laws. In the rest of the book, I will help you through some of the different kinds of mortgage loans and outline some of their features.

Section II

Chapter

The Types Of Loans Available For Purchases Or Refinancing

WHEN SHOPPING FOR A MORTGAGE LOAN to buy a home or to refinance your existing loan, you'll probably be offered a fixed rate mortgage with a thirty- or fifteen-year term at market rate with the normal closing costs and fees required. The fees are somewhat negotiable, as I discussed in Chapter Two. The type of mortgage you choose should fit your income and lifestyle, just as the home you chose fits your needs. There are several features of the loan that you must consider:

1. Interest rate: fixed versus nonfixed rate loan. A fixed interest rate with a fixed monthly payment, an adjustable rate loan or even a graduated payment loan, or any one of several other choices.

2. Assumability. The assumability of the loan should you decide to sell, including the fees required for the assumption, and the need for a future assumptor to qualify for the loan.
3. Prepayment penalty. The amount of any prepayment penalty should you pay off the loan early.
4. Term. The term of the loan, which will determine the size of your monthly payment.

Fit the Loan to Your Lifestyle

The features of your loan along with your income and expenses, other than the mortgage loan payment, must be considered. Your age and your future housing needs, if you are purchasing, may affect the type of mortgage you choose. If you live in a rural or urban area that has limited appeal to potential buyers, you may have fewer lender or program choices. However, if you are in a growing suburban area that lenders regularly lend in successfully, there may be more choices

Income

Start by considering the type and stability of your income. You may want a fixed rate mortgage that allows for a fixed payment monthly for thirty years. If you don't feel that you have the potential to increase your income more than the cost of living over the next three to five years, then the fixed rate will better fit your needs. Also, if you don't feel that your job is all that stable, or if you want to change careers soon with a lower starting income, the fixed rate plan offers a stable monthly payment. Lastly, for those who plan to stay in their home for many years to come or those who don't want to have to worry about the economy and how it will affect your monthly payments, the fixed rate is for you.

If, on the other hand, you have the potential for increasing your income, or you receive bonuses or commission income on a quarterly, semiannual, or annual basis, you may want to try an adjustable rate mortgage. It has a low interest rate to begin with, but has the potential to increase or decrease regularly, depending on the economy. While rates are low, your rate remains low, but should the lending market "tighten" and rates increase, your monthly payment will increase. You should have some source to increase your income accordingly, the type of flexibility that comes from commission or bonus income. The best feature of the adjustable rate mortgage is the low interest rate at the beginning. Some adjustable rate mortgages offer a *conversion option* to convert the rate to a fixed rate during a set period in your loan repayment. These types of loans may have a slightly higher beginning rate with a fee due upon conversion, but may be the answer for those who want the best of both worlds, fixed and adjustable. The drawback is knowing when to convert the rate and coordinating the conversion with the lender. If your income is fixed, such as retirement income, or you have an income that only increases by the cost of living index, then you may not feel comfortable with any type of loan that has the potential to increase more than your income.

If you're like most of us, on a salary subject to increases according to your ability to advance, then you'll need to rely on other factors to decide. Your type of income, stable or intermittent, will determine the amount of money you can allot to the mortgage payment monthly and should be an important factor. Check with your lender and ask that the loan officer compare the fixed rate mortgage loan with the alternative types of mortgages. Adjustable-type loans are certainly not risky loans, but they are tied to several economic conditions that you can't control, mainly the cost of savings funds or the bond market—all factors directly affected by the economic condition of the nation. Below I will outline the several types of mortgage loans available with adjustable-type payments.

Finally, your income must be adequate to provide some luxuries in addition to paying the bills. If you spend every cent on the house payment, the car payment, the charge cards, the utilities, child care, insurance, and food, with none left over for vacations, the occasional weekend trip, or the hobbies that you love, you'll feel strapped for money most of the time. If that is the case, maybe you should consider a lower priced home temporarily (until your income increases), or maybe you should wait until you have a larger down payment to decrease that mortgage payment. Your final investment in a home should be one that you can live comfortably with for about three to five years, the time it will take to build equity or save money for a down payment on a move-up home.

If you're looking for a mortgage loan to refinance your existing home loan, consider your income as an equally important factor when choosing the type of mortgage loan. Your potential for future earnings is important! Sit down and consider what you feel you'll be receiving over the next several years. Though you may have equity sufficient to receive cash out of the refinance, consider that you have to pay that loan back just like the previous loan. The cash received from the refinance should be designated for a specific purpose in order to justify the refinance. Consider refinancing carefully before drawing on your equity. If the purpose of your refinancing is to reduce the interest rate and your monthly payment as well as to draw on your equity and receive cash out of the transaction, you have the best of both worlds! There are still many people who are paying on their pre-1985 loans with interest rates exceeding 11 to 12 percent who should consider refinancing. We always think that a lower rate is right around the corner and may be right, but the time to refinance is in a stable economy when rates have remained the same (or varied no more than ½ of 1 percent) for six months or more. I cannot predict the rates any more than anyone else, so if you have an interest rate (fixed rate) higher than 11percent and you have equity in your property, check with your local lender to see the advantages of using that equity to make money for you while reducing your monthly payment.

Expenses

The bills you pay other than your mortgage payment need to be considered when choosing a mortgage loan. Your debts, for instance, may all be fixed payments, such as auto loans and furniture loans with a payment that will not change until paid in full. If the term on these loans is one year or less, then an adjustable rate mortgage might be logical. Your payments start out lower than a fixed rate and, in the worst case, your mortgage payment may increase at six months or one year from the start date, depending on the type you've chosen. Your payment could also remain the same or increase only slightly and, in the meantime, you will be paying off one or several of those short term loans, offsetting any potential mortgage payment increase.

Make a list of the monthly debts (installment or charge accounts) that you can control. This would not include utilities, commuting expenses, insurance or child care expenses, unless those expenses will be expected to change drastically soon: these are the constants in your total expenses. Determine which debts are short term (six months or less) and which are on-going. If your debts consist mostly of charge cards that you pay in full monthly, then you have total control of these expenses. However, if you normally pay the minimum monthly payment on your charge cards, you should consider this an on-going monthly debt. You're not likely to change your credit habits after buying a home or refinancing the home you have. Even if your bills will be paid in full from the proceeds of the refinance of your home, most homeowners get right back in debt within a year of their debt-consolidation refinance, unless they are more disciplined than the average. Sorry, this is a fact; we are a nation that uses credit as a way of life. There are exceptions, of course, but we've become accustomed to buying what we "need" now and paying later!

Your debts, then, may determine whether you have the flexibility for an adjustable rate mortgage with a low beginning rate and the potential for increasing payments or should choose a fixed rate, which will not change.

Age and Future Housing Needs

These two catagories may also be a factor in your choice of a mortgage loan. Your age won't be a factor in determining your qualifications for a mortgage loan but may affect your income or debts drastically. If you're approaching retirement, for instance, you'll need to consider what your income will be and compare it to your mortgage expense and all other expenses. If you are over fifty and have not done so already, you should send for a print-out from the Social Security office that will describe your current Social Security status and the projected income you can expect upon retirement. This is a free service and can be requested from your local office. Call the number in your telephone directory for the Social Security Administration, listed under Federal Offices or the U.S. Government and ask for the Personal Earnings and Benefit Estimate Statement. The statement uses the information on your earnings year-to-date and projects through age 62 to estimate what you can expect to earn. The statement only projects income, but will explain how Social Security benefits are calculated and includes a toll-free number to call for more information. If you pay into the Social Security system you may be curious about how it works and what you're actually entitled to upon retirement. So give them a call. Some federal, state and local government employees don't pay into the social security system, but an accounting is available with a phone call to the retirement plan office. Check with your employer.

After you've determined your future income, including retirement, investment, and interest earnings, you can better determine what payment you can afford. As a rule of thumb, a fixed income requires a fixed payment. Your normal employment expenses may also change. It's logical that many people later in life will have less commuting and employment costs and less need for "gadgets" due to a scaling down of household chores. On the other hand, many people have increased insurance costs or want to set more money aside for travel and hobbies, so expenses don't necessarily decrease as you retire. It's up to your individual needs what you want to set aside for a mortgage payment and how long you want to continue to pay. The term and potential for prepayment are particularly important to those contemplating retirement. Your tax situation is also important since you may be entitled to the one-time exclusion of taxable profit from the sale of your home at some time in the near future. If you are intending to take advantage of the exclusion by selling your home, your initial monthly payments are more important than a thirty-year, fixed term payment, and your assumability and prepayment penalties are important features of your loan.

On the other hand, if you're new to the work force, you may have the potential for increased income but may also be obligated to repay student loans during your first years of employment. If you're considering buying a home at the beginning of your career, your age is less of a factor than your ability to increase your income to cover your expenses during the first years of employment. Consider that the potential for increasing your income should coincide with any increases in your housing expense. Although a home is a great investment at the beginning of your career (particularly the interest deduction), your monthly payment on an adjustable rate loan may increase faster than your raises and certainly faster than the cost-of-iving increases we've experienced recently.

Your future housing needs may be a factor in the choice of a mortgage loan, especially when considering the features of the loan. If you're now buying a home that you expect to outgrow within a few years, your loan should feature an assumability clause to be attractive to future buyers. If your loan contains a prepayment penalty for early payoff and you expect to sell during the prepayment period, you may have to pay a substantial penalty, which will decrease the amount available to buy that move-up home. Many adjustable rate loans are assumable but have clauses that allow for a large increase in the rate or that convert the loan to a fixed rate at assumption. You need to be aware of these clauses. When asking about the features of your loan, don't stop with the question, "Is the loan assumable?"; ask what the conditions of assumption are and what fees are required. The assumption fee will be included in your legal documents and should be considered when choosing. Check with your lender on all the features of your loan.

If you're expecting to stay in your home longer than three to five years you might be smarter to get a fixed rate nonassumable loan in an area of increasing values. Even if you sell during the first few years, it is unlikely that you will find a buyer to pay you all of your equity in cash and assume the loan, no matter what the rate. The home you buy now may loose its attractive features to you sooner than you think because of increasing or decreasing family size, other outside factors such as the job, shopping, or school availability, or unexpected job opportunities. Prepare now by choosing features in your mortgage loan that you can live with now and in the future.

Features of Loan Types
Fixed Rate Mortgages

The obvious feature of the fixed rate mortgage loan is the stability of the monthly payments. Your principal and interest figure will not change over the term of the loan; though, of course, over the term the amount applied to principal increases and the amount paid for interest decreases. You may order an amortization schedule, which will show you exactly what portion of your payment goes to interest and what to principal for each payment, enabling you to keep track of your outstanding balance. At the end of each year you need to add up the interest you paid in order to report it on Schedule A of your income tax returns. You certainly may use the figure on the year end statement sent to you by the lender, which outlines the interest you paid and the disbursement of your impound account (the account that contains your property taxes, mortgage insurance if applicable, and fire and flood insurance monthly payments) if you have one. Lenders report to you what they have spent from the impound account on taxes, insurance, mortgage insurance or other fees they are collecting and paying on your behalf once a year. Of course, they'll also report to you any shortage in that account due to increases in your property taxes or your insurance premiums, or any extra in that account, which you may be entitled to receive or which you may apply to next year's tax or insurance bills. Your monthly payment may increase or decrease because of these impounds but never because of the interest rate on a normal fixed rate loan.

You do have several choices on a fixed rate loan other than the interest and fees you will pay. You may elect to pay off your loan in fifteen years instead of the customary thirty-year term. There are twenty-year and ten-year mortgage loans but they are rarely sold on the secondary market and may not be offered by many lenders. A certain volume is necessary to make a product attractive on the secondary market. You will want to compare the thirty- and the fifteen-year terms to see what fits your needs. Following is a comparison to use, including the twenty- year term in case you find a lender that offers all three.

Exhibit 11: Example of Monthly Prinicipal and Interest Payments Using a $72,000.00 Loan At 10 percent Interest

The factors used: 0.01075, 0.00966 and 0.00878 are from the Factor Sheet in the appendix.

15 Year	20 Year	30 Year
$72,000.00 x 0.01075 =	x 0.00966 =	x 0.00878 =
$774.00	$695.52	$632.16

When you are using the prequalifying sheets in the appendix, use all three terms to see how this affects your qualifying ratios. Obviously, the fifteen- and twenty-year loan will be paid off much sooner and with much less interest paid on the loan, so you may want this type of loan. You would have to qualify at the larger payment up front, so check your ratios to determine if you would still qualify. Another way to make the thirty-year loan a fifteen-year loan voluntarily without having to qualify for the larger payment, is to make a principal payment twice each month. Pay your regular payment with one check and issue a second check for a principal payment only. You must order an amortization schedule to do this but below is a sample of what it will look like and what you can do.

Exhibit 12: Example of an Amortization Schedule

For a loan of $71,518.00 at 10.50%—an FHA loan including the mortgage insurance premium financed.

Monthly payment of $654.20.

Payment #	Interest	Principal	Balance
1	625.78	28.42	71,489.58
2	625.53	28.67	71,460.91
3	625.28	28.92	71,431.99

And so on for thirty years. If on the second payment you sent a check for the total payment of $654.20 plus an extra check clearly marked with "a principal repayment of loan #0000" on it for $28.67 and on the third payment a principal check for $28.92 and so on, you would be paying your loan off in fifteen years instead of thirty without being required to do so. If you can't make those extra payments some months you won't be obligated to come up with the extra money. Some companies will do this for you for a fee—don't pay someone else to repay your loan early, do it yourself. Even by paying a minimal fee of fifteen dollars or so for the amortization schedule (though most are free), you're still ahead doing it yourself.

Of course, your own circumstances along with the availability of these types of loans will determine whether you choose a term of fifteen, twenty, or thirty years. You might also consider the assumable feature of your loan along with this choice. A fifteen-year loan that is assumable might not be as attractive to a future buyer because of the higher monthly payments. Most conventional fixed rate mortgages are not assumable or only assumable to a qualified buyer. All FHA loans after December 1989 are assumable only to a qualified buyer, and VA loans are no longer assumable except with restrictions. If you're intending to stay in your home for many years, a shorter term loan may be attractive to you. Should you decide to sell, you probably have built up many years of equity and will be selling only to someone who will put a new loan on your property. If you plan on being in your home for three to five years, though, you may want a thirty-year assumable loan with lower payments that would be attractive to potential buyers.

If you feel that this is property you'll be keeping as rental property after you move on (which is always my recommendation, if at all possible), the thirty-year loan will allow you lower payments that may be covered by the rents received. This will help to avoid a negative cash flow and still allow you tax benefits, such as deducting interest on the loan plus depreciation.

If you plan on living on the property until retirement, you may want it paid off at that point to allow more of your income to go for traveling or whatever you would rather do. The interest may no longer be an attractive deduction since you will have less income, and your home, owned free and clear, will be a wonderful inheritance for your children. You should consider a living trust for properties that you own when you are close to retirement in order to avoid unnecessary inheritance taxes. Pick up some books on how to do this yourself, or contact an attorney to accomplish this important task. Each state and circumstance is different, but for many, living trusts are a good way to pass on your assets and avoid paying excessive taxes for your heirs.

Adjustable Rate Mortgages (ARMS)

As I explained previously, the adjustable rate mortgage (ARM) is attractive to many people whose income and expenses allow for these adjustments in their housing payment. The attractive feature of the ARM is the beginning rate, especially when compared to the rate of a fixed rate loan. Generally, there is a gap of about 2 percent between the two. This looks dramatic, but it can also be misleading. Your lender may qualify you on the interest rate fully indexed to make sure that you can handle this type of payment in the future. This may be the rate after the first or even the second adjustment, depending on the change dates and adjustment caps. Ask your lender what rate will be used for prequalifying purposes before assuming that you'll be qualified on the lower rate. Also, expect the worse of your ARM loan from the outset (see the sample below) unless you have access to a crystal ball that will tell you what the market will be doing over the next several years!

The ARM loan is usually assumable with no prepayment penalty, but ask about available conversion options. If you can convert to a fixed rate at some point for a minimal fee, it may be worth several hundred dollars up front. Ask particularly what the fee will be at the conversion and what the rate will adjust to upon conversion. It will be based on the fixed rate at the time of the conversion "plus a certain percentage." Be sure to ask, and then follow up by reading your Note and Deed of Trust, including any riders or addendums. I know this is the "fine print" that you don't enjoy reading, but the only way to be sure you are getting what you paid for is to check the documentation. There will probably be five or six pages—split them up between you and your spouse and particularly check the paragraphs deleted or added by riders. If it looks too complicated, have your lender explain it and write it down.

Let's consider the particular features of an ARM loan. The terms *caps, margin,* and *index* are really not that complicated. Don't talk to a lender until you understand the features of the different ARM loans. You should know some of the basic terminology and features to arrive at the best loan for your circumstances.

Caps

If your loan is to adjust, there should be some limits to this adjustment, called caps. The caps are usually the maximum that the rate can increase or decrease for a particular period. Most ARMS have an adjustment period cap and a life cap, meaning that your rate cannot increase or decrease more than 0.5 to 2 percent (rate cap) for each individual adjustment and cannot increase or decrease more than 3 to 5 percent (lifetime cap) over the life of the loan. The cap is expressed in a percentage figure. Your interest rate may have a life cap of 5 percent, which means that your beginning rate on a 7.5 percent loan will never go over 12.5 percent or lower than 2.5 percent for the life of the loan. Your adjustment cap or rate cap may be 1 percent, which means that at each adjustment period, usually six or twelve months (though some written in the 1986 to 1987 era contained monthly adjustments), your rate will not be increased to more than 8.5 percent or less than 6.5 percent. Of course, at the next adjustment it can also increase or decrease the same amount, making the loan now 9.5 percent or 5.5 percent. Your adjustment period is sometimes called a *change date* in the legal documents you sign. The same type of caps can be placed on your monthly payment in addition to or in place of the interest rate caps. You'll need to ask whether the caps affect the interest rate or the monthly payment or both.

Margin

Your increase or decrease will be based on the current index plus a *margin*, an amount (expressed in a percentage rate) added to the index to determine your new interest rate, the same each adjustment within the limits of the caps. For instance, your beginning rate may be 7.5 percent and is to be adjusted according to an index, which is currently 6.5 percent but which increases to 7.0 percent after your first change date (the thirteenth month for a one-year ARM). Add 7.0 percent (index) to the margin 2.5 percent, which equals 9.5 percent. Your change date cap is 2.0 percent (2.0 percent cap plus 7.5 percent rate) so your first change cannot be more than 9.5 percent. In Exhibit 13 I have outlined a sample of adjustments.

Exhibit 13: Worst-Case Example of an ARM Loan

For a $72,000.00 one-year ARM loan for thirty years with a beginning rate of 8.0 percent, caps of 2 percent on the change date and a life cap of 5.0 percent. Assume that the index was 6.5 percent at the start and increases yearly 0.5 percent.

Months	Payment $	Rate %	Margin %	Index %	Cap %
1-12	$528.31	8.00	2.5	6.5	2/5
13-24	605.41	9.50	2.5	7.0	2/5
25-36	631.85	10.00	2.5	7.5	2/5
37-48	658.61	10.50	2.5	8.0	2/5
49-60	685.67	11.00	2.5	8.5	2/5

(Sample used without declining balance for comparison purposes.)

If you were paying the rates in Exhibit 13, after the fourth adjustment, your payment has increased from $503.43 to $679.85 per month, assuming the worst that could happen. You would have paid $37,318.82 in monthly payments over the sixty months; with a fixed rate of 9.5 percent for the same sixty months you would have paid $36,324.60—a difference of $994.22.

Index

There are many different indexes that lenders may use to base their changes on. Some of the common indexes are:

1. The Federal Home Loan Bank's (FHLB) District "Cost of Funds." This index reflects the interest that is being paid by savings and loan institutions on their various sources of mortgage money in one of the twelve districts in the country, the eleventh district being the one used most often (the 11th Dist. COF). The greatest source of mortgage money at most lending institutions is from money deposited in savings, though money can be "advanced" from the FHLB, borrowed by commercial banks, etc. This index is expressed as a percentage and is based on the "weighted average" interest rate being paid by savings and loan institutions on all of their sources of funds.
2. One-year treasury index. This index is the weekly average yield on U.S. Treasury securities adjusted to a constant maturity of one-year. It fluctuates with the bond market rather than the savings rate.
3. Quarterly T-bill. This index is the quarterly average of one-year Treasury bill discount rates rounded to the nearest quarter of a percent.
4. One-year T-bill. This index is the one-year Treasury bill discount rate.

Whichever index your lender uses, you'll receive a special ARM disclosure statement with a ten-year history of that index and a sample of how the changes in this index affect a sample loan. The T-bill index and the cost of funds index (the 11th Dist. COF) are the most common indexes currently used, but this may vary by area and by the market. You can bet that your lender will choose the index that will return the most on their loans within the guidelines of the Federal regulations. Your best hope is to compare the actual index offered by several lenders. Hopefully, you'll have a loan officer who understands the ARM program. If not, consider another lender. If you are offered an ARM loan be sure to ask what index is used for that program, what the current index is and how it will affect your first two adjustments (for the one year) or four adjustments (for the six month). The loan officer can only project, but the history of all the indexes is available to the lender and will be available to you if you ask!

Conversion Option

This feature of the ARM program is very attractive if you want to bail out at some point during the first few years of the loan. If you see a drastic, consistent increase in the rates, your index will soon reflect that increase, as will, eventually, your monthly payment. You need to ask up front during the loan interview for the special features and restrictions of the conversion option. First, ask what the conversion option fee is, and, second, ask during what period of the loan will you be able to convert. Usually the conversion period is between the first and fifth change date. Prior to each change date for your ARM loan you will receive a statement of the current index rate and your new rate. For conversion option loans, the statement will also include the current fixed rate that you may convert to and the time limit you have to pay the conversion fee if you choose to convert. This program, unfortunately, has caused snags in the servicing system and many homeowners are not being advised of the current fixed rate at each change date. Do not assume that the fixed rate is better or worse. Insist that your lender advise you of your options on each change date statement. Your lender should have a toll-free number to call for problems—call immediately since the rates change daily and you may save money over the life of your loan by converting quickly in an upward market. Of course, you take the chance of the rates going down, just like all of us, but you should always receive the choice during the conversion period.

The complete terms for conversion will be included in the ARM promissory note, the ARM advanced disclosure statement given to you at your initial application, and the disclosure statement given to you upon closing. You should take the time to read all of the features of your ARM prior to signing the note at the closing. Do not be rushed or you may miss the conversion dates because you weren't informed. Protect yourself by reading the closing documents and asking lots of questions.

Negative Amortization

One feature of the ARM loan and several other types of loans is the potential for *negative amortization*. This can occur when your monthly payment for principal and interest at the first low-interest rate years does not cover all the interest due on the loan. Your lender may add that unpaid interest to the original unpaid principal, and it becomes principal. Instead of normal amortization, which decreases your principal monthly, your principal balance actually increases. You have to make up for that new added-on principal by increasing the term of your loan or by increasing your payments at some point. Not a real good idea! This feature is rarely offered during a stable market, but during 1986-1988, when negative amortization was a feature of many ARM loans. Ask your lender about this feature first, then compare this ARM to others without negative amortization to see if you can avoid it. Negative amortization is normally allowed from 110 percent to 125 percent of the original loan balance, and your fees for mortgage insurance, title insurance, and hazard insurance will be more because the principal increases beyond the original loan amount. You can avoid some of the increase by prepaying the amount of the additional principal (most ARM loans do not contain prepayment penalties), but this could amount to a great deal of money on a large loan. If you are expecting a large lump sum to cover this added principal and want the lower initial payment, this may be the type of loan you need. This feature allows for a smaller initial monthly payment, attractive in a high-interest rate market, and can allow a buyer to buy a much more expensive home. If the home prices in your area are increasing dramatically enough to cover this risk, you may consider it, but the days of runaway inflation that cover our risks may be gone for awhile. Most lenders are now avoiding this type of lending practice. You may be attracted by the lower beginning rate but consider all the features before choosing this option.

FHA has an ARM program (251) that is allowed to owner-occupants only, has a thirty-year term, and uses an index based on the weekly average yield of U.S. Treasury Securities adjusted to a constant maturity of one year. FHA does not allow for negative amortization and only the one-year ARMS are allowed. Their yearly caps are not to exceed 1 percent, and their life caps, 5 percent. Ask your lender to compare the FHA ARM program with other programs.

Graduated Payment Mortgages (GPM)

This type of mortgage loan became popular during the early 1980's when interest rates caused mortgage payments to increase beyond the reach of most average homebuyers. The GPM loan has actually been around much longer, but is resurrected periodically during high interest rates. The term "graduated" describes the programs features. Your payment gradually increases during the first five to seven years, depending on the program, unlike the ARM loan which has the potential of increasing or decreasing depending on the market. GPMs can be an option for those who expect their income to increase along with the payments or their other expenses to decrease, making up for the larger payments.

Both the FHA and the VA offer graduated payment programs, as do conventional lenders. The FHA GPM program was reduced in 1987 but the FHA 245 (a) program is alive and well, though not in use much. Though this program has been offered less during the past several years, it is still attractive in areas where home prices are still soaring and homebuyers are not able to qualify for more conventional programs. The FHA offers five plans:

Plan I: monthly payments that increase 2 ½ percent each year for five years.
Plan II: monthly payments that increase 5 percent each year for five years.
Plan III: monthly payments that increase 7 ½ percent each year for five years.
Plan IV: monthly payments that increase 2 percent each year for ten years.
Plan V: monthly payments that increase 3 percent each year for ten years.

The FHA GPM allows for negative amorization so your principal balance may be larger at the end of the five or ten years of the program, so you will be expected to pay a larger down payment than the normal FHA loan to offset the risk. The factor to calculate the down payment is based on the amount of negative amortization remaining at the end of the monthly payment increases and can be an important factor when compared to a fixed rate FHA loan. Again, it is one option you should ask your loan officer about, especially for first-time homebuyers who have limited income but a larger down payment.

The VA also has a GPM program with increases of 7 ½ percent for five years but they require a down payment, unlike most of the VA programs. The interest rate may be 3 percent less than the VA regulated interest rate. You should check with your lender about this program since not all lenders offer it.

The 20-Year Mortgage

This is not another type of loan but a variation of the thirty-year and fifteen-year fixed loans. As stated earlier, most lenders do not offer this loan yet. Compared to the fifteen-year and thirty-year term mortgage loan, the twenty-year offers the best monthly payment with an amortization that allows the average forty-year-old borrower to be out of mortgage debt somewhere around retirement age. Most thirty-year-olds will never stay in their present home for the entire term of their loan, and many forty-year-olds will never stay either, however, this term can be very attractive to some forty-year-old and many fifty-year-old borrowers who would rather stay in their home and renovate it as needed or just plain stay put! Being over forty myself, I am aware that most people in their late forties are considering where they will be in the next twenty years and are beginning to plan seriously for their retirement. Usually, they are making their peak earnings and their potential for increase is now somewhat limited. Many are starting to dream of early retirement and are moving to the home they may make their permanent residence after retirement. They hope to own it free and clear, leaving them mortgage-free to travel or pursue hobbies. In the example in the fixed rate section, I have included an example of a twenty-year-term loan. You will note that for a loan amount of $72,000.00, the twenty-year-term loan is only $63.36 more than the thirty-year and only $78.48 less than the fifteen-year term. You could even make an extra principal payment each month and have the loan paid off in ten years! The problem with the twenty-year mortgage, which I believe will become quite attractive to the baby boomers soon, is that there are not enough to be sold on the secondary market. Computers are programmed to service fifteen-and thirty-year loans, mortgage insurance is quoted for only those programs, and loans are sold and traded in groups (pools) of loans with like terms. It will take some time before that type of loan is accepted and traded enough to be offered at an acceptable interest rate, so you may have to find this type of mortgage loan at a bank or savings and loan that can portfolio loans and does not need to sell them. They are out there, but difficult to find. Don't be discouraged if you get a "You want what!" look at first. Shop around for this product if you feel it is as attractive as I do and compare it to other term loans with your loan officer.

Fifteen-Year Equal Program

General Electric Mortgage Securities Corporation offers a unique program called the Equal program. It may be called another name by other lenders, so ask for a loan with the following specific features. It is a fixed rate loan that permits the monthly payments to start at a lower interest rate and increase gradually during the early years of the loan until they level off at a fixed rate for the duration of the loan. There are several types offered with different increases in payments. The low start rate coupled with the gradual increases makes this program very attractive. This is basically a conventional version of the GPM offered by the FHA and the VA. If you choose the program that increases for six-years or less you will pay a little more monthly (approximately thirty dollars), but you can avoid their buydown requirement. In order to avoid negative amortization, they require that someone put up the needed amount at the close of escrow in a third-party account, which they draw on until the payments level off. Ask your lender if they offer a program with graduated payments with a fifteen-year term similar to the Equal program offered by GEMSCO. It is another option to consider and may become very popular, particularly in areas of increasing home values and stable or increasing mortgage rates. FNMA only buys these loans by special arrangement with the buydown feature, and you may qualify at the lower start rate only if you occupy the single family residence. This program may also vary by lender according to the buydown terms, so check with your lender about the availability of such a program. Buydowns are simply putting money up front to cover the reduced mortgage payment caused by a lower interest rate at the first years of the loan to avoid negative amortization. Someone has to pay this fee and it is not always logical for a buyer to put up more money up front to reduce his payment. The seller may do so but that will cut into his profit and there are limitations established by FHA, VA, and conventional guidelines about the amount that the seller can contribute to the loan transaction in the form of buydowns or other seller's concessions.

The Thirty-Year Due In Seven Program

FNMA now offers a two-step mortgage: it has a thirty-year loan term that begins at a fixed rate. That rate continues for seven years, then adjusts once at the end of the seventh year to become a twenty-three-year fixed rate loan. The single adjustment cannot be more than 6 percent above the intital interest rate, and it is tied to the weekly average of ten-year Treasury securities adjusted to a constant maturity of ten years. This rate will be very similar to the current fixed rate available after the seventh year. Naturally the initial interest rate will not be as low as the normal ARM program, which allows for a quicker return to the lender because of more frequent adjustments in an upward market. However, the rate will be lower than a regular fixed rate loan. To qualify, you must be buying or refinancing an owner-occupied principal residence that is a single family dwelling, a condominium, or a planned unit development (PUD) unit. The loan-to-value cannot exceed 90 percent and mortgage insurance will be required for loans over 80 percent of the value.

The program started in March 1990, so it is relatively new and therefore somewhat slow to be accepted by all lenders. Ask your lender if they now offer it and, if so, to compare it to all the other programs.

Reverse Annuity Mortgages (RAMS)

This loan program was introduced several years ago as an alternative for elderly homeowners who were at risk of loosing their homes because of high taxes or decreased income. For those sixty-five years or older who live in single-family residences that they own free and clear, the lender will loan them (depending on the area) up to 80 percent of the value of their property. The area must be appreciating or be primarily homes that are being renovated or upgraded, with growth potential caused by adequate employment and transportation. Lenders are obviously not looking for old homes in run-down neighborhoods that do not show signs of changing for the better. When the borrower dies, moves, sells the home, or asks to terminate the agreement, the amount lent to the borrower must be repaid with a penalty or interest payment or the lender will exercise their right to take the home, sell it and pocket the profit. For a borrower with family to inherit the property or for a borrower who may want to move or sell the property at a later date, this is definitely not an appropriate program. Should the heirs want to keep the property after your death, they must pay back the payments advanced to you, along with interest and, if indicated by a reappraisal of the property, appreciation. However, for those elderly borrowers who have no one to leave their property to and would like an income for the remainder of their lives in order to live in their own home, it may be one option. HUD has pilot programs in several areas offered through local lenders to see how well it will be accepted. Check very carefully with your lender before committing to this program. Ask what fees are deducted from your monthly check for servicing this reverse loan, ask what fees are required up front and whether they can be included in the loan amount, and, lastly, ask what the interest rate is and whether it is fixed or adjustable. These programs vary by region and the fees can be very high. A preliminary counseling session is required to explain very carefully all the features of this program. The intent is good: a monthly income from their own equity, in cash, to elderly citizens who own their own homes. Every situation is different, but those considering this program should also contact a financial planner to consider a well-organized, diversified investment plan using the equity from a refinance of 50 to 60 percent of the value of your home. Loans with 50 percent LTVs require very little qualifying, especially in areas of increasing land values, and that money might be invested with an excellent return and very little risk in bonds or government securities. Your tax situation needs to be considered, so check first with your tax preparer to see what way is best, given your age and income status. Both options should be considered for the elderly contemplating this reverse annuity program.

Portable Mortgages

This program is not available as of this writing but may soon be a reality. I mention it here because any new program will only be accepted if the homeowners ask for it. The concept is to take your mortgage loan with you wherever you move. You qualify for the first mortgage loan on the house that you buy and the mortgage is simply transferred to another property should you move, with its interest rate, remaining balance and term intact. If a buyer is trading up, any appreciation on the first home or a second trust deed can fill the gaps. The lender will retain the homeowner's business for life and the process of applying for a mortgage loan need not be repeated. Some fees will still be required, like the appraisal, title searches and escrow fees, but homeowners will not have to pay costly origination fees and points. The rate will remain the same, which is good in a rising interest rate market but bad in a declining interest rate market. Several years ago this program was tried and did not succeed because of the lack of acceptance by secondary markets and technical problems such as coordinating the closing on both the sale and purchase transactions. Some lenders are considering reintroducing this type of program again and you may check with your lender to see if she has heard more about the program.

Chapter

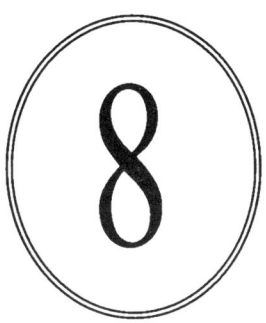

Refinancing Your Home

Before You Shop

If you own a home now with a mortgage loan or without any loan and are thinking about refinancing, you have several items to consider before shopping for a new mortgage loan, or even deciding that refinancing is appropriate for your particular case. Those factors include your tax bracket, the length of time you plan to stay in your home and the additional charges you must pay for the refinancing. When you refinance you usually pay off your original mortgage and sign a new loan. Your costs are much the same as the costs you paid for the original loan except *you* will have to pay them all. This can often run between 3 and 6 percent of the amount you borrow. The type of loan that you choose will depend on:

1. *Occupancy.* Is it a rental or do you intend to occupy it? The amount you can borrow will depend on the occupancy. Also, if you're living in the property now but plan to sell your home within the next three years, you may not have

time to realize the savings of the lower payments after paying for the refinance.
2. *Cash Back*. Do you want to refinance the existing debt plus closing costs to reduce your monthly payment or do you want your equity out of the transaction?
3. *Prepayment Penalty*. Does your existing mortgage loan contain a prepayment penalty clause and how much will it cost in prepayment penalties to refinance now? There are set times when the prepayment penalty may be charged, and you may find that you can wait for another period of time to avoid this penalty and save a great deal of money.
4. *Interest Rate*. Is your new rate going to require monthly payments that you can afford? Will the rate be less than you now have? Generally, a rate of two percent lower than the rate of your current mortgage is a good guideline if the purpose is to reduce your monthly payment. This will be enough to make up for the costs up front. Use the estimate of refinance closing costs in the appendix.
5. *Purpose*. Do you want to put yourself into a longer, more costly loan for a good purpose? Refinancing your existing loan with another thirty-year mortgage to pay short term debts may not be the best way to go. Refinancing can be a good idea if you have a profitable use for the borrowed money. Of course, profit can't be our only motive, our health and happiness are important too! So what if you want to blow your equity on a once-in-a-lifetime trip around the world—it's your equity!
6. *Assumability*. Is the new mortgage loan assumable so that you can sell the property easier later on?
7. *Costs*. How much will the new loan cost up front, and can you finance these charges over the term of the new loan or must you pay them out of your pocket at the closing? Generally, if the new loans costs can be repaid from the reduced monthly payments over thirty-six months you are ahead of the game.

You should also consider the tax benefits and drawbacks before you refinance. A refinance for a lower interest rate will reduce the amount of interest you can deduct on Schedule A of your tax returns and increase your tax liablility. Ask your lender to give you an amortization schedule to calculate the difference. Check last year's tax returns for the amount you were able to deduct and compare to the amount you can deduct on the new mortgage; then give your tax preparer a call and ask him to estimate what the difference will be in your tax liability. If you get less of a tax refund next year, for instance, you must consider this as part of your expense for the new loan.

Some of the closing costs associated with the new loan will be tax deductible, such as the title fees, appraisal, attorney's fees and recording costs, but the discount points can't be deducted all at once in the year of the refinance, as they can be when you buy a home. They must be deducted over the life of the loan instead. For the discount points to be deductible even on a purchase transaction, the amount must be paid by separate check at the closing rather than being deducted from the loan proceeds. A discount point is a tricky term when referring to tax deductible fees. Only when the discount point is charged to the borrower and paid to the lender for the use of the lender's money is it considered deductible at all. Check with your tax preparer about the tax implications to your own individual circumstances before considering a refinance.

Refinance Guidelines

The occupancy is very important to your search for the perfect mortgage loan. Owner-occupied properties can be refinanced with or without cash back at a relatively high loan-to-value ratio. Exhibit 14 lists the refinance programs and their limitations. Rental properties may be refinanced, but there are very few programs that allow for any cash back and the LTV is limited.

FHA One-To-Four Unit Properties

(The FHA allows a streamline refinance of an existing FHA loan on an investor property only when the property has been owned by the investor six months and the investor gets no cash out.)

If you are refinancing an existing FHA loan with financed MIP (that one-time mortgage insurance premium that you chose to finance at the time you purchased the property) the new loan amount will be based on the payoff of the old loan less the amount of the unused MIP. Take your old FHA loan papers in to your new lender and have that amount recalculated to arrive at a net mortgage insurance premium due on the new loan.

FHA offers a streamline refinance of some existing loans, which may save you an appraisal fee. Ask about using the streamline program if you do not want cash out and you only want your interest rate reduced on your existing FHA loan. If you assumed the FHA loan, you must wait six months to take advantage of the streamline refinance.

VA One-To-Four Unit Properties

For interest rate reduction loans only, the maximum loan-to-value is the amount of the balance of the previous loan plus closing costs, which means no cash back.

Streamline and interest rate reduction programs mean some savings in closing costs, so mention them to your lender if your only purpose is to reduce your monthly payments. They should take less time and be much easier to qualify for.

There are some programs other than the ones listed in Exhibit 14 available under the conventional programs by lenders who portfolio their loans and don't need to sell them on the secondary market. During periods of low interest rates many lenders create new refinance programs with reduced costs and negotiable interest rates, usually for newly originated loans rather than refinances of their own loans, so you may want to check with many lenders before finally choosing a refinance lender.

Exhibit 14: Refinance Loan-to-Value Ratios

	FHA 1-4 units	VA 1-4 units	Conventional 1-2 units	Conventional 3-4 units
Owner-occupied with cash out	85%	90%	75%	75%
Owner-occupied with no cash out	97/95%	90%	90%	80%
Nonowner-occupied no cash out	not allowed	90%[2]	70%[1] 70%[3]	70%[1] 70%[3]

Notes:
1. One unit only
2. If the veteran previously occupied the home
3. Fixed rate only

Closing Costs and Fees Required

I have included in the appendix an estimated closing costs worksheet for refinances to use when approaching your lender about the fees required.

Since there is quite a difference in the LTV for cash-out or no-cash-out refinances according to the previous chart let me give you some guidelines to follow to distinguish between the two. With a no-cash-out refinance, you may still receive up to $250 back for an FHA or VA refinance or up to $1000 for a conventional refinance transaction. This is only a guideline, but most lenders agree that closing costs and loan amounts cannot be accurately predicted prior to loan closing.

Before we determine your monthly savings with the new loan, let's see how much this may cost you. Let's say you have an old conventional loan with a balance of $72,000 and a home valued at $95,000 and you want a new conventional loan with no cash out, just a better interest rate. The maximum loan you can get would be $85,500., 90 percent of the value. Your fees may be as much as $2,200 to close this transaction, resulting in a new loan of $74,200 (These are only estimates; each area and lender is different. More information on closing costs is given in Chapter Two)

Exhibit 15: Example of Closing Costs

Loan fee	$1,113	(15% of the new loan of $74,200)
Appraisal fee	$250	
Credit report fee	$60	
Recording fees	$25	
Title insurance	$250	
Escrow fee	$150	Old loan of $72,000
Pest inspection	$60	Plus costs $2,253
Tax transfer fee	$35	New loan $74,200
Document fee	$300	(rounded off; you may have to
Notary fee	$10	come up with $100–$200 to keep
Total	$2,253	the no cash out)

Assuming that you wanted to finance the closing costs to avoid any cash out of your pocket, your new loan would have to be around $74,200 to cover all the costs.

Comparison of Your Old and New Loans

When comparing the monthly payment of your old loan to the one with your new loan, don't compare apples to oranges. If you have a fixed rate mortgage loan now and are applying for an ARM, use the principal and interest figure after the ARM loan has adjusted several times, at least through the first year of adjustments, to compare. Your loan officer should be able to provide you with this information as an estimate. Naturally, she won't know how the market will be one year from now, so ask that she use the worst case—the maximum caps for each adjustment and the lifetime maximum cap—then compare to your existing payments. The closing costs should be about the same for an ARM as for a fixed-rate except for the loan origination fee, which may be higher for an ARM.

Now your new loan in the example above is $74,200, including financed closing costs. Your old loan was a thirty-year fixed at 11.5 percent interest rate and your monthly payments were approximately $733. The old loan started at say $74,000 and you have paid it down to around $72,000. Ah, it appears we are right back where we started with a new loan of $74,200, so let's go further. The new loan will be $74,200 at 9.5 percent fixed for thirty years (within the 2 to 3 percent guideline to consider refinancing) and your monthly payment now will be $624, a savings of $109 per month. You've paid only a little cash up front but you have increased your loan amount by $2,200. You really need to consider this your expense for the transaction—you haven't paid it now but you will pay it later! The closing costs of $2,200 (financed portion) divided by your savings of $109 per month equals approximately twenty months. This means that it will take you almost two years of monthly payments to start realizing the savings. You are primarily paying off the costs of refinancing for those two years. This is well within the guidelines: Only consider refinancing if your monthly savings cover your closing costs within twenty-four to thirty-six months. You may want to go one step further. Get out the amortization schedule for your existing loan or order one from your lender to find out how much interest you will be paying on the old loan for next year, then ask your lender to run you an amortization schedule on your new loan, then compare the amount of interest you may deduct on Schedule A of your tax returns. This is important too—your interest is usually more during the first years of a mortgage loan (with less of your payment going toward the principal) and the tax deduction may be more even though the payments are lower. Check it out yourself or consult your tax preparer to do it for you to see if this refinance will be best for you in the next years for tax purposes. Some of the costs involved are deductible on that same Schedule A of your tax returns. The loan points paid to close a loan for a purchase or improvement of your primary residence are deductible in the year they are paid if you pay them separately by check to the lender. When you refinance for reasons other than home improvement, the points must be amortized over the life of the loan. The amount that remains unamortized at the sale of that property can be deducted during the year you sold it.

The example I used for closing costs was for a conventional loan with a 1.5 percent loan fee. If you are choosing an FHA or a VA loan you will have to pay approximately 1 percent for the loan fee and an additional amount for the discount points, depending on the interest rate you have chosen. (For more information on discount points see Chapter Two). You will want to choose the rate that has the fewest discount points to avoid more up-front closing costs, but that rate might not be 2 percent less than the one on your current loan, the amount needed to realize some savings. Call around to several lenders to determine if paying points in addition to the other closing costs is the best way to go for your refinance. Since one of the FHA and VA loans' best feature, assumability, is practically gone and since the down payment on a refinance is not a factor, FHA and VA refinances may not be a clear choice. You should compare the FHA and VA (if you are a veteran) rate with no discount points with the conventional rate. The loan fee other than discount points on the conventional loan may be higher—it is usually only 1 percent on FHA and VA loans, and may be as much as 1.5 percent or 2. percent on conventional.

Exhibit 16: Comparison of Loan Origination Fees and Discount Points

	FHA	VA	Conventional
Loan orig. fee	1.0 %	1.0%	1.5% to 2.0%
Discount points (to buy your rate down)	1.0%	1.0%	-0-
Total		2.0%	2.0%	2.0%

You need to compare the rate with and without discount points on the FHA or VA loan to see if it is actually cheaper than the conventional loan for a refinance.

Mortgage Insurance and Funding Fee
FHA

If you have an FHA loan originated since 1985 you had the option of paying the mortgage insurance premium (MIP) in cash at the closing or including the amount in your loan amount. Refinancing an FHA with a financed MIP and adding on the new MIP would result in two MIPs financed—a definite no-no to the

FHA. The loan officer will reduce your old FHA loan by the amount of the mortgage insurance premium that's to be refunded and add on the new MIP, if you choose to finance it, so you will only be financing the difference. To calculate the difference, first multiply your outstanding balance by the correct percentage from the MIP Refund Calculations Worksheet in the appendix, then calculate the new MIP using the percentage from the Factor Sheet in the appendix and subtract the difference. Or, better yet, let your loan officer do it for you! This amount will be added to your loan along with the closing costs you want to finance to arrive at a new loan amount.

If you're refinancing an FHA loan with financed MIP using another type of loan, conventional for instance, you will receive a refund of the unused portion of the MIP from the FHA about sixty days from the close of escrow. You must request the refund through your lender, so be sure to ask for the forms to complete along with the payoff of your old loan. Don't assume that your new lender will do so; mention it to them at the intitial application.

If you're refinancing an FHA or conventional loan with a VA loan you'll need to consider the 1.875 percent VA funding fee. You may pay it in cash or finance it like any other VA loan, but you must consider this in your loan amount if you finance it, or in your closing costs if you pay it in cash.

Prepaids or Impounds

Generally, if you already have an impound account for taxes and insurance on your previous loan, you'll also have one on your new loan if over 80 percent LTV. Some cash-out refinances are lower than 80 percent LTV, so you may not be required to pay in to an impound account. If that is the case, you'll be receiving back from the previous lender a refund of the impound account already established. Don't spend it though; you'll have to keep up the taxes and insurance yourself now and you'll be receiving those bills separately. If you do not have an impound account now and you'll need one on the new loan of over 80 percent LTV, you'll need more for the prepaids. Prepaids normally can't be financed and must either come out of the proceeds of the refinance or from you on a no-cash-out refinance. This will depend entirely on your LTV and on your new lender's requirements; more and more lenders are requiring the control that comes from the impound account for tax payments and insurance payments.

Prepaid Interest

When you refinance an existing loan or loans you may have to pay an additional amount of prepaid interest. Usually the escrow or title company will get the final interest amount on the old loan—the interest due to the date the new loan goes on the books with the new lender. If, for instance, you have made your payment on 1 April 1990, you have paid interest for the month of March—remember mortgage payments are in arrears, unlike rents, which are in advance. If your refinance closes on 15 April 1990, you owe interest at that time on the new loan from 15 April to 1 May on the old loan from 1 April thru 14 April; however, you don't have to make a payment again until 1 June 1990. This interest must be paid in cash up front, not financed, and needs to be considered at the closing. Some lenders do allow this to be financed, but since it may differ considerably depending on the closing date, it is difficult to include accurately. Check with your lender to see if you can have this financed along with the closing costs to avoid any out-of-pocket fees.

Prepayment Penalty

I haven't included in the estimate of the closing costs the prepayment penalty you may have to pay. This can wipe out the benefits of refinancing fast. If you didn't ask up front and don't know if you have a penalty for early repayment, your closing papers will tell you. It will state how much (usually a percentage of the balance) and when it applies (usually during the first one to three years of the loan). If you're still within that period and it amounts to over 2 percent of your loan, you may be over the thirty-six month guideline—that is, it may take you over thirty-six months of reduced monthly payments to realize any profit from the refinance. Add that prepayment figure to the closing costs and recalculate your monthly payment on the new loan and compare to the old loan as I did in my example to see if it will be a savings to you now. Maybe you would be wiser to pay the larger payment until you are out of the prepayment penalty period.

Cash-out Refinances

If your purpose in refinancing is to receive cash out, you first need to compare the advantages of the complete refinance of your existing debt with the *home equity loan* or *line of credit* discussed in Chapter Nine. The amount you want out of your equity and what you want to spend the money on are the major factors in determining the best program for you. There is no one answer for everyone, and the best source of information is a full-service lender who can provide you with both loans to compare. Your mortgage broker or mortgage banker may not be able to help you with both loans. They generally offer first mortgages rather than seconds, lines of credit or home equity loans. Your banker or your local savings and loan can probably provide you with the best choices for both types of loans and can compare for you. Your credit union may also have home equity loans but not necessarily first mortgages for the refinance should you choose that option.

If you want cash out and the resulting payment on the refinanced loan will be larger than your current payment, you should be making money with the cash out or at least improving what you now have (and thus making it more valuable). You should be refinancing to buy investments (either property or other investments in business ventures), to buy a second or vacation home, or to improve property you now own, either the subject property or other investment properties. Generally, these are the best reasons to refinance your existing loan other than to reduce the interest rate or to reduce the monthly payments. If you need money for short-term, nonincome-producing reasons, I would suggest that you consider a home equity loan, a second loan on your home, or a line of credit—all short-term loans. If you need money to consolidate your debts, you may not want to pay all those up-front fees required to refinance your existing first mortgage loan only to get right back into debt, which may happen unless you are more disciplined than most.

Secondary Financing

If you have a lien against the property, the new lender will require that you pay this in full. If you have subordinate financing (a second or even a third or fourth lien against the property) and want a cash-out refinance, the other liens must be paid. If the second lien is over one year and you don't want cash out, it can remain, subordinated to the new first lien (your new refinance), only if the first lien does not exceed 75 percent of the appraised value. The payments on the second lien must be considered in your qualifying and must be regular payments of principal and interest or interest only. There can be no negative amortization on the second, and the interest rate should not vary more than 2 percent from the new loan interest rate. So if you have taken out seconds, home equity loans, or lines of credit, you'll have to pay these off in the refinance transaction unless you want only 75 percent of the value. These guidelines vary greatly by lender and by program so ask up front if you want to keep your home equity line of credit active and want to refinance just the first lien with a new mortgage loan.

Refinancing your existing first lien for a lower interest rate, for cash out to invest either in property or business interests, or for a combination of both reasons makes sense in most cases. Refinancing for other reasons should be carefully considered. I've always thought that money (home equity) not making money is losing money. Your equity may be growing due to growth in your area and the increasing value of your property. If it isn't, then inflation is eating away at it and you may need to offset that by investing your equity in other ways. This is purely an editorial opinion. Don't rush out and refinance to invest in any business venture unless it is fully researched, but do consider that your money should be growing in some way. (On the other hand, that trip around the world mentioned earlier is sounding better and better!)

Chapter

Secondary Financing

Home Rich, Cash Poor

When it's time to use the equity in your home or in your investment properties, you'll have a wide variety of loan choices, and just like the first mortgage loan used to purchase or refinance, you'll have to choose the one that fits your needs. I've separated the types of subordinate or secondary financing you could use to draw on that equity into two categories: the *second mortgage installment loan* and the *home equity credit line*. There are some variations on these two types of loans, and each type of loan may be called something different due to the aggressive marketing now used to tap this new source of lending. You've probably heard of the tax advantages of using a second or home equity loan to purchase major personal items due to the gradual disappearance of the personal interest tax deduction, and it's true to a certain extent. The limitations to these deductions will be covered in each of the two categories below.

You'll have to qualify for either type of equity loan and must provide the same type of income and expense information that you provided for your original mortgage loan. You'll also have a good paying record on the first loan to add to your qualifications. The fact that you can only borrow up to 75 to 80 percent of the value will help to avoid mortgage insurance fees. Usually your credit limit on a home equity line is set by taking the percentage, say 75 percent, of the appraised value of the home and subtracting the balance owed on the existing mortgage.

Exhibit 17: Example of a Home Equity Line Limit

Appraised value of home	$100,000
Percentage	x 75%
Total available	$75,000
Less your current mortgage	– 50,000
Amount of Credit Line	$25,000

Your file will include the appraisal, a credit report, your income information (W-2s and paystubs or tax returns) and the mortgage loan history of your first lien.

Second Mortgages and Installment Loans

This type of mortgage loan is much like the first mortgage loan on your home but it's in second position on the title to the property or in "junior" position. The term of the second is usually three to twenty-five years with repayment at a fixed rate of interest and with fixed monthly payments throughout the term. Most seconds are called home improvement or home equity loans and are offered at banks and savings and loans (savings banks or thrifts), along with a wide range of other consumer loans. The difference between this type of equity loan and the others is that a second mortgage installment loan has one large advance of money with repayment on the original amount amortized over a set period of time.

If you have a specific need for a certain amount of money that you would like to repay in small regular payments, this type of loan may be for you. For instance, you may need to borrow $5,000 to $25,000 to repair or replace your roof, add on a bathroom, install new carpeting and generally increase the value of your home or your investment property. You have a bid by a contractor on all or a portion of the work and you need to be prepared to pay for the entire project by the time it's finished. Your monthly payments at say 12 percent for ten years will be around $144 per month for $10,000, but you've increased the value of your home, and when you sell it, you can pay off that loan. Cosmetic improvements (landscaping, carpeting, even upgrading appliances) don't always increase the value of your home substantially. Some room additions are not as valuable as others; for instance, an additional bedroom, making yours a five-bedroom home in a three-bedroom neighborhood, may not add too much to the value. A family room is great but not always valuable. A kitchen expansion and renovation or an additional bathroom add the most to your home in most areas.

Overimprovements can be costly and may increase the value only to you and your family. Check with some realtors or appraisers in the area to see what value they would place on your anticipated addition. Of course, be prepared for any realtor worth her salt to try to sell you another larger or already-improved home; that's her job!

If you secure this loan with your home, you can use the money for home improvements or for any other purpose, and the interest on the loan will be tax deductible, just like the interest on your first mortgage. You're entitled to deduct up to $100,000 of interest on that debt as long as the liens don't exceed the value of the property, no matter how the money is spent. You can use it for financing an education, paying bills, or investing in business, as long as the loan is secured by your primary residence or by a second home that you actually use the greater of at least fourteen days or 10 percent of its rental days each year. The up-front fees for a second lien are very similar to those for a first mortgage.

Exhibit 18 gives a sampling of the fees you may be required to pay.

Exhibit 18: Closing Costs For Typical Home Equity Installment Loans

Loan origination fees	Usually 1 to 3 percent of the loan amount
Appraisal fee	$200 to $250
Credit report fee	$20 to $60
Title policy and search or survey	$100 to $200
Recording fees	$10 to $20
Application fee or document fee	$100 to $250

Included in the appendix is a checklist with the basic features of these loans and questions to ask when considering any second lien on your property. Compare both the fees and repayment terms of several plans offered by your local bank or savings and loan before choosing one.

These fees can be deducted from the loan proceeds or paid in cash at the closing. Some or all of the fees may be waived or reduced if you are a customer of the bank or if the market dictates it. Home equity lines of credit are more popular these days and you stand a better chance of the fees being waived on those types of loans.

Remember that this is a lien against your home just like the first lien and should you default, the lender of the second loan will take your property just as fast. The difference is that the holder of the second will keep the first current if you don't to protect their "second" position. If you defaulted on the first and the lender foreclosed, the holder of the second would be out of luck. When you close a new second mortgage loan, the holder or lender will file a notice of default with the first lender to make sure they are notified of the second lien and both lenders are given the opportunity of protecting their interest. The point is, you could lose your home if you borrow money for any reason and can't repay the debt. I'd suggest that you borrow only what you need and use it wisely.

You pay for the money you borrowed whether you use it or not on this type of second mortgage loan, but it usually is a fixed rate and generally the interest rate is less than for a home equity line of credit—not always, so you need to compare the two. For this decision, you need to determine your needs for the money and the amount of money you need. Beginning in 1989, you're required to receive a disclosure statement on these types of loans similar to the disclosure statement on your first mortgage loan, outlining the fees involved and the terms and interest rate you'll be charged. You'll be expected to pay fees for the appraisal and credit report when you apply and it is likely that this will be nonrefundable. Ask before you write the check if you're not sure you're going to go through with this.

One drawback to some of the home equity installment loans offered is the balloon payment feature. In order to offer lower payments, your promissory note may include a balloon payment at the end. You may have the loan amortized over twenty years, with a large payment due at the end of five years. That means that your payments are calculated as if you were paying for the loan for twenty years (smaller payments) but the balance is actually due sooner, at a prearranged date. Be prepared to sell the property at the end of the five years or whenever the balloon payment is due, extend the mortgage term if allowed, or ask that the second mortgage be transferred to other property you own with more equity (called a transfer of security). Ask that these options be included in the promissory note before you sign it or you'll be at the lender's mercy come the due date. Look for the words "partial amortization," "balloon payment," or "remaining principal due" in the paperwork (either the note, the disclosure, or the deed) and make sure that the remaining principal due is actually at the end of the term you agreed upon. Understanding the terms of a second loan on your home is equally as important as on the first.

An "interest only" second mortgage loan may be offered by some lenders and may fit your needs. With this loan, you only pay interest until the term is up, when you must pay the entire principal. The interest is deductible as outlined previously, and for those who intend to sell their property upon completion of the improvements or have a large sum of money coming in, this can be a very attractive option. The snag (and there always is one!) is that the interest rate may be higher than on a fully amortized loan (with principal paid too) and, of course, you could loose your home just as easily. If you have chosen a private lender, whether it is a family member or friend, I would suggest that you have the paperwork reviewed by an attorney and have all the title searches, policies issued, and legal documents recorded just as you would do with a private lender on a first mortgage loan. It really is for everyone's protection.

Home Equity Line of Credit

Drawing out the equity on your home is becoming one of the fastest growing sources of lending. This type of loan is packaged differently by each lender, but the end result is pretty much the same. You have a second lien against your home just like the previously mentioned second mortgage installment loan, except you may have more choices on the rate, term, and the method of repayment.

If you need small amounts of money periodically to pay off revolving charge accounts and intend to pay the amount back quickly, the interest rate on the home equity credit line and the terms are not so important as the up-front fees. Home equity lines of credit sometimes have lower up-front fees because they are a hot item with lenders, and quick repayment reduces the interest paid no matter how high it is! In effect, the home equity loan can be used as a credit card that is secured by your home. For most home equity lines of credit, your up-front costs are about the same as the second mortgage installment loan. Loan fees, appraisal fees, credit report fees and even title fees can be waived if you are a regular customer or if the market warrants it (and it sure has lately). You may see the ads for a no fee line of credit. Naturally, you should take advantage of this offer if you are intending to use the equity anyway. Be aware, though, of some hidden costs that might offset those fees.

The home equity credit line is just that, a line of credit. You will be approved for a specified amount based on the value of your home and the amount of your first lien. Usually the lender will allow you a line of credit for up to 80 percent of the value of your home, although some lenders will allow only 70 to 75 percent LTV. That means that the first mortgage loan balance plus the maximum allowable line of credit cannot exceed 80 percent of the value of your property, the same as with a second mortgage. This varies by area and by lender. Since this type of loan is commonly held by the lender and not traded on the open market, they can pretty much make their own rules, within federal and state laws. You should be prepared to do some shopping for this type of loan just as you did for your first; there are many choices and your circumstances will determine the loan you choose. Let me outline some of the variables you may discover in your shopping and some of the drawbacks of those options.

Whether it's an annual fee, a renewal fee, a membership fee, or a participation fee, it is still a fee. Some lenders require a fee of twenty-five to one hundred dollars, depending on the line of credit terms. This means you pay yearly whether or not you use the line of credit. If it is based on the outstanding balance, you may get by with twenty-five to fifty dollars yearly for the privilege of having access to extra money. It must be extra if you haven't used it in a year! If the yearly fee is a flat fee of fifty dollars or more and you aren't using it, I'd suggest that you request a cancellation of this type of credit.

You may be charged a fee per transaction, called a transaction fee or participation fee, in addition to the interest charged on the money you borrow. Presumably this is a paperwork-type fee, over and above the application fee, the document fee, and the transfer fee; certainly it is one you should avoid if you plan on making small advances often.

Minimum/Maximum Advances

Make sure that you can advance yourself the proper amount for your purposes. If you will need only a hundred dollars or so at a time and the minimum is five hundred, you could advance five hundred dollars and repay the four hundred dollars immediately without paying interest, but why choose a program that doesn't fit your needs? Read the disclosure, which describes this important feature, and move on to another lender if your lender can't change the terms to accommodate you.

Terms For Repayment

Your loan may be repaid in a variety of ways. Usually you have a set term established for borrowing and repaying, say thirty-six to sixty months. During this period your note will allow you to borrow to the maximum as long as you meet the minimum payments required. You can repay in full and advance in full, many times over, as long as your payments are kept current and you are paying all the fees involved. At the end of the term, your note may provide for a renewal for another thirty-six to sixty months, or it may renew yearly after that with an adjustment in the rate, or it may become a closed end credit line that allows only for repayment on new installment terms, which amortize the debt over another three to five years. This is where you must be particularly careful. If you agree to a repayment schedule of the unpaid balance at a fixed rate, make sure it is a rate you can live with five years from now.

Some lenders require that you repay the entire balance due at the end of the line of credit. Check to see what other options you may have; perhaps you can refinance without extra fees or extend the term of the loan. This is a balloon payment just as on the second installment loan; you have to be prepared to repay the entire amount you borrowed or sell the property and pay off all the loans.

The amount you pay monthly is an important factor in your choice. Make sure that you understand the maximum and minimum you are required to pay before even considering a particular lender. You need to ask what the late penalties are, whether the payment includes principal and interest or interest only, and what fraction of the outstanding balance, plus interest, is due monthly.

Your loan payment is usually a percentage (usually 1.5 to 2.5 percent) of the outstanding balance, similar to the payments required on your revolving charge cards, with a minimum of fifty to one hundred fifty dollars depending on the size of your line of credit. For example, an outstanding balance of $5,000 at 12 percent interest (prime plus two—the prime at the time this is written happens to be 10 percent) would require a monthly payment of $100 (2 percent x $5000) plus interest of $50 (12 percent x $5000), for a total of $150. Obviously, paying off this debt early would save money in the long run. A second loan installment style for a five-year loan would be $111.22 per month on a fixed rate of 12 percent fully amortized. The difference may be that your second loan installment is applying some portion of the payment to principal, more in the later years.

You could also get a loan that requires interest-only payments for a shorter term. This loan may be more attractive for those who are in a short-term money crunch. You will want to check the terms of the balloon, or final payment, in order to determine your ability to repay this lump sum. Those on a yearly bonus or commission basis would benefit from the use of their own income in advance, as long as you can count on the bonus or commission! I know the best advice would be to suggest that you wait for that first commission check, put it in savings and then collect earnings while you spend a portion of it next year. Right! The fact is most of us are not that disciplined and are better at living for today. Just remember that this line of credit is secured by your rose-covered, cozy little cottage, which is home to your loved ones. I think you get the point.

Interest Rates

Most lenders use a type of adjustable rate loan; the rate is either tied to the prime lending rate as reported in the *Wall Street Journal* on a given day or it is taken from the same type of indexes used on other adjustable rate mortgage loans: the U.S. Treasury Bills yield or the FHLB district cost of funds. The term *tied to prime* means your rate is prime plus a set percentage—

prime plus 2 percent is common. For example, if prime as reported today is 10 percent (in the *Wall Street Journal*) then your interest rate is 12 percent today. (In the section of the *Wall Street Journal* Money and Investing you will find a page with federal home loan ARM rates and interest rate instruments for bond and treasury bill prices.) Usually the rate is determined at the end of the month on a set date for all loans tied to prime. If you choose an adjustable rate loan, your loan will have a cap, both a periodic (monthly, quarterly, yearly) cap and a term cap, and will have a margin to be added to the index to produce the current rate just like the ARM loan. Your periodic payment increases, monthly, quarterly, yearly or whatever, will be an important factor, too. If your loan has the potential of monthly increases in interest, you may want a loan with a conversion option to a fixed rate at a set time during the line of credit term. Your disclosure statement will give you the terms, conditions, and also a fifteen-year history of the index your lender will be using for your interest rate adjustments. Normally the U.S. Treasury Bill index changes more often with the market than the district cost of funds, but you will have to check in your area for the choices available. Your rate will be high, no doubt, so use this type of loan for short-term borrowing with minimal advances. You are still better off than using most revolving credit cards and better off than some other consumer loans for small household items or automobiles because the tax benefits for interest deduction offset some of the expense of the line of credit.

Concluding the Line of Credit

At the end of the term, assuming that your note allows for an installment-type payout, you will begin to retire the debt, with no more advances allowed, over a set period. You may still be paying 2 percent of the principal plus interest or $1/50$ of the balance, or your terms may convert to a fixed, fully amortized payment plan. You will have to read the disclosure to see which fits your needs.

You may also extend this line of credit or sell the home in the meantime and pay it off completely. Take the time to read the fine print for any special requirements: that you must notify the lender if you intend to sell the home, that you can't lease or rent the property, or any other special requirements. If you do sell the property and pay off all the loans, you may have to pay ten to fifty dollars to file and record the releases of this line of credit. Even without this requirement, you should notify the lender on your line of credit as soon as possible upon sale to avoid complications when you pay off the loan at the closing. Your line of credit could also contain a prepayment penalty, something to consider on any second installment loan or home equity line of credit.

One of the best ways to protect yourself is to ask for all the information concerning the terms and costs of the plan in writing. The federal requirements of disclosure will help, but discuss anything you don't understand with the loan officer and take notes. As mentioned in previous chapters, notes taken well at the outset can be used later to refresh your lender's memory. Use the checklist provided in the appendix for comparing features when you are shopping for this type of financing.

Section III

Chapter

Buying and Financing A Second (Vacation) Home

FINDING A MORTGAGE LOAN TO PURCHASE or refinance a second or vacation home may be somewhat more difficult than finding and qualifying for the first home. The qualifying guidelines are primarily the same. You must be able to qualify for your primary residence house payment, all other expenses and the housing expense of the second home. However, most lenders don't want to include any rents you may receive from that second home, since it moves the transaction into another category, the rental property category, a much more risky loan in the eyes of many lenders. The FHA and VA programs no longer allow for second home or vacation home financing except in "hardship" cases and your lender will be offering you a conventional loan. There are many more restrictions on the loans to purchase or refinance a rental or investment property, the basic restriction being a low loan-to-value or the maximum loan you can get with the least down payment. There is usually a loan-to-value restriction of 70 to 75 percent, depending on the program, for conventional first liens, on rental properties but as high as 85 percent on second home or vacation homes that are not rented. If you are going to qualify without rental income (be willing to state that you're not going to rent this home out, even though it sets vacant five months out of the year), then you're going to have to have the necessary income to qualify for both house payments.

In this chapter I will only cover the areas of qualifying and obtaining a mortgage loan for a vacation home that differ from the normal qualifying requirements I described in Part One. You need be able to prove your income, assets, and credit history, just as you did for the mortgage on the first home, and your resulting ratios must be the same, depending on the loan-to-value. You should review the qualifying guidelines for conventional programs to see first if you have the income to qualify for this type of loan. When using the conventional worksheets in the appendix, put the payment on this second or vacation home in the "other expenses" category, since your "bottom" ratio will determine your qualifications for this type of loan.

Shopping for the Mortgage Loan

From some lenders, you will get a "you want what!" attitude because they like to do only the "gravy" loans (the first mortgage loans on primary residences), mostly because they may not be familiar with other types of loans. If the lender you used for your home doesn't have an office or hasn't done business around a resort community they probably won't be the best choice; however, I would start there. Your first problem may be choosing a lender that can cross state lines. If your choice of a home is across the country, or even just in another state, you local bank, savings and loan, or thrift may not be licensed to do business there. Probably this is the first question you should ask if you want to do your shopping locally. Choosing a lender in the state or area where your second home is located makes more sense, although you may have to make an extra trip or two to close the transaction. Most companies who do business in a resort community know the limitations and have title companies, insurance companies, etc., who can accommodate you. Because we're a more mobile society now, owning and actually using a second home is less difficult. The little cabin at the lake has been replaced by the modern condo at Aspen or Hawaii. My lending experience has included mortgage loans on homes and condominiums in the Lake Tahoe region, one of the most popular spots to buy a vacation home for the California crowd, and it was taken for granted that originating loans for Tahoe properties would cause logistical problems. I trust your lender will take that into consideration when quoting your fees. Expect to pay a little, not a lot, more in mailing, fax, or miscellaneous fees, which may be added on to the loan fee, or expect to pay a larger loan origination fee to cover those costs. Mortgage loans for second or vacation homes are many times more expensive because of higher loan fees, more closing costs, and higher interest rates. The expense for this type of loan is halfway between that for owner-occupied and that for investment properties. Default rates are high in this area of lending, thus the added costs. FHA and conventional loan programs are available but the LTV is lower—and you'll have to put more of your own money into the transaction. Finding a mortgage loan to buy or refinance an existing condo or single family unit will be much easier than finding a loan to buy vacant land to build your own on.

Before you shop for that second home, consider the area for its resale values, rental potential, convenience for your family, and conformity with the rest of the area. If the area you've chosen is more than a few hours drive from your principal home, or if you're not familiar with the area, you should probably use the services of a realtor to represent you in this transaction. You can do-it-yourself using the same contracts and paperwork for a second home, with the same money saving advantages, except when you can't shop or don't know the area well enough to buy wisely. You're going to be obligated for a thirty- or fifteen-year mortgage loan in this area, so you should be very sure that the property will suit your family's needs for a long time to come or that you can sell it if you need to. Your realtor will probably know of lenders in the area who specialize in second homes if you can't use the same lender as on your primary residence. Ask him to shop around for you to get the best rate, term, and fees, just like he would shop for any other loan.

Programs Available

CLTV means the total of the first and any subordinate or second liens on the property. If there is going to be a second lien on the property then the first cannot be more than 75 percent LTV. Most conventional lenders require that the property be a single-family residence and that the property not be a rental. Since *not* renting this property is important to both of these programs, you'll probably have to submit a letter to the lender certifying that this will be your vacation home and that you don't intend to rent it. If you do intend to rent it, and most people do, then you'll need to shop for another lender who recognizes that most second homes are bought for the tax advantages and for some return on the investment. You may not be able to use the rental income to qualify, but there will be fewer restrictions. Banks and savings and loans in the area of the home will be able to help you, though, of course, you may pay more for this type of loan since they may not be able to be sold on the secondary market.

Exhibit 19: Second Home Maximum Loan-to-Value Ratios

	Conventional	
	LTV	CLTV
Purchase	80%	90%
Refinance with no cash out	70%	70%

Tax Advantages

The Tax Reform Act of 1986 changed the tax benefits of owning a second home as an investment and significantly changed the way buyers looked at the purchase of a second home. As more and more people begin to understand the limitations and the remaining tax benefits, the demand for mortgage loans to buy second or vacation homes is increasing, especially in certain areas. The time you occupy the home, the time you rent it, and the time the home will be vacant will all be factors in the tax deductions. First, let me suggest that you keep a log of your visits to the vacation home. Your personal record of your occupancy could help in a tax audit should you need to prove how many months of the year you used the second home. Our family has a log kept by everyone in the family who used the vacation spot while my children were growing up. It's a wonderful trip down memory lane for us old folks and contains some priceless comments on our family life. I ran across it recently and wasn't suprised to find that the main comments written in the log referred to food and the weather, evidently both important to our daily lives in those days! It does track the dates we were there also, and I'm confident that it would be acceptable evidence of our occupancy for tax purposes.

You'll need to be familiar with Schedule A and Schedule E of the federal tax returns, included in the appendix, or you need to be in touch with your tax preparer about those forms before you shop for a mortgage loan and especially before you shop for a vacation home. You should consult a tax accountant about all the rules of the IRS, but in this section I'll give you some of the basics so you'll know what to ask or what to look for on these forms. Schedule A contains a section for the deduction of mortgage interest on your homes, both your primary and your second home. Schedule E is used to calculate your taxable income or loss from rental properties (and trusts, partnerships, etc.).

When this second home is not rented at all or rented less than fifteen days a year, you may only report your tax deductible interest and property taxes (and any casualty loss you suffered) on the Schedule A. The limitations on deducting this interest, on property with up to $100,000 in mortgage debt, applies to both a primary and a second home, up to two residences. You can also deduct up to $100,000 interest paid on a home equity loan regardless of how you use the money. Interest paid during that year will be provided in a year-end statement from your lender. Property taxes are fully deductible on the second home in the year they are paid. Only the amount of property taxes the lender pays on your behalf or what you actually paid is deductible.

When this home is totally rented and no longer a second or vacation home, you can treat the income and expenses like any other investment or rental property by reporting mortgage interest, property taxes, insurance premiums, maintainence expenses, and depreciation on Schedule E. The maximum passive loss will be $25,000 of your ordinary income.

When you use the home part of the year and rent it the rest, it becomes tricky! This is the time to resort to the log, both to prove your occupancy and to keep a record for year-end tax time. If you use the property more than fourteen days or 10 percent of the rental days and you rent it more than fifteen days, you can deduct the interest, taxes, and expenses on Schedule E to offset the rental income. The amount of interest and taxes over the rental income can be carried over to your Schedule A and included in your home interest section but with no loss allowed, as is the case for rental loss. If you use the property less than fifteen days or 10 percent of the rental days and rent it over fifteen days per year, then it is considered a rental and you can deduct interest, taxes, and expenses (including depreciation) on Schedule E with the resulting tax loss limit of $25,000 of your ordinary income. Confusing, yes, but it must be considered in your decision to buy a second home. You may have heard from friends or relatives that a second home is a great write-off, and it used to be better than it is now. The rules have changed in the last four or so years and you need to be aware of them. If you don't want to get involved in all of this occupancy days and percentages, just decide up front that you won't rent it at all and that you and your family will occupy it exclusively. Of course, you will be losing out on the rental income that is so valuable in some areas, but, on the other hand, you may be able to get a mortgage loan of up to 80 percent of the value. To decide, call your tax preparer and go over the rules with a professional who is familiar with your tax situation. Not everyone needs the tax deductions still available. Although vacation or second homes are no longer great tax shelters, they are a wonderful investment in most geographical areas.

Types of Units

Conventional lenders limit the type of dwelling to a one-unit residential dwelling. This means a single family home, a unit in an approved condominium development, a unit in a planned unit development or any type of cluster, townhouse, or zero-lot-line-type dwelling, as long as it is not a duplex, triplex or fourplex. If you are buying a log cabin, an A-frame, or any unit without all the conveniences of home, because of the rustic quality, your lender may require that the property meet local codes for year round access and occupancy, may require more fire insurance for wooded areas, or may require community or private road maintainence agreements to prove the value of the property. Like any other property, the value is mostly determined by the sales in the area. You may be required to put a larger than normal down payment on nonconforming properties. Most lenders will not lend at all on homes that are not connected to a public power source—your water may come from a well, you may have a septic system, but your primary heat and light source will have to be from a dependable public or private system, though a butane or oil system is usually acceptable. Many lenders require a telephone (to call the fire department), and fire and emergency services must be reasonably close. Your fire and hazard insurance premiums will also reflect the emergency vehicle accessibility. Checking on local codes before purchasing in a nonresidential neighborhood is always best. You may want to improve, add on, or change the unit but can't because of restrictive building codes. More and more lands are subject to ecological controls, and yours may have restrictions about the use of the land as well as the size and type of improvements you can make. A lack of any utilities or any shopping and transportation services may affect the value of your home for resale, and your lender is always thinking about default rates in vacation homes caused by the lack of resale or rental value.

Timeshares

If you will be buying in a resort community, undoubtedly you will be offered a timeshare situation. The financing to purchase your share or interest in the partnership (timeshare) is usually offered through a private lender and most timeshare developments provide their own financing arrangements for those who need it. A timeshare is usually a type of partnership in the development. Make sure that you actually have some ownership in the unit, even just for your share of the time, whether it's a condominium or single family unit. Also, make sure it's a simple fee rather than a leasehold arrangement. Some timeshare agreements are actually memberships in a timesharing club, which gives you rights to use the property for your share of the year but which does not actually entitle you to ownership of any part of the property. Your tax deductions will differ according to the arrangement. Timeshares can be a good way to have the use of a resort unit for a part of the year, but you should be sure you'll be able to use it only those times or else make sure that your contract contains the option to float or exchange your share of use according to your needs. Make sure that the condominium or maintainence fees for the upkeep of the property are included in your yearly fees or in the costs of purchasing and that you pay only your share. Make sure that your share of the property taxes and insurance premiums are included in your yearly fees or in your costs of purchase. Property taxes and condominium or home-owners dues can become a lien against the property if unpaid and you could be left with a tidy sum should something happen to the partnership. It would be wise to use an attorney's services to review the contracts for you (usually for a flat fee) before you invest in this type of development. Some contracts that allow for actual ownership of the property result in property tax deductions come tax time. Check with your tax expert about your particular timeshare situation; do not assume that this type of second home purchase will fit your tax needs.

Qualifying

To determine your qualifications for the monthly payment of a second home you will be using the Conventional Prequalifying Worksheets in the appendix, depending on the type of program you choose with your lender. If your lender has their own program it will likely coincide closely with standard conventional underwriting guidelines for a loan-to-value ratio of 80 percent, or 28/36 percent. The top figure means that the housing expense on your primary residence (principal, interest, taxes, fire and flood insurance, and homeowners association dues if a condo or PUD) should not exceed 28 percent of your gross monthly income, and the bottom figure means that your housing expenses for both the primary and second residences plus all other expenses should not exceed 36 percent of your gross monthly income. More on those qualifying guidelines in Chapter Four. Since most lenders don't recognize the rental income (and don't want to know about it!) you'll need to qualify using your family's income alone. If you are self-employed or receive commission or bonus income, be prepared to supply tax returns, W-2s, paystubs, bank statements, a copy of the contract, and information on all of your outstanding debts. You will be required to pay the same closing costs as on your primary residence purchase or refinance and you must provide a check upon application for the appraisal and credit report fees. You should shop at all available lenders for this loan, though your choices may be limited to a few who understand this product. Ask your realtor, the neighbors in the resort community, or the local Chamber of Commerce to refer you to lenders who specialize in this type of financing. A mortgage broker in a resort community can be the most helpful by placing your loan quickly with the right lender. A mortgage broker charges approximately the same fees for her services but knows better how to package this special-needs loan, so check your telephone directory for a mortgage broker or mortgage banker in the area you've chosen.

Comparisons Before Buying a Second Home

Before you take the important step of buying a second home you should have already spent some time in the area you want to buy, and you should be convinced that you'll use the property or be able to rent it enough to make it worthwhile. Having done business in several resort communities, I have seen the best of intentions turn sour. Don't buy a property when you are fresh from a vacation—that might be when your vision is clouded. You've spent two glorious weeks in the sun and surf or in the mountains and don't want it to end. On the way out of town, you see a for sale sign, or a new timeshare development and are relaxed and very vulnerable. Go home and think about it through the winter. If it is a skiing retreat that you want, go back in the summer and do some thorough checking about the year-round use of the property and the area. Talk to neighbors about rental prices for comparable homes and talk to ski lodge employees about how they spend their summers. (If they leave town you may have a problem!) For beach communities, check the local newspapers for winter rental rates and check with hotel and motel employees about what the community is like during the off-season. If they say "dead," you may have to absorb the cost of this second home year round. If your intent is to use it year round as a retreat, be sure you pick an area that is accessible year round and, for mountain areas, make sure the roads are cleared by someone (preferrably not you) on a regular basis. Otherwise, do some checking for at least a year before you buy. I know most lenders would not like to hear this, but your family might be better off with a seasonal rental unit without the tax deductions but with less expense and less responsibility. Your needs will determine this. Sit down and calculate the cost both ways to see if your money could be better invested. If you choose an area with excellent rental possibilities, the worst than can happen is that you will own a rental unit too far away to keep up and you'll have the added expense of a rental service to take care of it for you.

While you are comparing the cost of a rental versus ownership of a vacation home, be sure to include the cost of commuting. If you own a unit, you may be inclined and able to stay longer, avoiding costly travel expenses. On the other hand, you may have to commute home to work more often and feel obligated to make use of the property rather than let it sit vacant, and your transportation expense may be greater. It could work both ways, depending on your work situation.

Lastly, consider your age and family needs. If you are new to the work force and are starting a family, this may just be the investment you need both for tax purposes and for continuity in the family. Your own retreat with your young family can bring you closer together, of course, the same family with older children can be a nightmare (come on you parents of teenagers, you know what I am saying). Spending two weeks with the old folks is not always attractive to "preadults." If you are approaching the empty-nest situation or, even better, retirement, this second home could be your retirement home and the investment in a mortgage loan to buy could be a good investment. Even if you don't use it all the time as a retirement home, the grown family and grandkids could take advantage of your wise investment until they're able to afford their own second home.

Chapter

Buying or Refinancing a Rental Property

Shopping for Financing

Shopping for a mortgage loan to buy or refinance an investment property will be similar to shopping for the loan needed to buy your primary residence or second home, except that you'll be limited to lenders who offer conventional loans or their own brand of portfolio loans.

FHA allows a refinance of nonowner-occupied properties if the existing lien is an FHA and if they have owned the property for at least six months. This is a streamline FHA loan to lower the monthly payments and cash back is not allowed. FHA has recently eliminated the individual investor from most of their purchase transaction programs. The maximum loan on the streamline refinance is limited to either the old loan balance not including closing costs if a new appraisal is not ordered, or the old loan balance with closing costs if a new appraisal shows it warrants the higher loan amount.

The VA only allows the refinance of a nonowner-occupied property if the veteran used to occupy it and if the existing loan is a VA loan that has a higher interest rate than the new loan. The VA does not allow any cash back from the transaction.

Conventional guidelines allow 70 percent LTV for the purchase of nonowner-occupied properties and 70 percent LTV for no-cash-out refinances of nonowner-occupied properties.

Some lenders allow for 80 percent, LTV and allow for cash out on refinances up to 80 percent but because this type of loan isn't easily traded on the secondary market you may have to shop a little more. FNMA will buy loans on investment properties, but only those with a borrower who has fewer than four properties that are currently being financed, including the borrower's principal residence. Shop at your local bank or your savings and loan first since they will have the option of portfolioing those loans that can't be sold. Private investors are out there but you will most likely be paying a premium both in interest and in the fees. The loan you choose will also depend on the type of property you own or want to buy, the rents you expect to receive and how much negative cash flow from the property you can afford. As a general rule of thumb, your loan payments should be covered by your rents, especially if you are buying your first rental property and haven't built up at least six months' payments in your savings account for a buffer after the purchase.

If you'd like to use the equity in your home to buy another home to live in, yet would like to keep your home for an investment, you might do better getting a home equity loan, a line of credit, or refinancing your existing lien with cash-out while you're still living in it before buying a new home. You may not be able to get cash out of your property after it's a rental with most programs. Cash-out refinances are usually limited to owner-occupied properties. Your lender may have you sign a statement that your property will be owner-occupied for a certain period of time and you'll have to comply with that agreement. If you approach a lender about an owner-occupied refinance with cash-out, you must play by their rules or find another lender.

Using the equity in your home for the investment in other property is best if the rent on the home will cover your expenses after you move, with no negative cash flow at first. The rent should cover the first lien, the second lien, and any utilities, taxes or insurance you must pay, especially if this is your first venture into "landlording." You should have a buffer of six months of expenses in the bank; that is, six times the principal, interest, taxes, and insurance (PITI), at least for your own peace of mind. If you are applying for a new loan you'll be expected to have that six months of reserves to qualify for a very good reason. Your qualifications are based on the rental income less a vacancy factor, and under extreme circumstances, you may actually have to absorb the rental housing expense with your income only. As with all other mortgage loans, lenders are very aware of the high default rate, and that rate is particularly high with nonowner-occupied properties. If you become delinquent on your home loan due to unforeseen circumstances, you have more incentive to find a way to keep your home (such as keeping a roof over your head!), but if you have a rental, and the market goes to pot, you might be inclined to walk away and take your losses. The lender ends up with a home to sell, and with the costs of selling and legal fees, rarely is anything left. The point is, you'll have to be prepared to make a larger down payment and have more cash reserves for this type of purchase, and you may not be able to get cash-out in a refinance.

Taxes, Taxes, Who Pays the Taxes

The tax advantages of this type of investment should far outweigh the difficulties with finding a lender who can help you with your mortgage loan needs. If you've been in your home for awhile, have built up some equity, or have come into some money lately, this type of investment can be a good long-term source of income, as well as offering a tax shelter for your ordinary income. You need to be prepared to do a lot of the work and research yourself to make it profitable, but the rewards are there for certain people. Some homeowners think they'll be able to see the financial results of property investment during the first year. You'll have to wait for your first set of tax returns to get the full benefit. A negative cash flow on the property is actually money out of your pocket each month until you realize the tax advantages at the end of the year. Several years and several properties later, you should begin to see the difference.

The form that you'll be using on your federal tax return is Schedule E, an all-purpose form to be used for income reported on rentals, trusts, partnerships and other types of income. For your purposes, the front of the schedule should be enough. I have included a blank Schedule E and a blank 4562 in the appendix, two forms that you or your tax preparer would be using if you buy a second home or a rental unit. If you've been thinking about buying a home or renting out your home, you might play with the figures to see what your profits or loss would be. Always consult your tax professional before taking the step, but the example below and a look at the forms may help you to decide. Line 27 will be the "bottom line" for you. If that line contains a positive figure you will carry it forward to line 18 of your 1040 (the front page of your returns) and pay tax based on that plus your salary, wages and nonpassive income. If it's a negative up to $25,000, it can be carried forward to offset your salary, wages and nonpassive income, assuming that you actively participated in the rental. There are passive activity and at-risk limits, so your own circumstances will determine your amount of deductible income. You must own a minimum of 10 percent of the property, you can't occupy the property yourself more than fourteen days each year, and you must have an adjusted gross income of $100,000 per year or less; over that amount you are subject to the phase-out rule. These tax rules are subject to change each year so you should consult a tax expert before you buy an investment property.

For an example, let's say that you bought a new home in February 1989 and rented your home for $1,100 a month. You have a mortgage loan on which you pay about $10,000 a year or $830 a month, and you bought a new appliance for $425. You would figure your expenses as shown in Exhibit 20.

Exhibit 20: Example of Rental Loss Calculated For Tax Purposes

Total rental income received 1989	$12,100
($1,100.00 x 11 months if you bought it 2/89)	
Fire insurance	$200
Mortgage interest	$8,500
General repairs	$175
Real Estate taxes	$800
Total expenses	$9,675
Minus depreciation:	
On the home	$3,500
(basis for depreciation cost $110,000 x 3.182% for the 11 months)	
On the appliance	$61
(basis for depreciation cost $425 x 14.28% for the 11 months)	
Total Depreciation	$3,561
Income	$12,100
Expenses	– $9,675
Depreciation	– $3,561
Net Rental Loss	$1,136 (for tax purposes)

The rental loss can be carried forward to the 1040 to offset ordinary income, subject to the $25,000 limitation and passive activity or at-risk limits, so, again, check with your tax advisor. The actual expenses can be seen in Exhibit 21.

Exhibit 21: Actual Rental Income Example

Fire insurance	$200		
Mortgage payment	$10,000		
(Principal *and* Interest)		Rental income	$12,100
Real estate taxes	$800	Less actual expenses	$11,600
General repairs	$175		
Appliance	$425	Actual income	$500
Total	$11,600		

The actual income realized was not great and you're probably not going to get rich off of one piece of rental property even in the best market. However, the tax write-offs can add up, and, while you are renting your property, it is usually increasing in value. Your property may actually be appreciating in value but the IRS allows you to deduct depreciation for tax purposes—the best of both worlds! The more properties you own, the more you may be able to write off, and you should be able to take advantage of many more tax deductions. The location of the property is extremely important to have the best of both worlds, so shop carefully for rental properties.

The obvious benefit is the depreciation deduction. The amount of depreciation you will be allowed will depend on the type of property you own and the date you placed it in service (began renting it). Property placed in service after 31 December 1987 is subject to the modified accelerated cost recovery (MACRS), which allows recovery periods of 5 years to 27.5 years. This means that a portion of the cost of the property you own can be deducted each year depending on the recovery period. Generally, the rental property itself can be deducted over 27.5 years and the appliances or equipment you buy for it can be deducted for 5 to 7 years, depending on its class life. The IRS will help you out even more by offering you free publications that further explain the depreciation. (You may have to use a stamp to request the forms. Look in your telephone book under IRS for a phone number to call for IRS offices in your area.) Publication #534 on depreciation is a good one, and Publication #527 on residential rental property is also good. These publications are written in fairly simple language and can be ordered through your Forms Distribution Center, depending on your state, or you can get copies at most public libraries or post offices. One last publication that I like and find very helpful is Publication #17, which is revised every year. It summarizes rules that have changed each year and what forms to use and how to complete them. If you're into that sort of thing or interested in doing it yourself, or just curious about what your tax professional is telling you, order these booklets. The depreciation booklet contains the tables to use for how much acutal money you can deduct yearly for your new rental property and how to calculate it, very helpful when contemplating becoming a successful landlord.

There are a few other tax benefits that you should consider but that you will have to review more carefully with your tax professional. You can trade or exchange your income property under the IRS Code 1031 for a tax deferred benefit (other than paying tax on the profit you receive from an actual sale) if you trade up to a more valuable "like" property without receiving any personal property such as cash or other seller's incentives. You can continue to exchange or trade properties and defer the tax on the profit with the so-called tax-free 1031 exchange for several years, or until the tax laws change. It isn't a tax-free exchange, just deferred, but a valuable tool when you get into bigger investments. You may have heard of the IRS 1034 "rollover residence replacement" rule; do not confuse the 1031 with the 1034. The 1034 applies to your primary residence and has to do with the sale and purchase, within twenty-four months, of a home of equal or greater value in order to avoid profit tax. You should discuss the 1031 if you are thinking of selling your rental property and the 1034 if you are thinking about selling your primary residence.

If you're not prepared to buy a rental on your own but still want the tax advantages, you should consider co-ownership with other friends or business acquaintances. You can set up a general partnership or a sub-chapter S corporation (another type of partnership) to share part of the profit and loss (subject to the same $25,000 loss deduction limitation). The income or loss will be included on the back of your Schedule E and carried forward to line #18 of the 1040. At this point, you and your partners will probably use the services of an attorney to set it up correctly and make sure you have properly written agreements about your benefits and responsibilities. Still, it might be the answer for your investments. My own personal opinion is that partnerships between relatives or friends don't always work out; I would stick to business associates that you know well enough to share financial information.

The Downside of Being a Landlord

The tax benefits can be calculated many times over to arrive at the "numbers" that make this a very attractive way to add to your income. However, landlording is not for everyone. If you're not prepared for the headaches as well as the advantages, you can lose money fast. For most people, hiring someone to do everything is costly and can quickly eat into your profit. You should be prepared to do some of the repairs and upkeep yourself with your spare time to save some expenses. Repairs and maintainence are tax deductible expenses but are also money out of your pocket. Make sure the house you rent is in good shape first; your renters will expect a safe, habitable home and many states have laws which require that you keep up the property. If you're going to rent the home you now live in, prepare it for renting by having furnaces serviced, roofs checked, and gutters cleaned to avoid costly repairs later from lack of maintainence. Make sure your renter understands that either they will do certain maintainence jobs or you will have access during certain times to do those items. Your investment is in the resale of the property as well as the rental and it only makes sense to take care of your investment. Your lease agreement should detail your responsibilities and the repairs and maintainence to be done by your tenants. Put it all in writing up front! Detail any additional responsibilities—upkeep of pool, yard, fences, etc—and the number of persons who may occupy the rental, as well as your restrictions for pets. Your attorney can draw up an agreement for a fee, but you can also buy rental or lease agreements at the local office supply and alter them according to your needs. Remember, if you delete or add to any agreement, all sections must be initialed by you and the lesser to protect everyone. Make sure your tenant understands where and when to pay the monthy rent, realizes their portion of the upkeep, and knows how to terminate the agreement. Now for the downside!

Even the best written agreement and the best of intentions can go bad. Prepare for a period of vacancy and for major repairs (remember you have that six months in reserve for this purpose) if you rent. Not that you'll have any problems but you should protect yourself. There are two sides to landlording and tenanting! If you don't repair the roof when asked, expect to repair water damage to the interior. If you don't help with the water bill during the summer, expect the lawn to dry up. Ask your tenant regularly if they have noticed signs of roof problems, termites, water heater or furnace noises, excessive water in the basement, or any signs that would require preventive maintainence; don't just assume that no news is good news. Ask your tenants how their jobs are going, how's the family, how they like their new area; you're not being nosy, just inquiring about future problems that could lead to vacancies. Take an interest in your house and your tenants but try not to be there too much. Just be prepared for the phone call in the middle of the night about the broken pipe, the roof leaking, or the unexpected move. It's all part of the price you pay to be a landlord.

Finally, if you and your spouse are landlords, or if you have a partnership landlording, decide who will be the contact person for the tenant. It is most frustrating to get two answers about a problem from a set of landlords, and can be very costly for you if your spouse gives a different answer than you. This is not the time to disagree—discuss it before taking on this investment. If you decide to sell the rental unit, allow your tenants ample time to move; don't sell it from underneath them! If they have a lease, you'll most likely be selling the home subject to the terms of the lease, which will be passed along to the new owner. All parties should be aware of the transfer. If they've been good tenants I think you should, at the least, let them know when you've sold. From the previous example, you should be able to calculate the advantages of investing in property, but you have to decide if the inconveniences outweigh the income. Again, contact your tax preparer or accountant to see how you would benefit from such an investment.

Chapter 12

Building Your Own Home

Construction Financing

I think all of us, at one time or another, have dreamed of building the perfect home. If we've owned several homes, we know the features we want in the perfect home. If this is your first home or if this is your first experience with the construction of a home, you should pay particular attention to the terminology in this section. If you're planning to do part of the construction yourself, you should have a working knowledge of home construction, have access to subcontractors who will complete the more technical aspects, have a good architect or designer or have purchased a good design package, and have a general contractor to oversee and help with the necessary permits and restrictions of home construction. There are several ways to handle the construction loan, depending on how much or how little you want to be involved, and the terms used in construction lending are very important to this transaction even for those who're going to be involved very little.

If you've already bought your land, chosen your plans, and have found a contractor who will be financing the construction, your only task is to start on the permanent or take-out financing to pay off the contractor and pay off the land loan, if you have one. Your escrow company or attorney will assist you in securing title to the completed home and property. You'll be following the steps outlined in Part One for a mortgage loan with two differences: the sales price will be the construction costs plus land and the appraised value will be based on the completed project compared to the other new homes in the area. The forms and terminology used in the financing and construction may be of interest to you since these terms will be tossed around by both the contractor and the lender throughout the transaction. You should understand how they may affect your transaction.

If you're thinking about being an owner-builder or are considering doing part of this yourself, you need to know the steps involved. Then you can better decide what part you want to do and what you want to pay others to do for you.

Let's start with the land to build on. If you've been shopping around for land in your area, you probably have a good idea of the size and location of the land you'd like to build on. Buying the piece of property can be the easy part; building on that land can be the hard part. If you're buying from a developer, he should provide you with the limitations for building on that land—but don't count on it. If the landowner is subdividing, he probably knows what the land can be used for; you'll need to get any limitations in writing in your land contract. But you still need to do some research to determine exactly what type of dwelling is allowed, what utilities are provided, what access or road requirements exist, what restrictions exist for sewer and wells, what county, city, or state geological requirements exist, and what financing is available to purchase this lot before you approach the seller, realtor, or developer about buying. Make an appointment with the county building department to discuss the land or lot you're considering buying to ask about: the size dwelling you can build, the placement of the dwelling on the property, the utilities provided by the city or county, the road maintainence, the zoning changes anticipated for that area, the type of improvements you can make, and what off-site improvements will be provided by the county, city, or state. Discuss the streets, gutters, storm drains, snow removal, sidewalks, street lights, limitations on driveways, and who will pay for what. If your property is not connected to public utilities, find out how much of the cost you'll have to pay to bring in the power, sewer and water lines from the street to your home. If you're buying in a developed area this may already be done, but before you decide on a price for the land, ask just to be sure everything can be connected by your contractor.

If you don't intend to build within two to three years of purchasing, hold off on the purchase. Purchasing land is a tricky business and your investment in unimproved land is not always the best way to invest capital. Just remember that it may be very difficult to sell unimproved land later, should you decide not to build.

Once you've found the land that suits your needs, you'll have to decide how to buy it. If you can pay it off in two to three years you might approach the owner about a land contract. The land contract states that you agree to pay the seller monthly, quarterly or whatever, a part of the purchase price along with interest until the land is paid for. The seller retains the title to the property until she has collected everything due her. An attorney can draw up such an agreement and have it recorded for a flat fee. This may be an option you.

If you have no other source, though, you'll have to go to a full service bank, a savings and loan, or savings bank most likely. FHA, VA, FNMA and FHLMC don't insure or purchase land loans, so you may need a portfolio lender who will have to keep this loan for the duration. The loan will usually be for 75 percent or less of the appraised value. ARM loans are available with a fifteen-year due date, but if you can afford the payments, I would suggest a shorter term loan. Many fixed rate loans amortize over fifteen years but have a "call" feature, which means the lender has the option of requiring the balance due be paid in as little as three years. You want as much of your own money in this land as possible when you go for the construction loan. Terms and rates vary by the area, by the market, and by the current building situation. Make sure that your land loan can be subordinated to the construction loan when you decide to build. That means that the lender who loans you the money to build on the land wants to have a first position on the title of the property. Obviously they're not going to lend you the money to improve someone else's property. The best of all worlds would be to get the land loan, the construction loan and the permanent or take-out loan all from the same lender; I would start with the bank or savings and loan that you now do business with. If their rates are comparable and their terms agreeable, you may not need to shop anywhere else. You might save yourself some money by choosing a lender who will convert your six-month construction loan to a permanent loan without any additional fees. The problem is that some lenders, banks, or savings and loans don't make unimproved land loans or even construction loans, and you may have to look a little for one who will. The rate on your land loan and on your construction loan will be high and the terms not too attractive because the risk is sometimes greater for the lender. Therefore, you want to buy the land and build quickly to avoid additional costs. If you buy the land from a private developer who provides financing, your terms won't necessarily be any better, so compare.

There are some lenders of construction money that require you to own the land with no liens before they'll consider advancing construction money. Some lenders prefer not to do FHA or VA loans because of the inspections and paperwork involved with new home construction. If you want a low-down-payment FHA or VA loan be sure you mention this before you start the construction loan. More on the steps for FHA and VA loans later.

If you've now bought a lot or some land and want to build on it, you'll need a set of plans for the home (called improvements) and a contractor to build. You need to decide just what you want to contribute to this project. If you don't need money to build the home, you may subcontract out what you can't do (electrical, plumbing, drywall, foundation, etc.) and do the rest yourself. You will need building permits and a whole series of inspections prior to occupancy, but your county or city inspectors will help along the way. You should have some building background, along with the time and money to complete the job. You need a set of plans, including a plot plan (where the buildings will set on the property), a floor plan, a foundation plan with cross sections and elevations and lots more, just to get the building permit (for a substantial fee in some areas). Unless you have bought a prepackaged deal on the home, you'll need to use the services of an architect to design some plans or provide you with predesigned plans. If this is truly a do-it-yourself project, you're going to need more than this book to get your home completed and you must have had some experience with building a complete home. There are many construction workers with friends that will share their talents to build a fine home, but the average nonconstruction worker will need some help. There are many videos on self-contracting and hundreds of books on how to build your home.

If you're like most of us and need the money to buy land *and* build a home, you'll need a professional builder for the project. Most lenders of construction money require that a state licensed general contractor oversee the entire project. However, you could save money by subcontracting out some of the work or by doing some of it yourself if your general contractor will allow it. Your contract to build should state what you want to do and what you want the contractor to do. Anyone who subcontracts to you or the general contractor for labor or materials can attach a lien to your property if they are not paid for their services, so deal with professionals in this important project.

To recap, you will need:

1. A trip to the building department of the local authority to determine what off-site improvements are included in your area, what limitations exist to the improvements you want to make, and how much of the costs will be yours for permits and off-sites.
2. Land, which you can purchase with a land contract, with a lot or land loan from a bank or savings bank, or which you can buy outright using a home equity or refinance on your

existing home. The lot/land loan must be able to be subordinated to the construction loan.
3. To check with the local building department about the improvements you can make to your property before you spend money on plans or hire a contractor.
4. A set of plans prepared by an architect or designer, or purchased from a developer or contractor and adjusted to fit you needs.
5. A contract between you and the general contractor to make specified improvements to your land, including a date of completion, a set fee, a cost breakdown and a description of materials. More on this later.
6. A building permit issued by the local authority (county or city).
7. A construction lender to advance you a set amount to build your home.
8. Permanent financing (sometimes called a take-out loan) to pay off the construction loan.
9. Lots of time, patience, and money to see you through this project!

Preparing Your Loan Package
Building Contract
The building contract between you and the contractor needs to specify the improvements the contractor will do for a specified amount of money with a time limit for the improvements to be completed. You'll need to sit down with the plans and go over the options you have for the layout of the outbuildings (garage, storage sheds), driveway, patios, wells, septic systems, connections to public utilities or any other preconstruction decisions you must agree on in addition to the actual building of the home. If you want fences, driveways, detached garages, or other buildings, you need to decide who will provide these. If you want to keep existing trees or special excavations you'll have to decide how to build around them, considering your foundation restrictions. Your building department will probably require a soils

report or geological report done by an engineering firm to determine the best and safest type of structure and foundation for your land. Decide who will pay for this and all other permits to avoid add-on costs later. Your initial trip to the building department should help with this. Your contractor can subcontract for any other additions but the cost will be added on to your contract. Also, the building permit will have to include all structures and their location on the property. All of this needs to be decided before one shovel of dirt is moved.

Fire Insurance

You will need a fire insurance policy in force before the structure is started so contact your agent now to prepare the policy. Give the insurance agent all the particulars: the cost, the contractor, the lender, the address and the expected completion date. You should include some additional liability coverage both for you and for the contractor for the construction period. Check with your agent for what's available and required in your area. Your construction lender will require evidence of a policy that is in effect.

Description of Materials

Before your contractor can decide on a price he needs to know the type of materials you want. You will discuss the features and choices you have to make. A copy of the FHA and VA Description of Materials is included in the appendix. You have twenty-seven areas to discuss, including special equipment for the on-site improvements. With a copy of this form ahead of time you can be better prepared for the questions he will ask. This completed form will accompany the contract and plans when you approach your lender for a construction loan. Your other on-site improvements (grading, retaining walls, fences, etc.) should be included on this form so your costs will be carried over to the contract—you don't want any surprises halfway through this project!

Construction Cost Breakdown

This form should be furnished, completed and signed by the contractor. It provides you and the lender with an itemized breakdown of costs and services for the project. Your off-site costs need to be discussed first since your contractor will include the subcontracting costs on your breakdown. A copy of a construction cost breakdown sheet is included in the appendix. Now is the time to discuss what portion of the building you want to do yourself and what you want your contractor to do. He will be certifying with the Building Department every aspect of construction so you and he will have to decide who does what. You'll notice at the bottom there is a place for the borrower's funds. You'll be expected to pay for some of the closing costs and down payment in cash, just as with any other loan. The construction cost breakdown, the description of materials, and the plans and specifications will determine the amount of your contract with the contractor or builder and, finally, the amount of the construction loan you need.

The Permanent, or Take-out, Loan

This may seem backwards, but you probably will have to have a permanent financing commitment to get a construction loan. Your construction lender and your contractor want to know where the money is coming from before they start. If you have plans and specifications, a building contract, including a cost breakdown and description of materials, you can start your permanent financing loan. This will be the thirty- or fifteen-year fixed rate or ARM loan you use to pay off your construction loan. You start just like you do with any other loan: you should prequalify yourself for any of the three programs in Part One, shop around for the best rates and terms, contact a loan officer, complete an application and have your income, assets, and credit history verified. The application fee needs to be paid and your appraisal will be based on the plans and specs your builder provides, with the cost breakdown and description of materials as supporting information. In the appendix I have included a checklist to use for preparing the information your lender will need.

The appraiser will give the lender a value based on the completed home as compared to other new homes in the area using the cost approach and the market data approach. The appraiser or a designated inspector will inspect at regular intervals for completion of the stages of construction and issue a Certificate of Completion or a final compliance inspection report at the finish. Armed with an approved take-out loan, or permanent financing, you can shop for a construction loan to start the project. Caution: don't start any part of the project, don't even move any dirt around before you get your construction money. You'll need to open escrow with a title or escrow company or hire an attorney to review the contracts, order the survey and handle the closing for you. You will need a title policy to protect your title to the property either from the title or escrow company or from the attorney. There are mechanic's liens that can be placed on your property for up to forty-five days after construction and your title company will record the notice of completion after the lien-free period. Your construction lender will require a title search to determine that there are no prior liens on the property before you begin construction, and the title company will be issuing a series of endorsements to the Construction Title Policy during construction. The FHA or VA appraisers and inspectors want to see an undisturbed piece of land before they issue the appraisal and start their series of inspections.

Construction Steps

With your permanent financing committed (usually you can get a six-month or one-year commitment for the financing) and your construction loan approved, you can proceed. The lender will place the money for the construction costs into a special account, using a voucher system, and advance a portion of the money at each step of construction. An estimated construction financing worksheet is included in the appendix to give you some idea about the costs. You will be paying closing costs very similar to the normal mortgage loan closing costs described in Section I. Notice the section for interest withheld: your construction loan will be interest-only payments for six months with a possible extention of from three to six months allowed. Normally you will pay interest only, usually a variable interest, such as the prime rate plus 1 to 3 percentage points, with four to six months collected up front or withheld from the construction loan proceeds. You are probably going to have to provide the down payment and your share of the closing costs up front at the start of the construction loan period and prior to building. In addition, your contractor will expect a good-faith deposit on his costs so prepare for cash expenses at the outset. This can be an expensive project even with the best financing.

The actual steps of construction will be decided by the size and type of project and your contractor's procedures. Some inspections will be done at different intervals (not including your own daily inspection, until you get tired of bugging the construction people or they run you off).

Your construction lender will probably have you and your builder execute a Building and Loan Agreement, agreeing to a series of advances using a voucher system during construction. They will want to inspect each step of the way to make sure the plans are being followed. In order to receive payments during construction the voucher and a lien release on the labor and materials used for this step will be completed by the contractor or subcontractors and submitted to the lender along with the receipts. When the building permit is issued the excavation and foundation will usually be completed first, including preliminary placing of power hook-ups, and then the first inspection will be done. Next will be exterior and floor framing, partition framing and then another inspection. Finally roof, finished floors, electrical, plumbing, heating, interior and exterior doors, trim, windows, cabinets, etc. and an inspection. There may be many more inspections due to noncompliance or weather-related delays. This is a brief description of the process, which is really much more involved. Most of the steps are out of your control and will be your contractor's problem, but you should use your set of plans, description of materials and cost breakdown to follow along and ask questions about anything that doesn't look right. Your money and time are also going into this project and though contractors are not wild about your inquiries, you need to protect your interest. One thing I would not do is ask questions of the subcontractors or construction workers. They work for your contractor and are usually paid hourly or per job. They may not take kindly to delays in their jobs, and ultimately you may be paying more for the questions. Decide up front when and where you and the contractor are going to meet regularly to discuss the project. Expect complete answers every step of the way. You most likely will be signing the vouchers or construction disbursements required by the lender, so you'll have some control.

When construction is complete, final inspections done, all liens released, a notice of completion filed and recorded, and the certificate of occupancy issued by the local authorities, your construction loan will roll-over to permanent financing or the take-out lender will disburse the permanent loan and pay off the construction loan. There may be additional closing costs at this time if you must use two different lenders; try to find one lender to do it all to avoid double closing costs.

FHA and VA New Construction Loans

If you have chosen conventional financing for the take-out loan, your appraiser needs the plans, specs, description of materials, and cost breakdown to complete the appraisal at the start of construction. She will do one final inspection and issue a #442, a final inspection form, stating that the improvements have been completed according to the plans. However, if you are using an FHA or VA permanent loan over 90 percent loan-to-value, there will be at least three inspections by the FHA or VA inspector during construction and a final inspection, a one year warranty, a termite soil treatment form and a certification that carpets meet FHA requirements (commonly called Bugs and Rugs!). You may also need Health Deptartment certifications if there is a well or septic tank and the builder must be on the FHA or VA's approved builder list. The paperwork and time involved is lengthy but the low down payment is attractive to most first-time homeowners, so shop around for a builder and lender who can offer this service. Of course, your interest rate and points may not be guaranteed for the entire construction period, so at the close of the permanent FHA or VA loan you may have to be flexible. Your plans must be approved by FHA or by an approved FHA underwriter prior to the start of construction to be eligible for the maximum FHA loan. It's going to be a little more difficult to find a construction lender who will do an FHA or VA loan.

There are some builders who are FHA and VA approved and who will issue a ten-year homeowner's warranty from an FHA approved warranty program (each area approves two or three of these programs). Many more builders are now using the ten-year warranty program to offer maximum FHA loans on their homes. FHA still requires approval of the plans and certain inspections, but the process is a little more simplified. As I have stated before, many builders state that they build FHA or VA quality homes but that is far different that building with FHA or VA inspections during construction.

Finally, if you have chosen building instead of buying a newly built home for your first or move-up property, be aware of the terminology that will be used, the forms that you need to complete, the role that your contractor will play and, above all, protect your own interests by following the project from beginning to end. The finished product should be a home that you can truly be proud of and well worth the time and effort.

Appendix

FHA Prequalifying Worksheet

*Use the factor tables on the next page to calculate the principal and interest and the Mortgage Insurance Premium to be included in the loan amount as well as for the monthly or annual mortgage Insurance payment.

Income Monthly

Borrowers base $ _____
Other Income _____
Co-Borrowers Base _____
Other Income _____

Total $ _____

Housing Expense

*Principal & Interest $ _____
Hazard Insurance _____
Property Tax _____
Mortgage Insurance _____
0.5% of loan divided by
12 mos. for estimate
Homeowners Assn. Dues _____
Total Housing $ _____

Liabilities

Creditor   Monthly payment
_____   _____
_____   _____
_____   _____
_____   _____
_____   _____
_____   _____

Other expenses _____
Total Liabilities** $ _____
                   _____
Plus Housing Expense _____
Total Fixed Expense $ _____

Ratios

Housing Expense divided by
Total Income
(guideline is 29%)   _____ %

Fixed Expense divided by
Total Income
(guideline is 41%)   _____ %

Total Income minus
Fixed Expense = Residual Income
(guideline varies by region)
                     $ _____

*Use debts with more
than 6 months remaining

Factor Sheet

For Principal and Interest

Multiply the Loan Amount by these for an estimate of the Principal and Interest for qualifying purposes only.

Rate %	15 years	20 years	30 years
7.50	.00928	.00806	.00729
8.00	.00956	.00837	.00734
8.50	.00985	.00886	.00769
9.00	.01015	.00900	.00805
9.50	.01045	.00933	.00841
10.00	.01075	.00966	.00878
10.50	.01106	.00999	.00915
11.00	.01137	.01033	.00981
11.50	.01169	.01067	.01017
12.00	.01201	.01102	.01054

Example: $72,000.00 x .00878 = $632.16 (30 yrs. at 10%)

Notes: Your principal and interest or Mortgage Insurance Premium figures may be off cents to your loan officers figures by close enough for pre-qualifying

Use the Principal and Interest factors for all three programs.

For One-Time Mortgage Insurance Premium (OTMIP on 203b FHA)

Use 3.8% of Loan amount for qualifying purposes, add to your loan amount to figure Principal and Interest if you choose to finance it.

Example: $72,000.00 x 3.800% = $2,736.00 (All MIP Financed for 30 year loan)

For Monthly Mortgage Insurance on Condos

Rate %	15 years	20 years	30 yeats
7.50	.004095	.04125	.004148
8.00	.004099	.04127	.004151
8.50	.004102	.04129	.004153
9.00	.004104	.04132	.004153
9.50	.004107	.04133	.004155
10.00	.004109	.04135	.004156
10.50	.004113	.04138	.004158
11.00	.004115	.04139	.004158
11.50	.004117	.04141	.004159
12.00	.004119	.04143	.004160

Example: $72,000.00 x .004148 = $29.86 (per month for Condominiums 234C only)

VA Prequalifying Worksheet

*Use the factors on the previous page for the principal and interest. Your VA funding fee may be included in your loan amount; refer to page 69 for calculating the funding fee, add to your loan and then figure the principal and interest. Manual calculations may be a few cents off from what the loan officer will use, but they'll be close enough for prequalifying.

Monthly Income

Borrower's Base $ _____
Other income _____
Co-borrowers base _____
Other income _____
Gross income $ _____
Less federal tax for both
(use paystubs) _____
*Less Social Security or
retirement for both _____
(use paystubs, FICA)
Less state income tax _____
_____
Net monthly income $ _____

Housing Expense

*Principal and interest $ _____
Hazard insurance _____
Property Tax _____
Homeowner's _____
Assn. dues _____

Total housing $ _____

Plus maintenance _____

Plus utilities _____
_____
Shelter expense $ _____

Debts and Obligations Monthly

Pay to   Amount
_____   _____
_____   _____
_____   _____
_____   _____

Total debts $ _____

Only include debts with more than six months remaining.

Ratio

Housing expense divided
by gross income _____ %

(guideline 41% or less)

Residual

Net income less shelter
expense and debts $ _____
(guideline varies by region)

The VA provides charts for maintenance and utilities; you will have to estimate for prequalifying.

*Social Security for 1991 is 7.65% of your monthly income.

Conventional Prequalifying Worksheet

*Use the factor tables on the Factor Sheet for the principal and interest calculations. Include the private mortgage insurance (PMI) in your loan amount, subject to limitations; see below. Figures may be off by cents but close enough for prequalifying.

Monthly Income

Borrower's base $ _____
Other income _____
Co-borrower's base _____
Other income _____
Rental income from Schedule
  of Real Estate Owned _____
  _____

Total monthly income $ _____

Housing Expense

*Principal and interest $ _____
Hazard insurance _____
Property tax _____
Homeowner's assn. dues _____
Secondary financing _____
**Mortgage Insurance _____
(if over 80% LTV) _____
Total housing expense $ _____

Debts Monthly

Creditor	Amount
_____	$ _____
_____	_____
_____	_____

Other expenses _____
Negative rental income from Schedule
of Real Estate Owned _____
Total debts $ _____

Ratios

Housing expanse divided by
total income _____ %

Housing expense plus debts with
over 10 mos. remaining divided
by total income _____ %

Top ratio should be no more than
28% for under 90% LTV and
25% for 90% and over LTV.

Bottom ratio should be no more
than 36% for under 90% LTV
and 33% for 90-95% LTV.

Use principal and interest at 2nd
adjustment for an ARM of over
80% LTV

Rations and guidelines vary
by lender; these are general
FNMA and FHLMC guidelines.

**Use 0.35% times the Loan Amount divided by 12 for prequalifying. Your first year's premium will be paid on the lender's required coverage, somewhere between 0.50% and 0.25% depending on the LTV. Your first year's premium will be paid in cash or financed and will be around 1% to 0.75% if you can finance it (on an owner - occupied 90% or less LTV purchase).

Mortgage Insurance Premium Refund Calculations

The FHA will refund to the borrower unearned mortgage insurance premiums if the contract of insurance is terminated before maturity of the mortgage.

Listed below are the percentages of the one-time mortgage insurance premiums (MIP) refunded to FHA borrowers when the loan is paid off during the first ten years.

Year Loan Is Payed Off	Percentage of MIP Refunded
1	90
2	78
3	63
4	50
5	39
6	31
7	25
8	20
9	17
10	14

Because the table's figures are calculated for the last month of each policy year, borrowers prepaying before the end of the policy year will receive slightly larger refund amounts.

Example: Original mortgage amount insured December 1983 for $80,000. The financed MIP was $3,040 ($80,000 x .3800). The property was sold and the mortgage insurance cancelled one year later on December 1984. The amount of the refund due the FHA borrower was $2,736 ($3,040 x 90%).

FHA Assumption Policy (As of December 1990)

The date your old FHA loan closed in very important to the new assumption changes. The guidelines below were set by the FHA but for each change of the policy there is some confusion about the weeks before and after the changes. Read your copy of the deed of trust, mortgage, or trust deed or have your lender explain your particular case if you closed your FHA loan around the dates below to be sure of the assumability of your FHA loan. The confusion is with the difference between the date your actually signed your loan application (FHA 2900) and the date you closed.

Prior to December 1, 1986	A simple assumption for either an owner-occupant or an investor, but the original borrower remains liable unless the new borrower qualifies and a substitute of liability is executed.
December 1, 1986 thru December 14, 1989	A simple assumption for an owner-occupant after 1 year. The original borrower is liable for 5 more years unless the new borrower qualifies and a release of liability is issued.
	A simple assumption for an investor after 2 years. The original borrower is liable for 5 more years unless the new borrower qualifies and a release of liability is issued.
February 5, 1988 thru December 14, 1989	Any investor who formally assumes a mortgage that was approved during these dates must pay down the principal balance to 75 percent of the appraised value at the time the loan closes.
After December 15, 1989	No investors may assume FHA loans. All new borrowers must qualify.

This is a simplification of the rules. Read the Attachment, Rider, or Exhibit attached to the Deed of Trust, Mortgage, or Trust Deed on any FHA loan closed around or after December 1, 1986 for any of the changes that may affect the sale of your current property with an existing FHA loan. You can also call your local FHA office for more help with this assumption policy.

Closing Costs Worksheet

Take this worksheet with you to the loan interview to ask what fees apply to your loan and to compare with the fees quoted. Experienced loan officers will prepare a statement similar to this at the loan interview to determine your costs in this transaction.

Closing Costs		**Impounds/Prepaids**	
Loan Origination Fee	$ _____	Property Taxes $ ____ per mo.	$ _____
Appraisal Fee	_____	Insurance/Fire &	
Inspection Fee/Survey	_____	Flood, $ ____ per mo.	_____
Credit Report Fee	_____	Private Mortgage Insurance $ ____ per mo.	_____
Recording Fee	_____	Per day interest	
Title Insurance	_____	$ ____ per day x 30	_____
Escrow Fee	_____	One-Year Fire Policy	
Pest Inspection	_____	One-Year Mortgage Ins.	_____
Tax Stamps/Transfer	_____	Total Closing Costs	$ _____
Underwriting Fee	_____	Total Prepaids	$ _____
Drawing/Document Fee	_____	Total Down payment	$ _____
Attorney Fee	_____		
Tax Contract/Service	_____	Cash required to close	$ _____
Homebuyer's Warranty	_____		
Notary Fee	_____		
Discount Fees @ ____ %	_____		
Other Fees	_____		
Total Closing Costs	$ _____		

Types of Closing Costs

Common Name	Paid To	Average Amount	Seller Fee
*Loan origination fee	lender	Conv.: 1–2.5% of loan FHA and VA: 1% of loan	no no
Appraisal fee	appraiser	$200–$350	no
Inspection/survey	survey co. or appraiser	$100–$200 $40–$65	no no
Credit report	credit agency	$50–$100	no
*Discount points	lender	1 percentage point of total loan for FHA and VA loans	FHA: negotiable VA: yes
Recording fees	county recorder	$18–$25	no
**Title insurance	title company	$150–$400	ALTA with lender's policy: no; seller's policy: yes
**Escrow fee	escrow company	$80–$200	varies by area
**Pest inspection/ Termite report	pest control co.	$45–$150	FHA and VA: no; conv.: either
Tax stamps/ transfer	county/state	$15–$65+	VA: no; FHA and conv.: varies
*Underwriting fee	lender	$100–$300, negotiate	FHA and VA: yes; conv.: either
*Document fee	lender	$100–$300	FHA and VA: yes
Drawing fee	title co.	$25–$75	FHA and VA: no conv.: varies
**Attorney fee	attorney	$100–$500	no
Tax contract/ tax service		$50–$100	FHA: yes VA: no conv.: either
Homebuyer's warranty	warranty co.	$100–$500 10 yr.	yes, builder
**Homebuyer's inspection	inspection co.	$50–$250	no
Notary fee	notary public, attorney	$10–$25	varies by area

*Possibly a negotiable fee with the lender — Ask.
**Shop around with competition in the area; compare rates.

Residential Mortgage Loan Application Checklist

I have included the following checklist of what to bring to assist you in preparing yourself and your spouse or co-borrowers for the loan application. The application is your opportunity to ask questions and you should read all the items to determine what you should ask and what you should bring with you to the interview. Allow ample time for the application and do not bring family, friends, or pets to this important event.

Personal Information

Picture ID (license, employee badge, etc.). _____
Evidence of Social Security number. _____
Residences for the last two years. _____

Debts

Credit cards: account numbers, payments, balances,
    copies of recent bills. _____
Installment debts (auto, furniture, etc.): bring the most recent
    bills for address and account numbers, balance, payments. _____
Mortgage loans: names of institutions, addresses, account numbers,
    payments and balances. _____
Be prepared to supply twelve months of cancelled checks
    for evidence of payment. _____

Income

Copy of last two years of W-2s or bring the originals to be copied. _____
Copy of last two paystubs or the original for copying. _____
Name and address of all employers for the last two years. _____
Commissioned earnings: Be prepared to supply two years of
    tax returns to prove expenses associated with earnings as well
    as a year-to-date income and expense statement. _____
If self-employed: Bring two years of tax returns with all schedules
    and attachments, as well as a profit and loss statement and a balance
    sheet completed year-to-date. (to within 90 days of the loan app.) _____
Retirement income: Bring the award letter showing length, source
    and amount received and copies of bank statements or copies of
    checks received. _____
Rental, note or interest income: Bring two years of tax returns
    and to prove receipt and for averaging. _____
Alimony and child support: Bring divorce decrees, including
    property disposition to determine length and amount. _____

continued on next page...

Residential Mortgage Loan Application Checklist (cont.)

Assets

Estimate of personal possessions (autos, jewelry,
household goods, boats, computers, RVs, etc.) _____
Value of life insurance (cash and face value) _____
Value of real estate, types and use (rental, vacation homes) _____
Stocks and bonds: Bring stock portfolio statement for
verification, including stock broker's name _____
Funds deposited in escrow, including name and address of
whoever hold the funds. _____
Retirement fund estimated value. _____
Checking and savings account information. _____
Names, addresses and account numbers of all depositories. _____
Miscellaneous items: Do not identify excessively
expensive items for insurance purposes; use general terms
(paintings instead of van Gogh). _____

VA Eligibility

Certificate of Eligibility, DD214, or other service record
information. Information on any other VA loans. _____

...If your property has a well, a septic system or an unusual utility system, advise your loan officer now.

...Advise your loan officer which title company, attorney, and escrow company you will use for the close.

...Ask what credit agency will be used and if they will be contacting you for verification.

...Ask what the fees are for the credit report and appraisals and if you may receive a copy of both.

...Bring all financial information you feel will be helpful to develop a complete loan application.

Appendix 213

ABC Mortgage
RESIDENTIAL LOAN APPLICATION

Married Applicants May Apply For A Separate Account

MORTGAGE APPLIED FOR	☑ Conventional ☐ FHA ☐ VA	Amount $	Interest Rate %	No. of Months	Monthly Payment Principal & Interest $	Escrow Impounds (to be collected monthly) ☐ Taxes ☐ Hazard Ins. ☐ Mtg. Ins.

Payment Option

SUBJECT PROPERTY

Property Street Address	City	County	State	Zip	No. Units

Legal Description (Attach description if necessary)   Year Built

Purpose of Loan: ☐ Purchase ☐ Construction-Permanent ☐ Construction ☐ Refinance ☐ Other (Explain)

Complete this line if Construction-Permanent or Construction Loan:
Lot Value Data — Year Acquired — Original Cost $ — Present Value (a) $ — Cost of Imps. (b) $ — Total (a + b) $ → ENTER TOTAL AS PURCHASE PRICE IN DETAILS OF PURCHASE

Complete this line if a Refinance Loan:
Year Acquired — Original Cost $ — Amt Existing Liens $ — Purpose of Refinance — Describe Improvements ☐ made ☐ to be made — Cost $

Title Will Be Held in What Name(s)   Manner In Which Title Will Be Held

Source of Down Payment and Settlement Charges

This application is designed to be completed by the Borrower(s) with the lender's assistance. The Co-Borrower Section and all other Co-Borrower questions must be completed and the appropriate box(es) checked if ☐ another person will be jointly obligated with the Borrower on the loan or ☐ the Borrower is relying on income from alimony, child support or separate maintenance or on the income or assets of another person as a basis for repayment of the loan, or ☐ the Borrower is married and resides, or the property is located, in a community property state.

BORROWER / CO-BORROWER

BORROWER				CO-BORROWER			
Name		Age	School Yrs	Name		Age	School Yrs
Present Address No. Years ___ ☐ Own ☐ Rent				Present Address No. Years ___ ☐ Own ☐ Rent			
Street				Street			
City State Zip				City State Zip			
Former Address if less than 2 years at present address				Former Address if less than 2 years at present address			
Street				Street			
City State Zip				City State Zip			
Years at former address				Years at former address			
Marital Status: ☐ Married ☐ Separated ☐ Unmarried (incl. single, divorced, widowed)		DEPENDENTS OTHER THAN LISTED BY CO-BORROWER NO / AGES		Marital Status: ☐ Married ☐ Separated ☐ Unmarried (incl. single, divorced, widowed)		DEPENDENTS OTHER THAN LISTED BY BORROWER NO / AGES	
Name and Address of Employer		Years employed in this line of work or profession? ___ years Years on this job ___ ☐ Self Employed		Name and Address of Employer		Years employed in this line of work or profession? ___ years Years on this job ___ ☐ Self Employed	
Position/Title	Type of Business			Position/Title	Type of Business		
Social Security Number***	Home Phone	Business Phone		Social Security Number***	Home Phone	Business Phone	

GROSS MONTHLY INCOME / MONTHLY HOUSING EXPENSE** / DETAILS OF PURCHASE

Item	Borrower	Co-Borrower	Total	Rent	Present	Proposed		Do Not Complete if Refinance	
Base Empl. Income	$	$	$	First Mortgage (P&I)	$	$	a. Purchase Price	$	
Overtime				Other Financing (P&I)			b. Total Closing Costs (Est.)		
Bonuses				Hazard Insurance			c. Prepaid Escrows (Est.)		
Commissions				Real Estate Taxes			d. Total (a + b + c)	$	
Dividends/Interest				Mortgage Insurance			e. Amount This Mortgage	(	)
Net Rental Income				Homeowner Assn. Dues			f. Other Financing	(	)
Other† (Before completing, see notice under Describe Other Income below)				Other			g. Other Equity	(	)
				Total Monthly Pmt	$	$	h. Amount of Cash Deposit	(	)
				Utilities			i. Closing Costs Paid by Seller	(	)
Total	$	$	$	Total	$	$	j. Cash Req'd for Closing (Est.)	$	

DESCRIBE OTHER INCOME

☐ B-Borrower C-Co-Borrower   NOTICE: † Alimony, child support, or separate maintenance income need not be revealed if the Borrower or Co-Borrower does not choose to have it considered as a basis for repaying this loan.

B/C		Monthly Amount
		$

IF EMPLOYED IN CURRENT POSITION FOR LESS THAN TWO YEARS COMPLETE THE FOLLOWING

B/C	Previous Employer/School	City/State	Type of Business	Position/Title	Dates From/To	Monthly Income

THESE QUESTIONS APPLY TO BOTH BORROWER AND CO-BORROWER

If a "yes" answer is given to a question in this column, explain on an attached sheet.

	Borrower Yes or No	Co-Borrower Yes or No		Borrower Yes or No	Co-Borrower Yes or No
Have you any outstanding judgments? In the last 7 years, have you been declared bankrupt?			Are you a U.S. citizen?		
Have you had property foreclosed upon or given title or deed in lieu thereof?			If "no," are you a resident alien?		
Are you a co-maker or endorser on a note?			If "no," are you a non-resident alien?		
Are you a party in a law suit?			Explain Other Financing or Other Equity (if any)		
Are you obligated to pay alimony, child support or separate maintenance?					
Is any part of the down payment borrowed?					

*FHLMC/FNMA require business credit report, signed Federal Income Tax returns for last two years, and, if available, audited Profit and Loss Statement plus balance sheet for same period
**All Present Monthly Housing Expenses of Borrower and Co-Borrower should be listed on a combined basis
***Optional for FHLMC

FHLMC 65 Rev. 10/86   Fannie Mae Form 1003 Rev. 10/86

How to Get a Mortgage

Appendix 215

Form Approved OMB No. 2900-0144

	USDA - FmHA Application For FmHA Guaranteed Loan	HUD/FHA Application For Commitment for Insurance Under the National Housing Act	1. AGENCY CASE NUMBER	2A. LENDER'S CASE NUMBER	2B SECTION OF THE ACT (HUD ONLY)
☐ VA Application For Home Loan Guaranty	☐	☐			

3A. NAME AND PRESENT ADDRESS OF BORROWER (Include ZIP Code)	3B. BORROWER'S SOCIAL SECURITY NO.	5A. BORROWER: If you do not wish to complete Items 5B or 5C, please initial in the space to the right.	INITIALS
		5B. RACE/NATIONAL ORIGIN ▲1☐ WHITE, NOT HISPANIC 4☐ ASIAN OR PACIFIC ISLANDER	5C. SEX ▲1☐ MALE
4A. NAME AND ADDRESS OF LENDER (Include ZIP Code)		2☐ BLACK, NOT HISPANIC 5☐ HISPANIC	2☐ FEMALE
		3☐ AMERICAN INDIAN OR ALASKAN NATIVE	
		6A. COBORROWER: If you do not wish to complete Items 6B or 6C, please initial in space to the right.	INITIALS
		6B. RACE/NATIONAL ORIGIN ▲1☐ WHITE, NOT HISPANIC 4☐ ASIAN OR PACIFIC ISLANDER	6C. SEX ▲1☐ MALE
4B. ORIGINATOR'S I.D. (HUD) OR LENDER I.D. CODE (VA)	4C. SPONSOR'S I.D. (HUD Only)	2☐ BLACK, NOT HISPANIC 5☐ HISPANIC	2☐ FEMALE
		3☐ AMERICAN INDIAN OR ALASKAN NATIVE	

7. PROPERTY ADDRESS INCLUDING NAME OF SUBDIVISION, LOT AND BLOCK NO., AND ZIP CODE	8A. LOAN AMOUNT $	8B. INTEREST RATE %	8C. PROPOSED MATURITY YRS. MOS.	8D. DISCOUNT AMT. (Only if borrower permitted to pay) $

VA ONLY: Veteran and lender hereby apply to the Administrator of Veterans Affairs for Guaranty of the loan described here under Section 1810, Chapter 37, Title 38, United States Code, to the full extent permitted by the veteran's entitlement and severally agree that the Regulations promulgated pursuant to Chapter 37, and in effect on the date of the loan shall govern the rights, duties, and liabilities of the parties.
HUD/FHA ONLY: Mortgagee's application for mortgage approval and commitment for mortgage insurance under the National Housing Act.

SECTION I — PURPOSE, AMOUNT, TERMS OF AND SECURITY FOR PROPOSED LOAN.

9A. PURPOSE OF LOAN — TO:	9B. TYPE OF AMORTIZATION	9C. HUD ONLY-BORROWER ▲ WILL BE	10 VA ONLY — TITLE WILL BE VESTED IN
▲1☐ PURCHASE EXISTING HOME PREVIOUSLY OCCUPIED 7☐ CONSTRUCT HOME-PROCEEDS TO BE PAID OUT DURING CONSTRUCTION	1☐ REG. FIXED PAYMENT 6☐ ARM	1☐ OCCUPANT 5☐ ESCROW COMMITMENT	☐ VETERAN
2☐ FINANCE IMPROVEMENTS TO EXISTING PROPERTY 8☐ PURCHASE PERMANENTLY SITED MANUFACTURED HOME	2☐ GPM LOAN BAL NEVER TO EXCEED REASONABLE VALUE	2☐ LANDLORD 6☐ FIRST TIME HOME BUYER	☐ VETERAN AND SPOUSE
4☐ PURCHASE NEW CONDO. UNIT 9☐ PURCHASE PERMANENTLY SITED MANUFACTURED HOME AND LOT	3☐ OTHER GPM 7☐ OTHER (Specify)	3☐ BUILDER	
5☐ PURCHASE EXISTING CONDO. UNIT 10☐ REFINANCE PERMANENTLY SITED MANUFACTURED HOME TO BUY LOT	4☐ GEM (GROWING EQUITY MORT.)	4☐ OPERATIVE BUILDER	☐ OTHER (Specify)
6☐ PURCHASE EXISTING HOME NOT PREVIOUSLY OCCUPIED 11☐ REFINANCE PERMANENTLY SITED MANUFACTURED HOME/LOT LOAN 12☐ HUD ONLY-FINANCE COOP PURCHASE	5☐ TEMPORARY BUY DOWN		

11. LIEN ☐ FIRST MORTGAGE ☐ OTHER (Specify)	12. ESTATE WILL BE ☐ FEE SIMPLE ☐ LEASEHOLD (Show expiration date)	13. IS THERE A MANDATORY HOMEOWNERS ASSOCIATION? ☐ YES ☐ NO (If "Yes," complete Item 14F)

14. ESTIMATED TAXES, INSURANCE AND ASSESSMENTS		15. ESTIMATED MONTHLY PAYMENT	
A. ANNUAL TAXES	$	A. PRINCIPAL AND INTEREST	$
B. AMOUNT OF HAZARD INSURANCE ON SECURITY		B. TAXES AND INSURANCE DEPOSITS	
C. ANNUAL HAZARD INSURANCE PREMIUM		C. OTHER	
D. ANNUAL SPECIAL ASSESSMENT PAYMENT			
E. UNPAID SPECIAL ASSESSMENT BALANCE			
F. ANNUAL MAINTENANCE ASSESSMENT		TOTAL	$

SECTION II — PERSONAL AND FINANCIAL STATUS OF APPLICANT

16. PLEASE CHECK APPROPRIATE BOXES: IF ONE OR MORE ARE CHECKED, ITEMS 18B, 21, 22 AND 23 MUST INCLUDE INFORMATION CONCERNING BORROWER'S SPOUSE (OR FORMER SPOUSE IF BOX "D" IS CHECKED). IF NO BOXES ARE CHECKED, NO INFORMATION CONCERNING THE SPOUSE NEED BE FURNISHED IN ITEMS 18B, 21, 22 AND 23.

A. ☐	THE SPOUSE WILL BE JOINTLY OBLIGATED WITH THE BORROWER ON THE LOAN	C. ☐	THE BORROWER IS RELYING ON THE SPOUSE'S INCOME AS A BASIS FOR REPAYMENT OF THE LOAN
B. ☐	THE BORROWER IS MARRIED AND THE PROPERTY TO SECURE THE LOAN IS LOCATED IN A COMMUNITY PROPERTY STATE	D. ☐	THE BORROWER IS RELYING ON ALIMONY, CHILD SUPPORT, OR SEPARATE MAINTENANCE PAYMENTS FROM A SPOUSE OR FORMER SPOUSE AS A BASIS FOR REPAYMENT OF THE LOAN.

17A. MARITAL STATUS OF ▲ BORROWER 1☐ MARRIED 3☐ UNMARRIED 2☐ SEPARATED	17B. MARITAL STATUS OF CO-BORROWER OTHER THAN SPOUSE 1☐ MARRIED 3☐ UNMARRIED 2☐ SEPARATED	17C. MONTHLY CHILD SUPPORT OBLIGATION $	17D. MONTHLY ALIMONY OBLIGATION $	18A. AGE OF BORROWER	18B. AGE OF SPOUSE OR COBORROWER	18C. AGE(S) OF DEPENDENT(S)

19. CURRENT MONTHLY HOUSING EXPENSE $	20. UTILITIES INCLUDED? ☐ YES ☐ NO	21. LIABILITIES (Itemize all debts)		
		NAME OF CREDITOR	MO. PAYMENT $	BALANCE $

22. ASSETS		JOB RELATED EXPENSE (Specify)		
A. CASH (Including deposit on purchase)	$			
B. SAVINGS BONDS — OTHER SECURITIES				
C. REAL ESTATE OWNED				
D. AUTO				
E. FURNITURE AND HOUSEHOLD GOODS				
F. OTHER (Use separate sheet, if necessary)		JOB RELATED EXPENSE (Specify)		
G. TOTAL	$		TOTAL	$

23. INCOME AND OCCUPATIONAL STATUS			24. ESTIMATED TOTAL COST	
ITEM	BORROWER	SPOUSE OR COBORROWER	ITEM	AMOUNT
A. OCCUPATION			A. PURCHASE EXISTING HOME OR CONSTRUCTION	$
			B. ALTERATIONS, IMPROVEMENTS, REPAIRS	
B. NAME OF EMPLOYER			C. LAND (If acquired separately)	
			D. REFINANCE (Attach list of debts to be paid)	
C. NUMBER OF YEARS EMPLOYED			E. PREPAID ITEMS	
			F. ESTIMATED CLOSING COSTS	
D. GROSS PAY	MONTHLY $ HOURLY $	MONTHLY ▲ $ HOURLY $	G. HUD MIP OR VA FUNDING FEE PAID IN CASH	
			H. DISCOUNT (Only if borrower permitted to pay)	
E. OTHER INCOME (Disclosure of child support, alimony and separate maintenance income is optional)	MONTHLY ▲ $	MONTHLY ▲ $	I. TOTAL COSTS (Add Items 24A through 24H)	
			J. LESS CASH FROM BORROWER	
			K. LESS OTHER CREDITS	
NOTE — If land acquired by separate transaction, complete Items 25A and 25B.			L. LOAN AMOUNT EXCLUSIVE OF MIP OR FUNDING FEE FINANCED	
25A. DATE ACQUIRED	25B. UNPAID BALANCE		M. MIP/FUNDING FEE FINANCED	
			N. LOAN AMOUNT INCLUDING MIP/FUNDING FEE	

VA FORM 26-1802a, FEB 1988
HUD FORM 92900.1

SUPERSEDES VA FORM 26-1802A AND HUD FORM 92900.1, JUN 1985, WHICH WILL NOT BE USED.

DELIVER TO BORROWER COPY 6

SECTION III – LENDER'S CERTIFICATION *(Must be signed by lender)*

The undersigned lender makes the following certifications to induce the Veterans Administration to issue a certificate of commitment to guarantee the subject loan under Title 38, U.S. Code, or to induce the Department of Housing and Urban Development - Federal Housing Commissioner to issue a firm commitment for mortgage insurance under the National Housing Act.

26A. The information furnished in Section I is true, accurate and complete.

26B. The information contained in Section II was obtained directly from the borrower by a full-time employee of the undersigned lender or its duly authorized agent and is true to the best of the lender's knowledge and belief.

26C. The credit report submitted on the subject borrower *(and coborrower, if any)* was ordered by the undersigned lender or its duly authorized agent directly from the credit bureau which prepared the report and was received directly from said credit bureau.

26D. The verification of employment and verification of deposits were requested and received by the lender or its duly authorized agent without passing through the hands of any third persons and are true to the best of the lender's knowledge and belief.

26E. This application was signed by the borrower after Sections I, II and V were completed.

26F. This proposed loan to the named borrower meets the income and credit requirements of the governing law in the judgment of the undersigned.

26G through 26I - TO BE COMPLETED OR APPLICABLE FOR VA LOANS ONLY.

26G. The names and functions of any duly authorized agents who developed on behalf of the lender any of the information or supporting credit data submitted are as follows:

	NAME	ADDRESS	FUNCTION *(e.g., obtained information in Sec. II: ordered credit report, verification of employment, verification of deposits, etc.)*
(1)			
(2)			
(3)			

If no agent is shown above, the undersigned lender affirmatively certifies that all information and supporting credit data were obtained directly by the lender.

26H. The undersigned lender understands and agrees that it is responsible for the acts of agents identified in item 26G as to the functions with which they are identified.

26I. The proposed loan conforms otherwise with the applicable provisions of Title 38, U.S. Code, and of the regulations concerning guaranty or insurance of loans to veterans.

27. DATE	28. NAME OF LENDER	29. TELEPHONE NUMBER *(Include Area Code)*	30. SIGNATURE AND TITLE OF OFFICER OR LENDER

SECTION IV – NOTICES TO BORROWERS

PRIVACY ACT INFORMATION - The information requested in this form *(except for social security number)* is authorized by 38 USC 1810 *(if VA)* and 12 USC 1701 et seq. *(if HUD/FHA)*. The Debt Collection Act of 1982, P.L. 97-365, requires persons applying for a federally insured or guaranteed loan to furnish his or her social security number. The information will be used to determine whether you qualify as a mortgagor. Any disclosure of information outside VA or HUD/FHA will be made only as permitted by law. Failure to provide any of the requested information, including social security number, may result in disapproval of your loan application.

NOTICE TO BORROWERS - This is notice to you as required by the Right to Financial Privacy Act of 1978 that the VA or HUD/FHA has a right of access to financial records held by financial institutions in connection with the consideration or administration of assistance to you. Financial records involving your transaction will be available to VA and HUD/FHA without further notice or authorization but will not be disclosed or released by this institution to another Government Agency or Department without your consent except as required or permitted by law.

CAUTION - Delinquencies, defaults, foreclosures and abuses of mortgage loans involving programs of the Federal Government can be costly and detrimental to your credit, now and in the future. The mortgagee *(lender)* in this transaction, its agents and assigns as well as the Federal Government, its agencies, agents and assigns, are authorized to take any and all of the following actions in the event loan payments become delinquent on the mortgaged loan described in the attached application; (1) Report your name and account information to a credit bureau; (2) Assess additional interest and penalty charges for the period of time that payment is not made; (3) Assess charges to cover additional administrative costs incurred by the Government to service your account; (4) Offset amounts owed to you under other Federal programs; (5) Refer your account to a private attorney, collection agency or mortgage servicing agency to collect the amount due, foreclose the mortgage, sell the property and seek judgment against you for any deficiency; (6) Refer your account to the Department of Justice for litigation in the courts; (7) If you are a current or retired Federal employee, take action to offset your salary, or civil service retirement benefits; (8) Refer your debt to the Internal Revenue Service for offset against any amount owed to you as an income tax refund; and (9) Report any resulting written-off debt of yours to the Internal Revenue Service as your taxable income. All of these actions can and will be used to recover any debts owed when it is determined to be in the interest of the lender and/or the Federal Government to do so.

SECTION V – BORROWER CERTIFICATION *(Must be signed by Borrower(s))*

31A. COMPLETE FOR APPLICATION FOR HUD/FHA INSURED MORTGAGE ONLY

SALES PRICE	ORIGINAL MORTGAGE AMT.
$	$

(1) Do you own or have you sold other real estate within the past 36 months?

☐ Yes ☐ No Is it to be sold? ☐ Yes ☐ No HUD/FHA Mortgage? ☐ Yes ☐ No

Address of Lender: ________ Name of Lender: ________

(2) If dwelling to be covered by this mortgage is to be rented, is it a part of, adjacent or contiguous to any project, subdivision or group of concentrated rental properties involving eight or more dwelling units in which you have any financial interest?

☐ Yes ☐ No If "Yes," please give details on a separate sheet.

Do you own four or more dwelling units with mortgages insured under any title of the National Housing Act? ☐ Yes ☐ No If "Yes" submit form HUD-92561.

31B. COMPLETE FOR VA-GUARANTEED MORTGAGE ONLY.

Have you ever had a VA home loan? ☐ Yes ☐ No

31C. APPLICABLE FOR BOTH VA AND HUD.

(1) During the past five years, have you directly or indirectly been obligated on any loan which resulted in foreclosure, transfer of title in lieu of foreclosure, or judgment? *(This would include such loans as home mortgage loans, SBA loans, home improvement loans, educational loans, manufactured (mobile) home loans, any mortgage, financial obligation, bond, or loan guarantee.)* ☐ Yes ☐ No If "Yes" provide details, including date, name and address of lender, FHA or VA case number, if any, and reasons for the action on a separate sheet

(2) Are you presently delinquent or in default on any debt to the Federal Government *(e.g., Public Health Service, U.S. Guaranteed Student Loan, GI Bill Education Benefits, etc.)* ☐ Yes ☐ No If "Yes" give details as described in (1) above.

31D. APPLICABLE FOR BOTH VA AND HUD. As a home loan borrower, you will be legally obligated to make the mortgage payments called for by your mortgage loan contract. The fact that you disposed of your property after the loan has been made WILL NOT RELIEVE YOU OF LIABILITY FOR MAKING THESE PAYMENTS. PAYMENT OF THE LOAN IN FULL IS ORDINARILY THE WAY LIABILITY ON A MORTGAGE NOTE IS ENDED. Some home buyers have the mistaken impression that if they sell their homes when they move to another locality, or dispose of it for any other reasons, they are no longer liable for the mortgage payments and that liability for these payments is solely that of the new owners. Even though the new owners may agree in writing to assume liability for your mortgage payments, this assumption agreement will not relieve you from liability to the holder of the note which you signed when you obtained the loan to buy the property. Also, unless you are able to sell the property to a buyer who is acceptable to the VA or to HUD/FHA and who will assume the payment of your obligation to the lender, you will not be relieved from liability to repay any claim which the VA or HUD/FHA may be required to pay your lender on account of default in your loan payments. THE AMOUNT OF ANY SUCH CLAIM PAYMENT WILL BE A DEBT OWED BY YOU TO THE FEDERAL GOVERNMENT. This debt will be the object of established collection procedures.

I, THE UNDERSIGNED BORROWER(S), CERTIFY THAT:

(1) I have read and understand the foregoing concerning my liability on the loan and Section IV, Notices to Borrowers.

(2) VA ONLY *(Check applicable box)* ☐ Purchase or Construction Loan. I now actually occupy the above-described property as my home or intend to move into and occupy said property as my home within a reasonable period of time. ☐ Home Improvement or Refinancing Loan. I own and personally occupy as my home, or intend to reoccupy after the completion of major alterations, repairs or improvements, the property described in Item 7 of the application.

(3) Check applicable box *(not applicable for Home Improvement or Refinancing Loan)*. I have been informed that $ ________ is ☐ the reasonable value of the property as determined by VA, ☐ the statement of appraised value as determined by HUD/FHA. IF THE CONTRACT PRICE OR COST EXCEEDS THE VA REASONABLE VALUE OR HUD/FHA STATEMENT OF APPRAISED VALUE, COMPLETE EITHER ITEM (a) OR (b), WHICHEVER IS APPLICABLE.

(a) ☐ I was aware of this valuation when I signed my contract and I have paid or will pay in cash from my own resources at or prior to loan closing a sum equal to the difference between the contract purchase price or cost and the VA or HUD/FHA established value. I do not and will not have outstanding after loan closing any unpaid contractual obligation on account of such cash payment;

(b) ☐ I was not aware of this valuation when I signed my contract but have elected to complete the transaction at the contract purchase price or cost. I have paid or will pay in cash from my own resources at or prior to loan closing a sum equal to the difference between contract purchase price or cost and the VA or HUD/FHA established value. I do not and will not have outstanding after loan closing any unpaid contractual obligation on account of such cash payment.

(4) Neither I, nor anyone authorized to act for me, will refuse to sell or rent, after the making of a bona fide offer, or refuse to negotiate for the sale or rental of, or otherwise make unavailable or deny the dwelling or property covered by this loan to any person because of race, color, religion, sex or national origin. I recognize that any restrictive covenant on this property relating to race, color, religion, sex or national origin is illegal and void and civil action for preventive relief may be brought by the Attorney General of the United States in any appropriate U.S. District Court against any person responsible for the violation of the applicable law.

(5) The Borrower certifies that all information in this application is given for the purpose of obtaining a loan to be insured under the National Housing Act or guaranteed by the Veterans Administration and the information in Sections II and V is true and complete to the best of his/her knowledge and belief. Verification may be obtained from any source named herein.

(6) HUD ONLY - For properties constructed prior to 1978-I have received information on lead paint poisoning. ☐ Yes ☐ Not applicable

(7) I AM AWARE THAT NEITHER HUD/FHA NOR VA WARRANTS THE CONDITION OR VALUE OF THE PROPERTY.

READ CERTIFICATIONS CAREFULLY— DO NOT SIGN UNLESS APPLICATION IS FULLY COMPLETED.	32. DATE	33. SIGNATURE(S) OF BORROWER(S) *(Before signing review accuracy of application and certifications)*

Federal statutes provide severe penalties for any fraud, intentional misrepresentation, or criminal connivance or conspiracy purposed to influence the issuance of any guaranty or insurance by the VA or USDA FmHA Administrator or the HUD/FHA Commissioner.

Reverse of the FHA or VA Loan Application

Read both of these sections to understand what your liability is for government insured loans before signing the final application. As with all forms, read and expect explanations of all the lines *before* signing and keep a copy for your records.

SECTION IV — NOTICES TO BORROWERS

PRIVACY ACT INFORMATION - The information requested in this form *(except for social security number)* is authorized by 38 USC 1810 *(if VA)* and 12 USC 1701 et seq. *(if HUD/FHA)*. The Debt Collection Act of 1982, P.L. 97-365, requires persons applying for a federally insured or guaranteed loan to furnish his or her social security number. The information will be used to determine whether you qualify as a mortgagor. Any disclosure of information outside VA or HUD/FHA will be made only as permitted by law. Failure to provide any of the requested information, including social security number, may result in disapproval of your loan application.

NOTICE TO BORROWERS - This is notice to you as required by the Right to Financial Privacy Act of 1978 that the VA or HUD/FHA has a right of access to financial records held by financial institutions in connection with the consideration or administration of assistance to you. Financial records involving your transaction will be available to VA and HUD/FHA without further notice or authorization but will not be disclosed or released by this institution to another Government Agency or Department without your consent except as required or permitted by law.

CAUTION - Delinquencies, defaults, foreclosures and abuses of mortgage loans involving programs of the Federal Government can be costly and detrimental to your credit, now and in the future. The mortgagee *(lender)* in this transaction, its agents and assigns as well as the Federal Government, its agencies, agents and assigns, are authorized to take any and all of the following actions in the event loan payments become delinquent on the mortgaged loan described in the attached application: (1) Report your name and account information to a credit bureau; (2) Assess additional interest and penalty charges for the period of time that payment is not made; (3) Assess charges to cover additional administrative costs incurred by the Government to service your account; (4) Offset amounts owed to you under other Federal programs; (5) Refer your account to a private attorney, collection agency or mortgage servicing agency to collect the amount due, foreclose the mortgage, sell the property and seek judgment against you for any deficiency; (6) Refer your account to the Department of Justice for litigation in the courts; (7) If you are a current or retired Federal employee, take action to offset your salary, or civil service retirement benefits; (8) Refer your debt to the Internal Revenue Service for offset against any amount owed to you as an income tax refund; and (9) Report any resulting written-off debt of yours to the Internal Revenue Service as your taxable income. All of these actions can and will be used to recover any debts owed when it is determined to be in the interest of the lender and/or the Federal Government to do so.

31D. APPLICABLE FOR BOTH VA AND HUD. As a home loan borrower, you will be legally obligated to make the mortgage payments called for by your mortgage loan contract. The fact that you disposed of your property after the loan has been made WILL NOT RELIEVE YOU OF LIABILITY FOR MAKING THESE PAYMENTS. PAYMENT OF THE LOAN IN FULL IS ORDINARILY THE WAY LIABILITY ON A MORTGAGE NOTE IS ENDED. Some home buyers have the mistaken impression that if they sell their homes when they move to another locality, or dispose of it for any other reasons, they are no longer liable for the mortgage payments and that liability for these payments is solely that of the new owners. Even though the new owners may agree in writing to assume liability for your mortgage payments, this assumption agreement will not relieve you from liability to the holder of the note which you signed when you obtained the loan to buy the property. Also, unless you are able to sell the property to a buyer who is acceptable to the VA or to HUD/FHA and who will assume the payment of your obligation to the lender, you will not be relieved from liability to repay any claim which the VA or HUD/FHA may be required to pay your lender on account of default in your loan payments. THE AMOUNT OF ANY SUCH CLAIM PAYMENT WILL BE A DEBT OWED BY YOU TO THE FEDERAL GOVERNMENT. This debt will be the object of established collection procedures.

FHA Appraisal (Conditional Commitment)

You will receive a copy of the appraisal, (a complete copy is on the previous page.) Some of the areas of interest are highlighted below.

Attention Homebuyers

This property is not FHA approved and FHA does not warrant the condition or the value of the property. However, FHA will insure a mortgage on the property if certain conditions are met.

Existing Houses - If you are buying a house which has been lived in before, be sure the house is in acceptable condition before signing a purchase contract. An appraisal is made only to estimate the value of the property. This appraisal does not guarantee that the house is free from defects. HUD cannot give you money for repairs so you must protect yourself before you buy. You should inspect the property carefully. If you need help a private inspection service can be hired in many localities. Look in the telephone book for such services.

New Homes - If you are buying a new home HUD requires the builder to provide a one year warranty. Please read carefully the information on the back of this form under the heading "new construction".

Fair Housing & Equal Opportunity Hotline: 800-424-8590

Advice to Homebuyers

Prepaid Items - These are charges that normally will be paid at closing and are recurring in nature. They include such items as funds for real estate taxes and hazard insurance. The amount of these items will vary depending upon the closing date. No estimate is provided with this statement.

Escrow Account - This is a special account that your lender will keep on your behalf to save the necessary funds to pay certain future bills. Your mortgage payment will include in addition to an amount for interest and principal, amounts to cover such items as property taxes, hazard insurance, and for certain FHA programs, the mortgage insurance premium. These charges are collected in advance so that your lender will have enough money in the account to apply the charge when it comes due. Generally, 1/12 of the next year's estimated charges will be the amount collected with each of your monthly mortgage payments. Bear in mind that in most communities taxes and other operating costs are increasing. The estimates should give some idea of what you can expect the costs to be at the beginning. In some areas the estimate of taxes may also include charges such as sewer charges, garbage collection fee, water rates, etc.

Mortgage Insurance Premium - The amount charged for insuring your mortgage. The premium may be in the form of a one-time charge or a monthly charge depending upon the section of the Housing Act under which your mortgage is insured. Your lender can provide you with specific information about your transaction.

Estimated Monthly Expenses - These are costs associated with homeownership which HUD believes the home-owners will have to pay when living in the property. Two examples of "Estimated Monthly Expenses" are fire insurance and taxes, which are paid to your lender each month as part of your mortgage payment. These are put into your escrow account.

Other Costs of Homeownership - Utilities are usually paid monthly to whomever provides the service. Also, you should save a certain amount each month to cover repair and maintenance costs which will come up while you own your home.

Late Payments - If you do not pay your mortgage payment within 15 days from the 1st day of the month, you can be charged a penalty. This may be 4 cents for each dollar of your payment.

New Construction - After specifications are accepted by HUD or a Direct Endorsement Lender before construction, the builder is required to warrant that the house substantially conforms to approved plans and specifications. This warranty is for 1 year following the date on which title is transferred to the original buyer or the date on which the house was first lived in which ever happens first. If, during the warranty period, you notice defects for which you believe the builder is responsible, ask him in writing to fix them. If he does not fix them, write the HUD Field Office. Include your FHA case number. If inspection shows the builder to be at fault, HUD will try to persuade him to fix the defect. If he does not, you may be able to obtain legal relief under the builder's warranty. Where a structural defect is involved HUD can provide money for corrections under certain conditions. You cannot expect the builder to fix damage caused by ordinary wear and tear or by poor maintenance. Keeping the house in good condition is your responsibility.

Appendix 219

UNIFORM RESIDENTIAL APPRAISAL REPORT

Valuation Section — File No. _____

Purpose of Appraisal is to estimate Market Value as defined in the Certification & Statement of Limiting Conditions.

COST APPROACH

BUILDING SKETCH (SHOW GROSS LIVING AREA ABOVE GRADE)
If for Freddie Mac or Fannie Mae, show only square foot calculations and cost approach comments in this space.

ESTIMATED REPRODUCTION COST – NEW – OF IMPROVEMENTS:

Dwelling	____ Sq. Ft. @ $ ____	= $ ____	
	____ Sq. Ft. @ $ ____	= ____	
Extras		= ____	
		= ____	
Special Energy Efficient Items		= ____	
Porches, Patios, etc.		= ____	
Garage/Carport	____ Sq. Ft. @ $ ____	= ____	
Total Estimated Cost New		= $ ____	
Less	Physical	Functional	External
Depreciation			= $ ____
Depreciated Value of Improvements			= $ ____
Site Imp. "as is" (driveway, landscaping, etc.)			= $ ____
ESTIMATED SITE VALUE			= $ ____
(If leasehold, show only leasehold value.)			
INDICATED VALUE BY COST APPROACH			= $ ____

(Not Required by Freddie Mac and Fannie Mae)
Does property conform to applicable HUD/VA property standards? ☐ Yes ☐ No
If No, explain: _____

Construction Warranty ☐ Yes ☐ No
Name of Warranty Program _____
Warranty Coverage Expires _____

The undersigned has recited three recent sales of properties most similar and proximate to subject and has considered these in the market analysis. The description includes a dollar adjustment, reflecting market reaction to those items of significant variation between the subject and comparable properties. If a significant item in the comparable property is superior to, or more favorable than, the subject property, a minus (–) adjustment is made, thus reducing the indicated value of the subject. If a significant item in the comparable is inferior to, or less favorable than, the subject property, a plus (+) adjustment is made, thus increasing the indicated value of the subject.

SALES COMPARISON ANALYSIS

ITEM	SUBJECT	COMPARABLE NO. 1		COMPARABLE NO. 2		COMPARABLE NO. 3	
Address							
Proximity to Subject							
Sales Price	$		$		$		$
Price/Gross Liv. Area	$	$		$		$	
Data Source							
VALUE ADJUSTMENTS	DESCRIPTION	DESCRIPTION	+(–)$ Adjustment	DESCRIPTION	+(–)$ Adjustment	DESCRIPTION	+(–)$ Adjustment
Sales or Financing Concessions							
Date of Sale/Time							
Location							
Site/View							
Design and Appeal							
Quality of Construction							
Age							
Condition							
Above Grade Room Count	Total / Bdrms / Baths	Total / Bdrms / Baths		Total / Bdrms / Baths		Total / Bdrms / Baths	
Gross Living Area	Sq. Ft.	Sq. Ft.		Sq. Ft.		Sq. Ft.	
Basement & Finished Rooms Below Grade							
Functional Utility							
Heating/Cooling							
Garage/Carport							
Porches, Patio, Pools, etc.							
Special Energy Efficient Items							
Fireplace(s)							
Other (e.g. kitchen equip., remodeling)							
Net Adj. (total)			+ ☐ – ☐ $		+ ☐ – ☐ $		+ ☐ – ☐ $
Indicated Value of Subject			$		$		$

Comments on Sales Comparison: _____

INDICATED VALUE BY SALES COMPARISON APPROACH .... $ ____
INDICATED VALUE BY INCOME APPROACH (If Applicable) Estimated Market Rent $ ____ /Mo. x Gross Rent Multiplier ____ = $ ____
This appraisal is made ☐ "as is" ☐ subject to the repairs, alterations, inspections or conditions listed below ☐ completion per plans and specifications.
Comments and Conditions of Appraisal: _____

RECONCILIATION

Final Reconciliation: _____

This appraisal is based upon the above requirements, the certification, contingent and limiting conditions, and Market Value definition that are stated in
☐ FmHA, HUD &/or VA instructions.
☐ Freddie Mac Form 439 (Rev. 7/86)/Fannie Mae Form 1004B (Rev. 7/86) filed with client _____ 19 ____ ☐ attached.
I (WE) ESTIMATE THE MARKET VALUE, AS DEFINED, OF THE SUBJECT PROPERTY AS OF _____ 19 ____ **to be** $ ____
I (We) certify: that to the best of my (our) knowledge and belief the facts and data used herein are true and correct; that I (we) personally inspected the subject property, both inside and out, and have made an exterior inspection of all comparable sales cited in this report; and that I (we) have no undisclosed interest, present or prospective therein.

Appraiser(s) SIGNATURE _____   Review Appraiser SIGNATURE _____   ☐ Did ☐ Did Not
NAME _____   (if applicable) NAME _____   Inspect Property

Freddie Mac Form 70 10/86 12Ch.   Forms and Worms Inc.® 315 Whitney Ave., New Haven, CT 06511 1(800) 243-4545   Fannie Mae Form 1004 10/86

UNIFORM RESIDENTIAL APPRAISAL REPORT

Property Description & Analysis — File No. _____

SUBJECT
- Property Address
- City / County / State / Zip Code / Census Tract
- Legal Description
- Owner/Occupant / Map Reference
- Sale Price $ / Date of Sale
- Loan charges/concessions to be paid by seller $
- R.E. Taxes $ / Tax Year / HOA $/Mo.
- Lender/Client

PROPERTY RIGHTS APPRAISED: Fee Simple / Leasehold / Condominium (HUD/VA) / De Minimis PUD

LENDER DISCRETIONARY USE:
- Sale Price $
- Date
- Mortgage Amount $
- Mortgage Type
- Discount Points and Other Concessions Paid by Seller $
- Source

NEIGHBORHOOD

LOCATION	Urban	Suburban	Rural
BUILT UP	Over 75%	25-75%	Under 25%
GROWTH RATE	Rapid	Stable	Slow
PROPERTY VALUES	Increasing	Stable	Declining
DEMAND/SUPPLY	Shortage	In Balance	Over Supply
MARKETING TIME	Under 3 Mos.	3-6 Mos.	Over 6 Mos.

PRESENT LAND USE % / LAND USE CHANGE / PREDOMINANT OCCUPANCY / SINGLE FAMILY HOUSING PRICE $(000) AGE (yrs)
- Single Family — Not Likely — Owner — Low
- 2-4 Family — Likely — Tenant — High
- Multi-family — In process — Vacant (0-5%) — Predominant
- Commercial — To: — Vacant (over 5%)
- Industrial
- Vacant

NEIGHBORHOOD ANALYSIS (Good / Avg / Fair / Poor):
- Employment Stability
- Convenience to Employment
- Convenience to Shopping
- Convenience to Schools
- Adequacy of Public Transportation
- Recreation Facilities
- Adequacy of Utilities
- Property Compatibility
- Protection from Detrimental Cond.
- Police & Fire Protection
- General Appearance of Properties
- Appeal to Market

Note: Race or the racial composition of the neighborhood are not considered reliable appraisal factors.
COMMENTS: _____

SITE
- Dimensions
- Site Area / Corner Lot / Topography
- Zoning Classification / Zoning Compliance / Size
- HIGHEST & BEST USE: Present Use / Other Use / Shape / Drainage

UTILITIES Public/Other — SITE IMPROVEMENTS Type Public/Private — View / Landscaping / Driveway
- Electricity / Street
- Gas / Curb/Gutter
- Water / Sidewalk — Apparent Easements
- Sanitary Sewer / Street Lights — FEMA Flood Hazard Yes* No
- Storm Sewer / Alley — FEMA* Map/Zone

COMMENTS (Apparent adverse easements, encroachments, special assessments, slide areas, etc.):

IMPROVEMENTS

GENERAL DESCRIPTION:
- Units
- Stories
- Type (Det./Att.)
- Design (Style)
- Existing
- Proposed
- Under Construction
- Age (Yrs.)
- Effective Age (Yrs.)

EXTERIOR DESCRIPTION:
- Foundation
- Exterior Walls
- Roof Surface
- Gutters & Dwnspts
- Window Type
- Storm Sash
- Screens
- Manufactured House

FOUNDATION:
- Slab
- Crawl Space
- Basement
- Sump Pump
- Dampness
- Settlement
- Infestation

BASEMENT:
- Area Sq. Ft.
- % Finished
- Ceiling
- Walls
- Floor
- Outside Entry

INSULATION:
- Roof
- Ceiling
- Walls
- Floor
- None
- Adequacy
- Energy Efficient Items

ROOM LIST

ROOMS	Foyer	Living	Dining	Kitchen	Den	Family Rm	Rec. Rm	Bedrooms	# Baths	Laundry	Other	Area Sq Ft
Basement												
Level 1												
Level 2												

Finished area **above** grade contains: Rooms; Bedroom(s); Bath(s); Square Feet of Gross Living Area

INTERIOR

SURFACES — Materials/Condition:
- Floors
- Walls
- Trim/Finish
- Bath Floor
- Bath Wainscot
- Doors

Fireplace(s) #

CAR STORAGE:
- Garage — Attached
- No. Cars — Carport — Detached
- Condition — None — Built-In

HEATING: Type / Fuel / Condition / Adequacy / COOLING / Central / Other / Condition / Adequacy

KITCHEN EQUIP.: Refrigerator / Range/Oven / Disposal / Dishwasher / Fan/Hood / Compactor / Washer/Dryer / Microwave / Intercom

ATTIC: None / Stairs / Drop Stair / Scuttle / Floor / Heated / Finished

AUTOS: Adequate / Inadequate / House Entry / Outside Entry / Basement Entry

IMPROVEMENT ANALYSIS (Good / Avg / Fair / Poor):
- Quality of Construction
- Condition of Improvements
- Room Sizes/Layout
- Closets and Storage
- Energy Efficiency
- Plumbing-Adequacy & Condition
- Electrical-Adequacy & Condition
- Kitchen Cabinets-Adequacy & Cond.
- Compatibility to Neighborhood
- Appeal & Marketability
- Estimated Remaining Economic Life ___ Yrs.
- Estimated Remaining Physical Life ___ Yrs.

Additional features: _____

COMMENTS

Depreciation (Physical, functional and external inadequacies, repairs needed, modernization, etc.): _____

General market conditions and prevalence and impact in subject/market area regarding loan discounts, interest buydowns and concessions: _____

Freddie Mac Form 70 10/86 12Ch — Forms and Worms Inc.,® 315 Whitney Ave., New Haven, CT 06511 (800) 243-4545 — Item # III/10 — Fannie Mae Form 1004 10/86

Appendix 221

Conditional Commitment
Direct Endorsement
Statement of Appraised Value

U.S. Department of Housing
and Urban Development
Office of Housing
Federal Housing Commissioner

OMB No. 2502-0111 (Exp. 10/31/89)

It is required by law that borrowers who are using HUD insured financing must receive a copy of this form prior to the purchase of property. The following definitions refer to phrases used in the Commitment Terms sections below. **The Estimated Value of Property** (Est. Value of Prop.) is defined as the amount HUD considers the property to be worth. The estimated value of the property does not fix a sales price except under HUD's section 235 homeownership subsidy program. The Estimated Closing Cost is the estimated amount to be paid in order to complete the mortgage loan transaction. These costs may be paid by the seller or buyer. They normally include items such as fees for preparing the mortgage documents, title insurance, loan origination fees, and transfer and recording of the deed. The **Maximum Mortgage Amount** (Max. Mort. Amt.) is the highest amount HUD can insure for a non-veteran and is based on the sum of the "Estimated Value of the Property" and the "Estimated Closing Costs". **There is additional information on the reverse side which also should be read carefully.**

Attention Homebuyers

This property is not FHA approved and FHA does not warrant the condition or the value of the property. However, FHA will insure a mortgage on the property if certain conditions are met.
Existing Houses - If you are buying a house which has been lived in before, be sure the house is in acceptable condition before signing a purchase contract. An appraisal is made only to estimate the value of the property. This appraisal does not guarantee that the house is free from defects. HUD cannot give you money for repairs so you should protect yourself before you buy. You should inspect the property carefully. If you need help a private inspection service can be hired in many localities. Look in the telephone book for such services
New Homes - If you are buying a new home HUD requires the builder to provide a one year warranty. Please read carefully the information on the back of this form under the heading "new construction".

Fair Housing & Equal Opportunity Hotline: 800-424-8590

Commitment Terms

☐ Conditional Commitment for mortgage insurance under the National Housing Act, Sec	Est. Value of Prop. $ Est. Closing Cost $	Max. Mort. Amt. $ No. Mos.
☐ See below	Property Address	
By	Action Date	
	☐ Existing ☐ Proposed	MONTHLY EXPENSE ESTIMATE Fire Ins . . . . $
Lender ID FHA Case No.	(See Gen. Cond. 3)	Taxes . . . . $
	Commitment Issued	Maint & Repairs . . . . $
INST Case	Commitment Expires	Heat & Utilities . . . . . $
Sponsor ID Ref. No.	Improved Living	Condo. Com. Exp. . . . $
Mortgagee	Area Sq. Ft.	Total . . . . $

Specific Commitment Conditions (Applicable when checked)

HUD's commitment to insure a mortgage on this property is dependent on the completion of the conditions listed below. **HUD Does Not Guarantee** the work done to comply with the conditions.

Estimated Remaining Economic Life of this property is _____ years.

☐ **Manufactured Housing**

1. ☐ **Subdivision Requirements:** Comply with Requirements No. _____ from Report dated _____ for _____ Subdivision.
2. ☐ **Section 221 (d) (2):** The maximum insurable mortgage for a mortgagor other than a displaced family presenting a Certificate of Eligibility, Form FHA 3476, is $
3. ☐ **Assurance of Completion:** If the required repairs cannot be completed prior to submission of closing papers, Form HUD 92300 in the amount of $ _____ (or such additional amount as the lender desires) may be established as the means to assure completion.

☐ **See Indicated Additional Items on Attached:**
☐ **See the Following Additional Conditions on Reverse:**

"Contact your local utility company or other qualified person or firm for a home energy audit. If energy-related improvements are required, the value of your property may be increased to include the following: Thermostats * Insulation Wrap for Water Heaters * Insulation of Ducts and Pipes in Unheated Spaces of Heating/Cooling Systems * Attic Insulation * Insulation for Floors and Foundation Walls * Installation of Weather-Stripping/Caulking * Installation of Storm Windows/Doors. The value may be increased by up to (a) $2,000 without a separate value determination; (b) $3,500, if supported by a value determination by an approved appraiser; or (c) more than $3,500, subject to a value determination by the VA or HUD, as applicable, and subsequent endorsement of the VA Certificate of Reasonable Value, HUD Conditional Commitment, or Statement of Appraised Value."

This must be delivered to the borrower promptly, but no later than at the time of borrower's signing of the Application for Commitment and Insurance, Form HUD 92900.

Previous Edition is obsolete.
Homebuyer Copy

HUD-92800.5B (3-87)
HB4115.1

VMP MORTGAGE FORMS • (313)293-8100 • (800)521-7291

Specific Commitment Conditions *(Applicable when indicated on reverse)*

B. Proposed Construction: The builder or mortgagee must notify the assigned Fee Inspector as appropriate (See Items 11, 12 and 13 below).
C. Warranty: Form HUD-92544 and one-year performance guarantee on labor and materials shall be executed between builder and purchaser.
D. Section 223: This commitment is issued pursuant to Section 223(e).
E. Health Authority Approval: Local Health Authority shall complete HUD-92573 indicating acceptable installation of individual water supply and/or sewage disposal system. (Approval by letter or Health Authority form may be used.)
F. Reserved
G. Prefabricator's Certificate: Lender shall provide Prefabrication Certificate required by related Engineering Bulletin.
H. Termite Control: Proposed Construction: Builder shall complete Form HUD-92052, Termite Soil Treatment Guarantee, and transmit a copy to HUD.

An original and a copy are sent to the mortgagee who provides the mortgagor with the original at closing.

1. Lead Paint Notice: This house was constructed before 1978. There is a possibility that it may contain lead paint that was in use before that time. The lender is required to provide information on LEAD PAINT POISONING to the buyer
2. Flood Insurance Requirement: This property is located in a flood hazard area and must be covered by flood insurance in accordance with HUD Regulation 24CFR 203.16a
3. Carpet identification: (as listed in Certified Products Directory) and manufacturer recommended maintenance program must be provided to the homebuyer.
4. Termite Control - Existing Construction: A recognized termite control operator shall furnish a certificate that the house and other structures within the legal boundaries of the property indicate no evidence of active termite infestation.
5. Code Enforcement: Lender shall submit a statement from the public authority that the property meets local code requirements. If the mortgage on the property is to be insured under Section 221(d)(2), a code compliance inspection is required.
6. Repairs: Lender shall notify the original appraiser upon completion of required repairs, unless otherwise instructed.
7. Certificate of Completion: Lender shall furnish a certificate that required repairs have been examined and were satisfactorily completed.
8. Manufactured Warranties: must be provided to homebuyer covering Heating/Cooling systems, Hot Water Heaters, Ranges, etc.
9. Initial Inspection (2 working days) is requested before "beginning of construction" with forms in place.
10. Frame Inspection (1 working day) is requested when building is enclosed and framing, plumbing, heating, electrical and insulation is complete and visible.
11. Final inspection is requested when construction is completed and the property is ready for occupancy.
12. Insulation Certificate must be posted in a conspicuous location in the dwelling.
13. The Insured Protection Plan Warranty Agreement shall be executed between builder and purchaser.
14. Borrower Notification: At the time of the application for firm commitment, the mortgagee must include a certificate that the borrower was notified that the property was not approved by HUD prior to the start of construction and the Department does not have authority to provide financial relief for any future property repairs under Section 518(a) of the National Housing Act.

Advice to Homebuyers

Prepaid Items - These are charges that normally will be paid at closing and are recurring in nature. They include such items as funds for real estate taxes and hazard insurance. The amount of these items will vary depending upon the closing date. No estimate is provided with this statement.

Escrow Account - This is a special account that your lender will keep on your behalf to save the necessary funds to pay certain future bills. Your mortgage payment will include in addition to an amount for interest and principal, amounts to cover such items as property taxes, hazard insurance, and for certain FHA programs, the mortgage insurance premium. These charges are collected in advance so that your lender will have enough money in the account to apply the charge when it comes due. Generally, 1/12 of the next year's estimated charges will be the amount collected with each of your monthly mortgage payments. Bear in mind that in most communities taxes and other operating costs are increasing. The estimates should give some idea of what you can expect the costs to be at the beginning. In some areas the estimate of taxes may also include charges such as sewer charges, garbage collection fee, water rates, etc.

Mortgage Insurance Premium - The amount charged for insuring your mortgage. The premium may be in the form of a one-time charge or a monthly charge depending upon the section of the Housing Act under which your mortgage is insured. Your lender can provide you with specific information about your transaction.

Estimated Monthly Expenses - These are costs associated with homeownership which HUD believes the home-owners will have to pay when living in the property. Two examples of "Estimated Monthly Expenses" are fire insurance and taxes, which are paid to your lender each month as part of your mortgage payment. These are put into your escrow account.

Other Costs of Homeownership - Utilities are usually paid monthly to whomever provides the service. Also, you should save a certain amount each month to cover repair and maintenance costs which will come up while you own your home.

Late Payments - If you do not pay your mortgage payment within 15 days from the 1st day of the month, you can be charged a penalty. This may be 4 cents for each dollar of your payment.

New Construction - After specifications are accepted by HUD or a Direct Endorsement Lender before construction, the builder is required to warrant that the house substantially conforms to approved plans and specifications. This warranty is for 1 year following the date on which title is transferred to the original buyer or the date on which the house was first lived in which ever happens first. If, during the warranty period, you notice defects for which you believe the builder is responsible, ask him in writing to fix them. If he does not fix them, write the HUD Field Office. Include your FHA case number. If inspection shows the builder to be at fault, HUD will try to persuade him to fix the defect. If he does not, you may be able to obtain legal relief under the builder's warranty. Where a structural defect is involved HUD can provide money for corrections under certain conditions. You cannot expect the builder to fix damage caused by ordinary wear and tear or by poor maintenance. Keeping the house in good condition is your responsibility.

If you signed your sales contract prior to receiving this statement or appraised value, the sales contract must include or be changed to include the following language:

"It is expressly agreed that notwithstanding any other provisions of the contract, the purchaser shall not be obligated to complete the purchase of the property described herein or to incur any penalty by forfeiture of earnest money deposits or otherwise unless the seller has delivered to the purchaser a written statement issued by the Federal Housing Commissioner or a Direct Endorsement Lender setting forth the appraised value of property (excluding closing costs) of not less than $_____ (estimated value of property listed on reverse) which statement the seller hereby agrees to deliver to the purchaser promptly after such appraised value statement is made available to the seller. The purchaser shall, however, have the privilege and option of proceeding with the consummation of the contract without regard to the amount of the appraised valuation. The appraised valuation is arrived at to determine the maximum mortgage the Department of Housing and Urban Development will insure. HUD does not warrant the value nor the condition of the property. The purchaser should satisfy himself/herself that the price and condition of the property are acceptable".

Amount to be Borrowed

When you borrow to buy a home, you pay interest and other charges which add to your cost. A larger downpayment will result in a smaller mortgage. Borrow as little as you need and repay in shortest time.

Types of Self-Employed Borrowers

All tax returns and financial statements need to be signed by all borrowers. Financial statements need to be prepared and signed by an accountant.

1. Types of Borrowers
   Individual with sole-proprietorship income or business (Schedule C)
   Individual with rental income (Schedule E)
   Individual with partnership income (K-1s and 1065s)
   Individual with sub-chapter S corporation income (K-1s and 1120s)
   Individual with corporate income (1120s) (a corporate officer whose sole income is from a small corporation)

   You will note that loans are made to private individuals who have businesses or income from businesses; most residential loans cannot be made to a business directly.

2. Types of Tax Forms Needed

   Complete tax returns are required for two full years. Underwriters start with the 1040 and determine income from:
   A. W-2s for all wages listed
   B. If a partnership is indicated from:
      1. a general partner: K-1s, 1065, and a partnership agreement
      2. limited partner (with recourse indicated on K-1): K-1s, 1065 and/or partnership agreement depending on recourse risk
      3. limited partner (without recourse indicated on K-1): K-1s
   C. If a sub-chapter S corporation:
      1. K-1s
      2. 1120s
   D. If a corporate officer:
      1. verification of employment completed by an accountant or controller for officer's compensation
      2. complete corporate returns if available and majority of income (over 50 percent)
   E. If rental income:
      1. rental or lease agreements on all properties
      2. mortgage ratings on all liens
      3. schedule of real estate owned summarizing net cash flow if under ten properties; for over ten use two years of tax returns only

If tax returns are over ninety days old, financial statements will be required:
   1. balance sheet
   2. year-to-date profit and loss or income statement (to within ninety days of application)

Underwriting Analysis of the Self-Employed Borrowers

Lenders vary with this analysis according to allowable add-backs, allowable capital gains rules, and the treatment of depreciation. Use the most conservative approach when analyzing your own returns, then average the cash flow for the best results. In 1990 we would analyze 1989 and 1988 returns as well as a year-to-date profit and loss statement. Even with the acceptable averaged cash flow, a history of decreasing net income might be cause for rejection. Self-employed borrowers must meet the test of "stable, continuing income."

Start with the adjusted gross income at the bottom of the 1040 and adjust for nontangible deductions from income, money not actually spent. No two underwriters analyze tax returns the same and most will use a more conservative approach when in doubt. Finally, taxes and the forms used change each year so you may have to look for these items.

	Year	Year
Adjusted gross income	$ _____	$ _____
Add back alimony deducted and use actual monthly debt from divorce papers	_____	_____
Add back penalty on early savings withdrawal	_____	_____
Add back Keogh deduction	_____	_____
Add back IRA deduction	_____	_____
Adjust additional employee expenses (Form 2106) *Actual* employee expense, this is deductible portion	_____	_____
Other income or loss must be adjusted according to its likelihood of continuation; take out if not ongoing, five years FHA, three years VA and conv.	_____	_____
Net operating loss carryover (NOLC): fifteen years allowed on some income; if not an actual loss in this year add back	_____	_____
Social Security and retirement: add in any amount received not subject to taxes from info	_____	_____
Unemployment income: only use if you have a history with it and if it is likely to continue; on FHA and VA only	_____	_____
Farm Income or Loss: if ongoing leave and adjust for depreciation/depletion	_____	_____
Schedule E: Adjust income or loss and go to form 4562Y	_____	_____
Part I Add rents received	_____	_____
Subtract total expenses w/o depreciation	_____	_____
Add/subtract partnership/sub-S from reverse if ongoing	_____	_____

...continued on next page

Underwriting Analysis of the Self-Employed Borrowers (cont.)

Pensions, IRA dist. Annuities: adjust and use actual amount from proof of income, total income, future income (rarely acceptable) _____ _____

Schedule C business income: leave in only if on-going and likely to continue: adjust if not _____ _____

Add depletion/depreciation if 3 yrs. left _____ _____

In-home office interest (if subject, add) _____ _____

Other interest (add if used as monthly debt) _____ _____

Pension/profit sharing: add back _____ _____

Travel/entertainment: add back 20% exclusion _____ _____

Jobs credit: subtract, real expense is total _____ _____

Casualty loss: one-time add back _____ _____

Amortization: one-time add back _____ _____

Other nontangible expenses: add back _____ _____

Net Adjusted Gross Income $ _____ _____

Analyze partnership income/loss, sub-chapter S corporation income/loss, and corporation income/loss separately if borrower is 10 to 25 percent invested in these businesses.

Form 1040 — U.S. Individual Income Tax Return (1990)

Department of the Treasury—Internal Revenue Service

For the year Jan.–Dec. 31, 1990, or other tax year beginning _____, 1990, ending _____, 19__   OMB No. 1545-0074

Label (See Instructions on page 8.)

Use IRS label. Otherwise, please print or type.

- Your first name and initial | Last name | Your social security number
- If a joint return, spouse's first name and initial | Last name | Spouse's social security number
- Home address (number and street). (If you have a P.O. box, see page 9.) | Apt. no.
- City, town or post office, state, and ZIP code. (If you have a foreign address, see page 9.)

For Privacy Act and Paperwork Reduction Act Notice, see Instructions.

Presidential Election Campaign (See page 9.)
- Do you want $1 to go to this fund? Yes / No
- If joint return, does your spouse want $1 to go to this fund? Yes / No

Note: Checking "Yes" will not change your tax or reduce your refund.

Filing Status

Check only one box.

1. Single. (See page 10 to find out if you can file as head of household.)
2. Married filing joint return (even if only one had income)
3. Married filing separate return. Enter spouse's social security no. above and full name here. ▶
4. Head of household (with qualifying person). (See page 10.) If the qualifying person is your child but not your dependent, enter this child's name here. ▶
5. Qualifying widow(er) with dependent child (year spouse died ▶ 19). (See page 10.)

Exemptions (See Instructions on page 10.)

6a ☐ **Yourself** If your parent (or someone else) can claim you as a dependent on his or her tax return, do not check box 6a. But be sure to check the box on line 33b on page 2

b ☐ **Spouse**

c **Dependents:**
(1) Name (first, initial, and last name) | (2) Check if under age 2 | (3) If age 2 or older, dependent's social security number | (4) Dependent's relationship to you | (5) No. of months lived in your home in 1990

No. of boxes checked on 6a and 6b ____

No. of your children on 6c who:
- lived with you ____
- didn't live with you due to divorce or separation (see page 11) ____

No. of other dependents on 6c ____

If more than 6 dependents, see Instructions on page 11.

d If your child didn't live with you but is claimed as your dependent under a pre-1985 agreement, check here ▶ ☐
e Total number of exemptions claimed

Add numbers entered on lines above ▶ ____

Income

Attach Copy B of your Forms W-2, W-2G, and W-2P here.

If you do not have a W-2, see page 8.

Attach check or money order on top of any Forms W-2, W-2G, or W-2P.

7 Wages, salaries, tips, etc. (attach Form(s) W-2) ... 7
8a Taxable interest income (also attach Schedule B if over $400) ... 8a
b Tax-exempt interest income (see page 13). DON'T include on line 8a | 8b |
9 Dividend income (also attach Schedule B if over $400) ... 9
10 Taxable refunds of state and local income taxes, if any, from worksheet on page 14 ... 10
11 Alimony received ... 11
12 Business income or (loss) (attach Schedule C) ... 12
13 Capital gain or (loss) (attach Schedule D) ... 13
14 Capital gain distributions not reported on line 13 (see page 14) ... 14
15 Other gains or (losses) (attach Form 4797) ... 15
16a Total IRA distributions | 16a | 16b Taxable amount (see page 14) 16b
17a Total pensions and annuities | 17a | 17b Taxable amount (see page 14) 17b
18 Rents, royalties, partnerships, estates, trusts, etc. (attach Schedule E) ... 18
19 Farm income or (loss) (attach Schedule F) ... 19
20 Unemployment compensation (insurance) (see page 16) ... 20
21a Social security benefits | 21a | 21b Taxable amount (see page 16) 21b
22 Other income (list type and amount—see page 16) ... 22
23 Add the amounts shown in the far right column for lines 7 through 22. This is your **total income** ▶ 23

Adjustments to Income

(See Instructions on page 17.)

24a Your IRA deduction, from applicable worksheet on page 17 or 18 . 24a
b Spouse's IRA deduction, from applicable worksheet on page 17 or 18 . 24b
25 One-half of self-employment tax (see page 18) ... 25
26 Self-employed health insurance deduction, from worksheet on page 18 . 26
27 Keogh retirement plan and self-employed SEP deduction ... 27
28 Penalty on early withdrawal of savings ... 28
29 Alimony paid. Recipient's SSN ▶ ... 29
30 Add lines 24a through 29. These are your **total adjustments** ▶ 30

Adjusted Gross Income

31 Subtract line 30 from line 23. This is your **adjusted gross income**. If this amount is less than $20,264 and a child lived with you, see page 23 to find out if you can claim the "Earned Income Credit" on line 57 ▶ 31

Appendix 227

Form 1040 (1990) — Page 2

Tax Computation	32	Amount from line 31 (adjusted gross income)	32
If you want IRS to figure your tax, see Instructions on page 19.	33a	Check if: ☐ You were 65 or older ☐ Blind; ☐ Spouse was 65 or older ☐ Blind. Add the number of boxes checked above and enter the total here ▶ 33a ☐	
	b	If your parent (or someone else) can claim you as a dependent, check here ▶ 33b ☐	
	c	If you are married filing a separate return and your spouse itemizes deductions, or you are a dual-status alien, see page 19 and check here ▶ 33c ☐	
	34	Enter the larger of: • Your **standard deduction** (from the chart (or worksheet) on page 20 that applies to you), **OR** • Your **itemized deductions** (from Schedule A, line 27). If you itemize, attach Schedule A and check here ▶ ☐	34
	35	Subtract line 34 from line 32	35
	36	Multiply $2,050 by the total number of exemptions claimed on line 6e	36
	37	**Taxable income.** Subtract line 36 from line 35. (If line 36 is more than line 35, enter -0-.)	37
	38	Enter tax. Check if from: a ☐ Tax Table, b ☐ Tax Rate Schedules, or c ☐ Form 8615 (see page 21) (If any is from Form(s) 8814, enter that amount here ▶ d _____.)	38
	39	Additional taxes (see page 21). Check if from: a ☐ Form 4970 b ☐ Form 4972	39
	40	Add lines 38 and 39 ▶	40
Credits (See Instructions on page 21.)	41	Credit for child and dependent care expenses (attach Form 2441) — 41	
	42	Credit for the elderly or the disabled (attach Schedule R) — 42	
	43	Foreign tax credit (attach Form 1116) — 43	
	44	General business credit. Check if from: a ☐ Form 3800 or b ☐ Form (specify) — 44	
	45	Credit for prior year minimum tax (attach Form 8801) — 45	
	46	Add lines 41 through 45	46
	47	Subtract line 46 from line 40. (If line 46 is more than line 40, enter -0-.) ▶	47
Other Taxes	48	Self-employment tax (attach Schedule SE)	48
	49	Alternative minimum tax (attach Form 6251)	49
	50	Recapture taxes (see page 22). Check if from: a ☐ Form 4255 b ☐ Form 8611	50
	51	Social security tax on tip income not reported to employer (attach Form 4137)	51
	52	Tax on an IRA or a qualified retirement plan (attach Form 5329)	52
	53	Advance earned income credit payments from Form W-2	53
	54	Add lines 47 through 53. This is your **total tax** ▶	54
Payments Attach Forms W-2, W-2G, and W-2P to front.	55	Federal income tax withheld (**If any is from Form(s) 1099, check** ▶ ☐). — 55	
	56	1990 estimated tax payments and amount applied from 1989 return — 56	
	57	**Earned income credit** (see page 23) — 57	
	58	Amount paid with Form 4868 (extension request) — 58	
	59	Excess social security tax and RRTA tax withheld (see page 24) — 59	
	60	Credit for Federal tax on fuels (attach Form 4136) — 60	
	61	Regulated investment company credit (attach Form 2439) — 61	
	62	Add lines 55 through 61. These are your **total payments** ▶	62
Refund or Amount You Owe	63	If line 62 is more than line 54, enter amount **OVERPAID** ▶	63
	64	Amount of line 63 to be **REFUNDED TO YOU** ▶	64
	65	Amount of line 63 to be **APPLIED TO YOUR 1991 ESTIMATED TAX** ▶ 65	
	66	If line 54 is more than line 62, enter **AMOUNT YOU OWE.** Attach check or money order for full amount payable to "Internal Revenue Service." Write your name, address, social security number, daytime phone number, and "1990 Form 1040" on it.	66
	67	Estimated tax penalty (see page 25). — 67	

Sign Here
Keep a copy of this return for your records.

Under penalties of perjury, I declare that I have examined this return and accompanying schedules and statements, and to the best of my knowledge and belief, they are true, correct, and complete. Declaration of preparer (other than taxpayer) is based on all information of which preparer has any knowledge.

Your signature	Date	Your occupation
Spouse's signature (if joint return, BOTH must sign)	Date	Spouse's occupation

Paid Preparer's Use Only

Preparer's signature	Date	Check if self-employed ☐	Preparer's social security no.
Firm's name (or yours if self-employed) and address		E.I. No.	
		ZIP code	

☆ U.S. Government Printing Office: 1990 — 265-152

SCHEDULES A&B (Form 1040) Department of the Treasury Internal Revenue Service (0)	Schedule A—Itemized Deductions (Schedule B is on back) ▶ Attach to Form 1040. ▶ See Instructions for Schedules A and B (Form 1040).	OMB No. 1545-0074  Attachment Sequence No. 07
Name(s) shown on Form 1040		Your social security number

Medical and Dental Expenses		Caution: *Do not include expenses reimbursed or paid by others.*		
	1	Medical and dental expenses. (See page 27 of the Instructions.)	1	
	2	Enter amount from Form 1040, line 32 . [2]		
	3	Multiply the amount on line 2 by 7.5% (.075). Enter the result .	3	
	4	Subtract line 3 from line 1. Enter the result. If less than zero, enter -0- . . . . ▶		4
Taxes You Paid	5	State and local income taxes	5	
	6	Real estate taxes	6	
(See Instructions on page 27.)	7	Other taxes. (List—include personal property taxes.) ▶	7	
	8	Add the amounts on lines 5 through 7. Enter the total . . . . ▶		8
Interest You Paid	9a	Deductible home mortgage interest paid to financial institutions and reported to you on Form 1098. Report deductible points on line 10 . .	9a	
(See Instructions on page 27.)	b	Other deductible home mortgage interest. (If paid to an individual, show that person's name and address.) ▶		
		. . . .		
		. . . .	9b	
	10	Deductible points. (See Instructions for special rules.) . . .	10	
	11	Deductible investment interest (attach Form 4952 if required). (See page 28.)	11	
	12a	Personal interest you paid. (See page 28.) [12a]		
	b	Multiply the amount on line 12a by 10% (.10). Enter the result .	12b	
	13	Add the amounts on lines 9a through 11, and 12b. Enter the total . . . . ▶		13
Gifts to Charity		Caution: *If you made a charitable contribution and received a benefit in return, see page 29 of the Instructions.*		
(See Instructions on page 29.)	14	Contributions by cash or check	14	
	15	Other than cash or check. (You **MUST** attach Form 8283 if over $500.)	15	
	16	Carryover from prior year.	16	
	17	Add the amounts on lines 14 through 16. Enter the total . . . . ▶		17
Casualty and Theft Losses	18	Casualty or theft loss(es) (attach Form 4684). (See page 29 of the Instructions.) . ▶		18
Moving Expenses	19	Moving expenses (attach Form 3903 or 3903F). (See page 30 of the Instructions.). ▶		19
Job Expenses and Most Other Miscellaneous Deductions	20	Unreimbursed employee expenses—job travel, union dues, job education, etc. (You **MUST** attach Form 2106 if required. See Instructions.) ▶	20	
	21	Other expenses (investment, tax preparation, safe deposit box, etc.). List type and amount ▶		
(See Instructions on page 30 for expenses to deduct here.)		. . . .	21	
	22	Add the amounts on lines 20 and 21. Enter the total	22	
	23	Enter amount from Form 1040, line 32. [23]		
	24	Multiply the amount on line 23 by 2% (.02). Enter the result .	24	
	25	Subtract line 24 from line 22. Enter the result. If less than zero, enter -0-. . . . . ▶		25
Other Miscellaneous Deductions	26	Other (from list on page 30 of Instructions). List type and amount ▶		
		. . . .		
		. . . . ▶		26
Total Itemized Deductions	27	Add the amounts on lines 4, 8, 13, 17, 18, 19, 25, and 26. Enter the total here. Then enter on Form 1040, line 34, the **LARGER** of this total or your standard deduction from page 20 of the Instructions . . . . ▶		27

For Paperwork Reduction Act Notice, see Form 1040 Instructions.   Schedule A (Form 1040) 1990

Appendix 229

Schedules A&B (Form 1040) 1990
OMB No. 1545-0074 Page **2**
Name(s) shown on Form 1040. (Do not enter name and social security number if shown on other side.)
Your social security number

Schedule B—Interest and Dividend Income
Attachment Sequence No. **08**

Part I Interest Income

(See Instructions on pages 13 and 30.)

If you received more than $400 in taxable interest income, or you are claiming the exclusion of interest from series EE U.S. savings bonds issued after 1989 (see page 31), you must complete Part I. List ALL interest received in Part I. If you received more than $400 in taxable interest income, you must also complete Part III. If you received, as a nominee, interest that actually belongs to another person, or you received or paid accrued interest on securities transferred between interest payment dates, see page 31.

Interest Income		Amount
1	Interest income. (List name of payer—if any interest income is from seller-financed mortgages, see Instructions and list that interest first.) ▶	
	....	
	....	
	....	

Note: If you received a Form 1099-INT, Form 1099-OID, or substitute statement, from a brokerage firm, list the firm's name as the payer and enter the total interest shown on that form.

	....	1
	....	
	....	
2	Add the amounts on line 1. Enter the total	2
3	Enter the excludable savings bond interest, if any, from Form 8815, line 14. Attach Form 8815 to Form 1040	3
4	Subtract line 3 from line 2. Enter the result here and on Form 1040, line 8a . . ▶	4

Part II Dividend Income

(See Instructions on pages 13 and 31.)

If you received more than $400 in gross dividends and/or other distributions on stock, you must complete Parts II and III. If you received, as a nominee, dividends that actually belong to another person, see page 31.

Dividend Income		Amount
5	Dividend income. (List name of payer—include on this line capital gain distributions, nontaxable distributions, etc.) ▶	

Note: If you received a Form 1099-DIV, or substitute statement, from a brokerage firm, list the firm's name as the payer and enter the total dividends shown on that form.

	....	5
6	Add the amounts on line 5. Enter the total	6
7	Capital gain distributions. Enter here and on Schedule D* .	7	
8	Nontaxable distributions. (See the Inst. for Form 1040, line 9.)	8	
9	Add the amounts on lines 7 and 8. Enter the total	9
10	Subtract line 9 from line 6. Enter the result here and on Form 1040, line 9 . . ▶	10

*If you received capital gain distributions but do not need Schedule D to report any other gains or losses, see the Instructions for Form 1040, lines 13 and 14.

Part III Foreign Accounts and Foreign Trusts

(See Instructions on page 31.)

If you received more than $400 of interest or dividends, OR if you had a foreign account or were a grantor of, or a transferor to, a foreign trust, you must answer both questions in Part III. | Yes | No

11a At any time during 1990, did you have an interest in or a signature or other authority over a financial account in a foreign country (such as a bank account, securities account, or other financial account)? (See page 31 of the Instructions for exceptions and filing requirements for Form TD F 90-22.1.) . . . .

  b If "Yes," enter the name of the foreign country ▶ ....

12 Were you the grantor of, or transferor to, a foreign trust that existed during 1990, whether or not you have any beneficial interest in it? If "Yes," you may have to file Form 3520, 3520-A, or 926 . . . .

For Paperwork Reduction Act Notice, see Form 1040 Instructions. Schedule B (Form 1040) 1990

☆ U.S. Government Printing Office: 1990 — 265-183

SCHEDULE E (Form 1040)	**Supplemental Income and Loss**	OMB No. 1545-0074
Department of the Treasury Internal Revenue Service (0)	(From rents, royalties, partnerships, estates, trusts, REMICs, etc.) ▶ Attach to Form 1040 or Form 1041. ▶ See Instructions for Schedule E (Form 1040).	1990 Attachment Sequence No. 13
Name(s) shown on return		Your social security number

Part I Income or Loss From Rentals and Royalties Note: *Report farm rental income or loss from* **Form 4835** *on page 2, line 39.*

1 Show the kind and location of each **rental property**:
  A ....
  B ....
  C ....

2 For each rental property listed on line 1, did you or your family use it for personal purposes for more than the greater of 14 days or 10% of the total days rented at fair rental value during the tax year? (See Instructions.)

	Yes	No
A		
B		
C		

Rental and Royalty Income:		Properties			Totals
		A	B	C	(Add columns A, B, and C)
3 Rents received	3				3
4 Royalties received	4				4
Rental and Royalty Expenses:					
5 Advertising	5				
6 Auto and travel	6				
7 Cleaning and maintenance	7				
8 Commissions	8				
9 Insurance	9				
10 Legal and other professional fees	10				
11 Mortgage interest paid to banks, etc. (see Instructions)	11				11
12 Other interest	12				
13 Repairs	13				
14 Supplies	14				
15 Taxes	15				
16 Utilities	16				
17 Wages and salaries	17				
18 Other (list) ▶	18				
19 Add lines 5 through 18	19				19
20 Depreciation expense or depletion (see Instructions)	20				20
21 Total expenses. Add lines 19 and 20	21				
22 Income or (loss) from rental or royalty properties. Subtract line 21 from line 3 (rents) or line 4 (royalties). If the result is a (loss), see Instructions to find out if you must file **Form 6198**	22				
23 Deductible rental loss. **Caution:** Your rental loss on line 22 may be limited. See Instructions to find out if you must file **Form 8582**	23	( )	( )	( )	
24 **Income.** Add rental and royalty income from line 22. Enter the total income here					24
25 **Losses.** Add royalty losses from line 22 and rental losses from line 23. Enter the total losses here					25 ( )
26 Total rental and royalty income or (loss). Combine amounts on lines 24 and 25. Enter the result here. If Parts II, III, IV, and line 39 on page 2 do not apply to you, enter the amount from line 26 on Form 1040, line 18. Otherwise, include the amount from line 26 in the total on line 40 on page 2.					26

For Paperwork Reduction Act Notice, see Form 1040 Instructions.   Schedule E (Form 1040) 1990

Appendix 231

Schedule E (Form 1040) 1990 — Attachment Sequence No. 13 — Page 2

Name(s) shown on return. (Do not enter name and social security number if shown on other side.) — Your social security number

Note: *If you report amounts from farming or fishing on Schedule E, you must include your gross income from those activities on line 41 below.*

Part II — Income or Loss From Partnerships and S Corporations

If you report a loss from an at-risk activity, you MUST check either column (e) or (f) of line 27 to describe your investment in the activity. See Instructions. If you check column (f), you must attach **Form 6198**.

27	(a) Name	(b) Enter P for partnership; S for S corporation	(c) Check if foreign partnership	(d) Employer identification number	Investment At Risk? (e) All is at risk	(f) Some is not at risk
A						
B						
C						
D						
E						

	Passive Income and Loss		Nonpassive Income and Loss		
	(g) Passive loss allowed (Attach **Form 8582** if required)	(h) Passive income from **Schedule K-1**	(i) Nonpassive loss from **Schedule K-1**	(j) Section 179 expense deduction from **Form 4562**	(k) Nonpassive income from **Schedule K-1**
A					
B					
C					
D					
E					
28a Totals					
b Totals					

29 Add amounts in columns (h) and (k) of line 28a. Enter the total income here **29**
30 Add amounts in columns (g), (i), and (j) of line 28b. Enter the total here . . . . **30** (   )
31 Total partnership and S corporation income or (loss). Combine amounts on lines 29 and 30. Enter the result here and include in the total on line 40 below **31**

Part III — Income or Loss From Estates and Trusts

32	(a) Name	(b) Employer identification number
A		
B		
C		

	Passive Income and Loss		Nonpassive Income and Loss	
	(c) Passive deduction or loss allowed (Attach **Form 8582** if required)	(d) Passive income from **Schedule K-1**	(e) Deduction or loss from **Schedule K-1**	(f) Other income from **Schedule K-1**
A				
B				
C				
33a Totals				
b Totals				

34 Add amounts in columns (d) and (f) of line 33a. Enter the total income here **34**
35 Add amounts in columns (c) and (e) of line 33b. Enter the total here . . . . **35** (   )
36 Total estate and trust income or (loss). Combine amounts on lines 34 and 35. Enter the result here and include in the total on line 40 below **36**

Part IV — Income or Loss From Real Estate Mortgage Investment Conduits (REMICs)—Residual Holder

37	(a) Name	(b) Employer identification number	(c) Excess inclusion from **Schedules Q**, line 2c (see Instructions)	(d) Taxable income (net loss) from **Schedules Q**, line 1b	(e) Income from **Schedules Q**, line 3b

38 Combine amounts in columns (d) and (e) only. Enter the result here and include in the total on line 40 below **38**

Part V — Summary

39 Net farm rental income or (loss) from **Form 4835**. (Also complete line 41 below.) **39**
40 TOTAL income or (loss). Combine amounts on lines 26, 31, 36, 38, and 39. Enter the result here and on Form 1040, line 18 . . . . ▶ **40**
41 **Reconciliation of Farming and Fishing Income:** Enter your **gross** farming and fishing income reported in Parts II and III, and on line 39 (see Instructions) **41**

☆ U.S. Government Printing Office: 1990 — 265-196

Form 4562 — Depreciation and Amortization (Including Information on Listed Property)

Department of the Treasury — Internal Revenue Service
► See separate instructions.   ► Attach this form to your return.

OMB No. 1545-0172

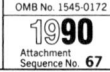

Attachment Sequence No. **67**

Name(s) shown on return | Identifying number

Business or activity to which this form relates

Part I — Election To Expense Certain Tangible Property (Section 179) (Note: If you have any "Listed Property," also complete Part V.)

1	Maximum dollar limitation (see instructions)	$10,000
2	Total cost of section 179 property placed in service during the tax year (see instructions)	
3	Threshold cost of section 179 property before reduction in limitation	$200,000
4	Reduction in limitation—Subtract line 3 from line 2, but do not enter less than -0-	
5	Dollar limitation for tax year—Subtract line 4 from line 1, but do not enter less than -0-	

(a) Description of property	(b) Cost	(c) Elected cost
6		

7	Listed property—Enter amount from line 26	
8	Total elected cost of section 179 property—Add amounts in column (c), lines 6 and 7	
9	Tentative deduction—Enter the lesser of line 5 or line 8	
10	Carryover of disallowed deduction from 1989 (see instructions)	
11	Taxable income limitation—Enter the lesser of taxable income or line 5 (see instructions)	
12	Section 179 expense deduction—Add lines 9 and 10, but do not enter more than line 11	
13	Carryover of disallowed deduction to 1991—Add lines 9 and 10, less line 12 ► 13	

Note: *Do not use Part II or Part III below for automobiles, certain other vehicles, cellular telephones, computers, or property used for entertainment, recreation, or amusement (listed property). Instead, use Part V for listed property.*

Part II — MACRS Depreciation For Assets Placed in Service ONLY During Your 1990 Tax Year (Do Not Include Listed Property)

(a) Classification of property	(b) Mo. and yr. placed in service	(c) Basis for depreciation (Business use only—see instructions)	(d) Recovery period	(e) Convention	(f) Method	(g) Depreciation deduction
14 General Depreciation System (GDS) (see instructions):						
a 3-year property						
b 5-year property						
c 7-year property						
d 10-year property						
e 15-year property						
f 20-year property						
g Residential rental property			27.5 yrs.	MM	S/L	
			27.5 yrs.	MM	S/L	
h Nonresidential real property			31.5 yrs.	MM	S/L	
			31.5 yrs.	MM	S/L	
15 Alternative Depreciation System (ADS) (see instructions):						
a Class life					S/L	
b 12-year			12 yrs.		S/L	
c 40-year			40 yrs.	MM	S/L	

Part III — Other Depreciation (Do Not Include Listed Property)

16	GDS and ADS deductions for assets placed in service in tax years beginning before 1990 (see instructions)	
17	Property subject to section 168(f)(1) election (see instructions)	
18	ACRS and other depreciation (see instructions)	

Part IV — Summary

19	Listed property—Enter amount from line 25	
20	Total—Add deductions on line 12, lines 14 and 15 in column (g), and lines 16 through 19. Enter here and on the appropriate lines of your return. (Partnerships and S corporations—see instructions)	
21	For assets shown above and placed in service during the current year, enter the portion of the basis attributable to section 263A costs (see instructions)	

For Paperwork Reduction Act Notice, see page 1 of the separate instructions.   Form **4562** (1990)

Appendix

Form 4562 (1990) — Page 2

Part V Listed Property.—Automobiles, Certain Other Vehicles, Cellular Telephones, Computers, and Property Used for Entertainment, Recreation, or Amusement

If you are using the standard mileage rate or deducting vehicle lease expense, complete columns (a) through (c) of Section A, all of Section B, and Section C if applicable.

Section A.—Depreciation (Caution: *See instructions for limitations for automobiles.*)

22a Do you have evidence to support the business use claimed? ☐ Yes ☐ No | 22b If "Yes," is the evidence written? ☐ Yes ☐ No

(a) Type of property (list vehicles first)	(b) Date placed in service	(c) Business use percentage	(d) Cost or other basis	(e) Basis for depreciation (business use only)	(f) Recovery period	(g) Method/ Convention	(h) Depreciation deduction	(i) Elected section 179 cost
23 Property used more than 50% in a trade or business:								
		%						
		%						
		%						
24 Property used 50% or less in a trade or business:								
		%				S/L –		▓▓▓
		%				S/L –		▓▓▓
		%				S/L –		▓▓▓

25 Add amounts in column (h). Enter the total here and on line 19, page 1 . . . . **25**
26 Add amounts in column (i). Enter the total here and on line 7, page 1 . . . . **26**

Section B.—Information Regarding Use of Vehicles—*If you deduct expenses for vehicles:*
- Always complete this section for vehicles used by a sole proprietor, partner, or other "more than 5% owner," or related person.
- If you provided vehicles to your employees, first answer the questions in Section C to see if you meet an exception to completing this section for those vehicles.

	(a) Vehicle 1		(b) Vehicle 2		(c) Vehicle 3		(d) Vehicle 4		(e) Vehicle 5		(f) Vehicle 6	
27 Total business miles driven during the year (DO NOT include commuting miles)												
28 Total commuting miles driven during the year												
29 Total other personal (noncommuting) miles driven												
30 Total miles driven during the year—Add lines 27 through 29												
	Yes	No	Yes	No	Yes	No	Yes	No	Yes	No	Yes	No
31 Was the vehicle available for personal use during off-duty hours?												
32 Was the vehicle used primarily by a more than 5% owner or related person?												
33 Is another vehicle available for personal use?												

Section C.—Questions for Employers Who Provide Vehicles for Use by Their Employees
(*Answer these questions to determine if you meet an exception to completing Section B.* **Note:** *Section B must always be completed for vehicles used by sole proprietors, partners, or other more than 5% owners or related persons.*)

	Yes	No
34 Do you maintain a written policy statement that prohibits all personal use of vehicles, including commuting, by your employees?		
35 Do you maintain a written policy statement that prohibits personal use of vehicles, except commuting, by your employees? (See instructions for vehicles used by corporate officers, directors, or 1% or more owners.)		
36 Do you treat all use of vehicles by employees as personal use?		
37 Do you provide more than five vehicles to your employees and retain the information received from your employees concerning the use of the vehicles?		
38 Do you meet the requirements concerning qualified automobile demonstration use (see instructions)?		

Note: *If your answer to 34, 35, 36, 37, or 38 is "Yes," you need not complete Section B for the covered vehicles.*

Part VI Amortization

(a) Description of costs	(b) Date amortization begins	(c) Amortizable amount	(d) Code section	(e) Amortization period or percentage	(f) Amortization for this year
39 Amortization of costs that begins during your 1990 tax year:			▓▓▓		▓▓▓
40 Amortization of costs that began before 1990. . . . . **40**					
41 Total. Enter here and on "Other Deductions" or "Other Expenses" line of your return **41**					

☼ U.S. Government Printing Office: 1990 — 265-331

Home Equity Line of Credit Checklist

	Lender 1	Lender 2	Lender 3
Basic Features			
Fixed rate	_____	_____	_____
Adjustable rate (start rate)	_____	_____	_____
Index used	_____	_____	_____
Current index	_____	_____	_____
Margin	_____	_____	_____
Change caps/frequency	_____	_____	_____
Life cap	_____	_____	_____
Length of Plan			
Draw period	_____	_____	_____
Renewal period	_____	_____	_____
Repayment term	_____	_____	_____
Fees/Closing Costs			
Appraisal fee	_____	_____	_____
Credit report fee	_____	_____	_____
Application fee	_____	_____	_____
Discount points	_____	_____	_____
Title fees	_____	_____	_____
Recording/notary fees	_____	_____	_____
Continuing Costs			
Membership fees	_____	_____	_____
Transaction fees	_____	_____	_____
Repayment			
Principal and interest	_____	_____	_____
Penalty for lates	_____	_____	_____
Interest only	_____	_____	_____
During draw period	_____	_____	_____
Final balloon payment	_____	_____	_____
Refinance options	_____	_____	_____
Extension terms	_____	_____	_____
Conversion to a fixed rate	_____	_____	_____

Before you sign the loan papers, use this checklist to compare loan features for several lenders with this highly competitive product. Call around to find the features, then visit one or two for current rates and points.

Refinance Worksheet

To help decide when a refinance makes sense, use this worksheet. When your existing interest rate is 2 percent more than the going rate consider refinancing.

Existing Mortgages _____
1st lien estimated payoff $ _____
2nd lien estimated payoff _____

Total mortgages to refinance $ _____
_____

FHA Refinance _____
_____

Total existing mortgages $_____
Less MIP refund (if financed) _____
Add closing costs _____
Add new MIP (if financed) _____
_____

Total loan with no cash out $ _____

VA Refinance _____

Total existing mortgages $ _____
Add VA funding fee _____
Add closing costs _____

Total loan with no cash out $ _____

Conventional Refinance _____
_____

Total existing mortgages $ _____
Add closing costs _____
_____

Total loan with no cash out $ _____

*Closing Costs to be included
Discount Points (FHA & VA) _____
Origination fee (all loans) _____

Appraisal Fee _____
Credit Report fee _____
Recording Fees _____
Title Policy
Escrow fee _____
Misc. local fees _____
(Pest Inspection, Transfer
Tax, Doc. Fee, Notary Fee)
Total Closing Costs $ _____

**Prepaids/Impounds $ _____

Property taxes _____
One-year fire policy _____
Prepaid interest _____

Total prepaids/impounds _____ $

(If lender does not require an impound account this may be less, but use this in case.)
Add MIP or VA funding fee $ _____
if you are paying in cash

Refinance Worksheet (cont)

Comparison note: Assume you are going to live on this property for five years or sixty months more. To compare the payments but remember you also need to compare the additional interest deduction from Schedule A. The new loan may decrease this interest amount; you'll need your old amortization schedule and a new one to compare.

Old loan monthly payment $ _____   Your new loan monthly payment $ ___
x 60 months = $ _____   x 60 months = $ _____

You saved yourself $ _____ over 60 months
    (Old monthly payment minus new)
Less your costs (Total closing costs plus total prepaids) $ _____
Total Savings $ _____ but you may pay more income taxes as explained in the comparison note above.

*See Types of Closing Costs for estimate.
**Use explanation of prepaids/impounds in Section I, if your conventional loan is over 80 percent LTV you will need to use the mortgage insurance (MI) estimates on the Factor Sheet.

Construction Loan Checklist

_____	Application #1003 completed and signed
_____	Check for $ _____ for appraisal and credit report
_____	Plans (2 sets) signed and dated on front page by borrower and contractor, and including:
	_____ plot plan
	_____ floor plan
	_____ foundation plan
	_____ cross section
	_____ elevations
_____	Description of materials to be signed and dated by borrower and contractor
_____	Completed cost breakdown to be signed and dated by contractor and including contractor's license number
_____	Evidence of contractor's license with limit sufficient to cover the contract amount
_____	Copy of contract between borrower and contractor
_____	Purchase contract for land, including date purchased and amount paid
_____	Evidence of any liens on land and name and addresses of lienholders
_____	Name and address of title company, escrow company and/or attorney
_____	Legal description of property
_____	Hazard insurance company to issue construction policy
_____	Building permits (if issued, photocopy)
_____	List or subcontractors and copy of subcontracts)

Estimated Construction Financing Worksheet

1. Land costs or land value $ _____
   If land has been owned one year or longer, use value from appraisal

2. Cost breakdown
   Profit for owner or builder is not allowed, or for nonowner-occupied properties

3. Total costs $ _____

   Closing Costs and Prepaids

   Loan fees _____ % of loan amount   _____
   Voucher control fee (_____ % of the costs)   _____
   Recording fees
      (estimate $25–$50 on construction loans)   _____
   Title policy
      (with rewrite and inspections could by $350+)   _____
   Escrow fee ($65–$200)   _____
   Property taxes
      (Call the county tax assessor
      for rate on your undeveloped land for now)   _____
   Hazard/fire/flood insurance
      (Call your agent for a quote
      on construction policy with extra liability if necessary)   _____
   Document preparation fee ($150–$300)   _____
   Tax service ($50 $100)   _____

4. Total of closing costs and prepaids $ _____

5. Interest withheld (use total cost breakdown x interest rate
   divided by 12, multiplied by 4–6 months)   _____

Total of costs (#3, 4, 5) $ _____
Appraised value   _____
Maximum loan amount
   (usually 80 percent of appraisal
   or 80 percent of costs, whichever is less)   _____

Total cash required from borrower $ _____
   (the difference between the costs and the loan amount)

This is a typical way of calculating the loan amount and the cash required for a construction loan; these figures vary with different lenders and areas.

VETRANS ADMINISTRATION U.S.D.A. FARMERS HOME ADMINISTRATION, AND
U.S. DEPARTMENT OF HOUSING AND URBAN DEVELOPMENT
HOUSING – FEDERAL HOUSING COMMISSIONER

Form Approved
OMB No. 2502-0192

(For accurate register of carbon copies, form may be separated along above fold. Staple completed sheets together in original order.)

☐ Proposed Construction

☐ Under Construction

DESCRIPTION OF MATERIALS

No. _____
(To be inserted by FHA, VA or FmHA)

Property address _____ City _____ State _____

Mortgagor or Sponsor _____
                                     (Name)   (Address)

Contractor or Builder _____
                                     (Name)   (Address)

INSTRUCTIONS

1. For additional information on how this form is to be submitted, number of copies, etc., see the instructions applicable to the HUD Application for Mortgage Insurance, VA Request for Determination of Reasonable Value, or FmHA Property Information and Appraisal Report, as the case may be.
2. Describe all materials and equipment to be used, whether or not shown on the drawings, by marking an X in each appropriate check-box and entering the information called for each space. If space is inadequate, enter "See misc." and describe under Item 27 or on an attached sheet. THE USE OF PAINT CONTAINING MORE THAN THE PERCENTAGE OF LEAD BY WEIGHT PERMITTED BY LAW IS PROHIBITED.
3. Work not specifically described or shown will not be considered unless required, then the minimum acceptable will be assumed. Work exceeding minimum requirements cannot be considered unless specifically described.
4. Include no alternates, "or equal" phrases, or contradictory items. (Consideration of a request for acceptance of substitute materials or equipment is not thereby precluded.)
5. Include signatures required at the end of this form.
6. The construction shall be completed in compliance with the related drawings and specifications, as amended during processing. The specifications include this Description of Materials and the applicable Minimum Property Standards.

1. EXCAVATION:
    Bearing soil, type _____

2. FOUNDATIONS:
    Footings: concrete mix _____ ; strength psi _____ Reinforcing _____
    Foundation wall: material _____ Reinforcing _____
    Interior foundation wall: material _____ Party foundation wall _____
    Columns: material and sizes _____ Piers: material and reinforcing _____
    Girders: material and sizes _____ Sills: material _____
    Basement entrance areaway _____ Window areaways _____
    Waterproofing _____ Footing drains _____
    Termite protection _____
    Basementless space: ground cover _____ ; insulation _____ ; foundation vents _____
    Special foundations _____
    Additional information: _____

3. CHIMNEYS:
    Material _____ Prefabricated *(make and size)* _____
    Flue lining: material _____ Heater flue size _____ Fireplace flue size _____
    Vents *(material and size)*: gas or oil heater _____ ; water heater _____
    Additional information: _____

4. FIREPLACES:
    Type: ☐ solid fuel; ☐ gas-burning; ☐ circulator *(make and size)* _____ Ash dump and clean-out _____
    Fireplace: facing _____ ; lining _____ ; hearth _____ ; mantel _____
    Additional information: _____

5. EXTERIOR WALLS:
    Wood frame: wood grade, and species _____ ☐ Corner bracing. Building paper or felt _____
    Sheathing _____ ; thickness _____ ; width _____ ; ☐ solid; ☐ spaced _____ " o. c.; ☐ diagonal; _____
    Siding _____ ; grade _____ ; type _____ ; size _____ ; exposure ____ "; fastening _____
    Shingles _____ ; grade _____ ; type _____ ; size _____ ; exposure _____ "; fastening _____
    Stucco _____ ; thickness _____ ". Lath _____ ; weight _____ lb.
    Masonry veneer _____ Sills _____ Lintels _____ Base flashing _____
    Masonry: ☐ solid ☐ faced ☐ stuccoed; total-wall thickness _____"; facing thickness _____"; facing material _____
        Backup material _____ ; thickness _____"; bonding _____
    Door sills _____ Window sills _____ Lintels _____ Base flashing _____
    Interior surfaces: dampproofing, _____ coats of _____ ; furring _____
    Additional information: _____
    Exterior painting: material _____ ; number of coats _____
    Gable wall construction: ☐ same as main walls; ☐ other construction _____

6. FLOOR FRAMING:
    Joists: wood, grade, and species _____ ; other _____ ; bridging _____ ; anchors _____
    Concrete slab: ☐ basement floor; ☐ first floor; ☐ ground supported; ☐ self-supporting; mix _____ ; thickness _____";
    reinforcing _____ ; insulation _____ ; membrane _____
    Fill under slab: material _____ ; thickness _____". Additional information: _____

7. SUBFLOORING: *(Describe underflooring for special floors under item 21.)*
    Material: grade and species _____ ; size _____ ; type _____
    Laid: ☐ first floor; ☐ second floor; ☐ attic _____ sq. ft.; ☐ diagonal; ☐ right angles. Additional information: _____

8. FINISH FLOORING: *(Wood only. Describe other finish flooring under item 21.)*

Location	Rooms	Grade	Species	Thickness	Width	Bldg. Paper	Finish
First floor							
Second floor							
Attic floor		sq. ft					

    Additional information: _____

Previous Edition May Be Used Until Supply Is Exhausted

DESCRIPTION OF MATERIALS
HUD-92005 (6-79)
VA Form 26-1852, Form FmHA 424-2

DESCRIPTION OF MATERIALS

9. PARTITION FRAMING:
Studs: wood, grade, and species _____ size and spacing _____ Other _____
Additional information: _____

10. CEILING FRAMING:
Joists: wood, grade, and species _____ Other _____ Bridging _____
Additional information: _____

11. ROOF FRAMING:
Rafters: wood, grade, and species _____ Roof trusses (see detail): grade and species _____
Additional information: _____

12. ROOFING:
Sheathing: wood, grade, and species _____ ; ☐ solid; ☐ spaced _____" o.c.
Roofing _____ ; grade _____ ; size _____ ; type _____
Underlay _____ ; weight or thickness _____ ; size _____ ; fastening _____
Built-up roofing _____ ; number of plies _____ ; surfacing material _____
Flashing: material _____ ; gage or weight _____ ; ☐ gravel stops; ☐ snow guards
Additional information: _____

13. GUTTERS AND DOWNSPOUTS:
Gutters: material _____ ; gage or weight _____ ; size _____ ; shape _____
Downspouts: material _____ ; gage or weight _____ ; size _____ ; shape _____ ; number _____
Downspouts connected to: ☐ Storm sewer; ☐ sanitary sewer; ☐ dry-well. ☐ Splash blocks: material and size _____
Additional information: _____

14. LATH AND PLASTER
Lath ☐ walls, ☐ ceilings: material _____ ; weight or thickness _____ Plaster: coats _____ ; finish _____
Dry-wall ☐ walls, ☐ ceilings: material _____ ; thickness _____ ; finish _____ ;
Joint treatment _____

15. DECORATING: *(Paint, wallpaper, etc.)*

Rooms	Wall Finish Material and Application	Ceiling Finish Material and Application
Kitchen		
Bath		
Other		

Additional information: _____

16. INTERIOR DOORS AND TRIM:
Doors: type _____ ; material _____ ; thickness _____
Door trim: type _____ ; material _____ Base: type _____ ; material _____ ; size _____
Finish: doors _____ ; trim _____
Other trim *(item, type and location)* _____
Additional information: _____

17. WINDOWS:
Windows: type _____ ; make _____ ; material _____ ; sash thickness _____
Glass: grade _____ ; ☐ sash weights; ☐ balances, type _____ ; head flashing _____
Trim: type _____ ; material _____ Paint _____ ; number coats _____
Weatherstripping: type _____ ; material _____ Storm sash, number _____
Screens: ☐ full; ☐ half; type _____ ; number _____ ; screen cloth material _____
Basement windows: type _____ ; material _____ ; screens, number _____ ; Storm sash; number _____
Special windows _____
Additional information: _____

18. ENTRANCES AND EXTERIOR DETAIL:
Main entrance door: material _____ ; width _____ ; thickness _____"; Frame: material _____ ; thickness _____"
Other entrance doors: material _____ ; width _____ ; thickness _____"; Frame: material _____ ; thickness _____"
Head flashing _____ Weatherstripping: type _____ ; saddles _____
Screen doors: thickness _____"; number _____ ; screen cloth material _____ Storm doors: thickness _____"; number _____
Combination storm and screen doors: thickness _____"; number _____ ; screen cloth material _____
Shutters: ☐ hinged; ☐ fixed. Railings _____ , Attic louvers _____
Exterior millwork: grade and species _____ Paint _____ ; number coats _____
Additional information: _____

19. CABINETS AND INTERIOR DETAIL:
Kitchen cabinets, wall units: material _____ ; lineal feet of shelves _____ ; shelf width _____
Base units: material _____ ; counter top _____ ; edging _____
Back and end splash _____ Finish of cabinets _____ ; number coats _____
Medicine cabinets: make _____ ; model _____
Other cabinets and built-in furniture _____
Additional information: _____

20. STAIRS:

Stair	Treads		Risers		Strings		Handrail		Balusters	
	Material	Thickness	Material	Thickness	Material	Size	Material	Size	Material	Size
Basement										
Main										
Attic										

Disappearing: make and model number _____
Additional information: _____

Appendix 241

21. SPECIAL FLOORS AND WAINSCOT. *(Describe Carpet as listed in Certified Products Directory)*

	LOCATION	MATERIAL, COLOR, BORDER, SIZES, GAGE, ETC.	THRESHOLD MATERIAL	WALL BASE MATERIAL	UNDERFLOOR MATERIAL
FLOORS	Kitchen _____				
	Bath _____				

	LOCATION	MATERIAL, COLOR, BORDER, CAP. SIZES, GAGE, ETC.	HEIGHT	HEIGHT OVER TUB	HEIGHT IN SHOWERS (FROM FLOOR)
WAINSCOT	Bath _____				

Bathroom accessories: ☐ Recessed; material _____ ; number _____ ; ☐ Attached; material _____ ; number _____
Additional information: _____

22. PLUMBING:

FIXTURE	NUMBER	LOCATION	MAKE	MFR'S FIXTURE IDENTIFICATION NO.	SIZE	COLOR
Sink _____						
Lavatory _____						
Water closet _____						
Bathtub _____						
Shower over tub △						
Stall shower △						
Laundry trays _____						

△☐ Curtain rod   △☐ Door   ☐ Shower pan: material _____
Water supply: ☐ public; ☐ community system; ☐ individual (private) system. ★
Sewage disposal: ☐ public; ☐ community system; ☐ individual (private) system. ★
★ *Show and describe individual system in complete detail in separate drawings and specifications according to requirements.*
House drain (inside): ☐ cast iron; ☐ tile; ☐ other _____   House sewer (outside): ☐ cast iron; ☐ tile; ☐ other _____
Water piping: ☐ galvanized steel; ☐ copper tubing; ☐ other _____   Sill cocks, number _____
Domestic water heater: type _____ ; make and model _____ ; heating capacity _____
_____ gph. 100° rise. Storage tank: material _____ ; capacity _____ gallons.
Gas service: ☐ utility company; ☐ liq. pet. gas; ☐ other _____   Gas piping: ☐ cooking; ☐ house heating.
Footing drains connected to: ☐ storm sewer; ☐ sanitary sewer; ☐ dry well. Sump pump; make and model _____
_____ ; capacity _____ ; discharges into _____

23. HEATING:
☐ Hot water. ☐ Steam. ☐ Vapor. ☐ One-pipe system. ☐ Two-pipe system.
☐ Radiators. ☐ Convectors. ☐ Baseboard radiation. Make and model _____
Radiant panel: ☐ floor; ☐ wall; ☐ ceiling. Panel coil: material _____
☐ Circulator. ☐ Return pump. Make and model _____ ; capacity _____ gpm.
Boiler: make and model _____   Output _____ Btuh.; net rating _____ Btuh.
Additional information: _____
Warm air: ☐ Gravity. ☐ Forced. Type of system _____
Duct material: supply _____ ; return _____   Insulation _____ , thickness _____   ☐ Outside air intake.
Furnace: make and model _____   Input _____ Btuh.; output _____ Btuh.
Additional information: _____
☐ Space heater; ☐ floor furnace; ☐ wall heater. Input _____ Btuh.; output _____ Btuh.; number units _____
Make, model _____   Additional information: _____
Controls: make and types _____
Additional information: _____
Fuel: ☐ Coal; ☐ oil; ☐ gas; ☐ liq. pet. gas; ☐ electric; ☐ other _____ ; storage capacity _____
Additional information: _____
Firing equipment furnished separately: ☐ Gas burner, conversion type. ☐ Stoker: hopper feed ☐; bin feed ☐
Oil burner: ☐ pressure atomizing; ☐ vaporizing _____
Make and model _____   Control _____
Additional information: _____
Electric heating system: type _____   Input _____ watts; @ _____ volts; output _____ Btuh.
Additional information: _____
Ventilating equipment: attic fan, make and model _____ ; capacity _____ cfm.
kitchen exhaust fan, make and model _____
Other heating, ventilating, or cooling equipment _____

24. ELECTRIC WIRING:
Service: ☐ overhead; ☐ underground. Panel: ☐ fuse box; ☐ circuit-breaker; make _____ AMP's _____ No. circuits _____
Wiring: ☐ conduit; ☐ armored cable; ☐ nonmetallic cable; ☐ knob and tube; ☐ other _____
Special outlets: ☐ range; ☐ water heater; ☐ other _____
☐ Doorbell. ☐ Chimes. Push-button locations _____   Additional information: _____

25. LIGHTING FIXTURES:
Total number of fixtures _____   Total allowance for fixtures, typical installation, $ _____
Nontypical installation _____
Additional information: _____

DESCRIPTION OF MATERIALS

26. INSULATION:

Location	Thickness	Material, Type, and Method of Installation	Vapor Barrier
Roof			
Ceiling			
Wall			
Floor			

27. MISCELLANEOUS: *(Describe any main dwelling materials, equipment, or construction items not shown elsewhere; or use to provide additional information where the space provided was inadequate. Always reference by item number to correspond to numbering used on this form.)* _____

_____
_____
_____
_____
_____
_____
_____
_____
_____

HARDWARE: *(make, material, and finish.)* _____
_____

SPECIAL EQUIPMENT: *(State material or make, model and quantity. Include only equipment and appliances which are acceptable by local law, custom and applicable FHA standards. Do not include items which, by established custom, are supplied by occupant and removed when he vacates premises or chattels prohibited by law from becoming realty.)* _____
_____
_____
_____
_____
_____
_____
_____

PORCHES: _____
_____

TERRACES: _____
_____

GARAGES: _____
_____

WALKS AND DRIVEWAYS:
Driveway: width _____ ; base material _____ ; thickness _____ "; surfacing material _____ ; thickness _____ "
Front walk: width _____ ; material _____ ; thickness _____ ". Service walk: width _____ ; material _____ ; thickness _____ "
Steps: material _____ ; treads _____ "; risers _____ ". Cheek walls _____

OTHER ONSITE IMPROVEMENTS:
(Specify all exterior onsite improvements not described elsewhere, including items such as unusual grading, drainage structures, retaining walls, fence, railings, and accessory structures.)
_____
_____

LANDSCAPING, PLANTING, AND FINISH GRADING:
Topsoil _____ " thick: ☐ front yard; ☐ side yards; ☐ rear yard to _____ feet behind main building.
Lawns *(seeded, sodded, or sprigged)*: ☐ front yard _____ ; ☐ side yards _____ ; ☐ rear yard _____
Planting: ☐ as specified and shown on drawings; ☐ as follows:
_____ Shade trees, deciduous, _____ " caliper.   _____ Evergreen trees, _____ ' to _____ ', B & B.
_____ Low flowering trees, deciduous, _____ ' to _____ '.   _____ Evergreen shrubs, _____ ' to _____ ', B & B.
_____ High-growing shrubs, deciduous, _____ ' to _____ '.   _____ Vines, 2-year
_____ Medium-growing shrubs, deciduous, _____ ' to _____ '.
_____ Low-growing shrubs, deciduous, _____ ' to _____ '.

IDENTIFICATION.—This exhibit shall be identified by the signature of the builder, or sponsor, and/or the proposed mortgagor if the latter is known at the time of application.

Date _____   Signature _____

Signature _____

DESCRIPTION OF MATERIALS
HUD-92005 (6-79)
VA Form 26-1852, Form FmHA 424-2

Maximum FHA Loan Amount Worksheet

Use the lesser of the frst or second method of calculating the maximum loan amount.

First Calculation:

1. Sales price or FHA appraised value $ _____
   (lesser of the two)
2. Add on closing costs paid by buyer $ _____
   (Use 1.5% of sales price for prequalifying; you may only use actual closing costs paid within variance of $250.)
3. Total is amount used to determine loan $ _____
4. Deduct the first $25,000.00 $\underline{\hphantom{xx} -25,000.00}$
5. Equals $ _____
6. Multiply #5 by 95% $ _____
7. Add $24,250.00 $\underline{\hphantom{xx} +24,250.00}$
   (97% of the first $25,000.00)
8. Maximum base loan amount $ _____
   (Round down to $50. increments)

Second Calculation:

1. Sales price or FHA appraised value $ _____
   (Lesser of the two)
2. Multiply #1 by 97.75% if value exceeds $50,000.00
   or by 98.75% if value $50,000.00 and under
3. Maximum base loan amount (Round to $50) $ _____
   (Do not add any closing costs.)

CONSTRUCTION COST BREAKDOWN

OWNER_____ CONTRACTOR_____

Job Address_____ Phone_____

Any voucher issued for more than the cost breakdown bid will be returned to the payee unless there is sufficient money remaining in the miscellaneous funds to cover the difference.

NO VOUCHERS will be paid until foundation is complete.

No.	ITEM	BID		NAME OF SUB-CONTRACTOR
1.	PLANS & SPECS.			
2.	BUILDING PERMIT			
3.	SURVEY & ENGINEERING			
4.	TEMPORARY WATER POWER			
5.				
6.				
7.	EXCAVATING & GRADING			
8.	WATER LINE			
9.	GAS LINE			
10.	SEWER			
11.	DRIVEWAY			
12.	LANDSCAPE			
13.	MISCELLANEOUS			
14.				
15.				
16.	FOUNDATIONS			
17.	HARDWARE, ROUGH			
18.	LUMBER, ROUGH			
19.	PLUMBING GROUND			
20.				
21.	CARPENTRY, ROUGH			
22.	ELECTRIC, ROUGH			
23.	PLUMBING, TOP OUT			
24.	FIREPLACE			
25.	ROOFING			
26.				
27.				
28.	EXTERIOR SIDING			
29.	FRAMES & WINDOWS			
30.	INSULATION			
31.	DRYWALL			
32.	MASONRY			
33.				
34.				
35.	HEATING			
36.	KITCHEN APPLIANCES			
37.	CABINETS			
38.	DOORS			
39.	COUNTER TOPS			
40.	FLOORING			
41.	ELECTRIC, FINISH			
42.	PLUMBING, FINISH			
43.	TILE			
44.				
45.	LUMBER, FINISH			
46.	CARPENTRY, FINISH			
47.	HARDWARE, FINISH			
48.	FLOORING, FINISH			
49.	PAINTING			
50.	GARAGE DOOR			
51.	EXTERIOR FLATWORK			
52.	CLEAN UP			
53.				
54.	CONTROL FEE OR BOND			
55.	INTEREST, INSURANCE, ETC.			
56.	PROFIT & OVERHEAD			
Total Required Construction funds				

DISPOSITION OF LOAN FUNDS / FOR BANK USE ONLY

Amount of Loan $_____

Less:
  A. Loan Fee $_____
  B. Land or Lot Payoff $_____
  C. Title and Escrow $_____
  D. Other $_____ − $_____

Subtotal $_____

Plus:
  A. Borrowers Funds + $_____

Total Available Construction Funds (must equal required funds above) $_____

I certify that the above is to the best of my knowledge, a true and correct statement of the estimated cost of the job.

Signed:_____ Date:_____

Appendix

A.	B. TYPE OF LOAN
	1. ☐ FHA 2. ☐ FMHA 3. ☐ CONV. UNINS.
	4. ☐ VA 5. ☐ CONV. INS.
	6. File Number: 7. Loan Number:
SETTLEMENT STATEMENT U.S. DEPARTMENT OF HOUSING AND URBAN DEVELOPMENT	8. Mortgage Insurance Case Number:

C. NOTE: This form is furnished to give you a statement of actual settlement costs. Amounts paid to and by the settlement agent are shown. Items marked "(p.o.c.)" were paid outside the closing; they are shown here for informational purposes and are not included in the totals.

D. NAME OF BORROWER:
   ADDRESS:

E. NAME OF SELLER:
   ADDRESS:

F. NAME OF LENDER:
   ADDRESS:

G. PROPERTY LOCATION:

H. SETTLEMENT AGENT:
   ADDRESS:

I. SETTLEMENT DATE:

PLACE OF SETTLEMENT:
   ADDRESS:

J. SUMMARY OF BORROWER'S TRANSACTION		K. SUMMARY OF SELLER'S TRANSACTION	
100. GROSS AMOUNT DUE FROM BORROWER:		**400. GROSS AMOUNT DUE TO SELLER:**	
101. Contract sales price		401. Contract sales price	
102. Personal property		402. Personal property	
103. Settlement charges to borrower (line 1400)		403.	
104.		404.	
105.		405.	
Adjustments for items paid by seller in advance		*Adjustments for items paid by seller in advance*	
106. City/town taxes to		406. City/town taxes to	
107. County taxes to		407. County taxes to	
108. Assessments to		408. Assessments to	
109.		409.	
110.		410.	
111.		411.	
112.		412.	
120. GROSS AMOUNT DUE FROM BORROWER		420. GROSS AMOUNT DUE TO SELLER	
200. AMOUNTS PAID BY OR IN BEHALF OF BORROWER:		**500. REDUCTIONS IN AMOUNT DUE TO SELLER:**	
201. Deposit or earnest money		501. Excess deposit (see instructions)	
202. Principal amount of new loan(s)		502. Settlement charges to seller (line 1400)	
203. Existing loan(s) taken subject to		503. Existing loan(s) taken subject to	
204.		504. Payoff of first mortgage loan	
205.		505. Payoff of second mortgage loan	
206.		506.	
207.		507.	
208.		508.	
209.		509.	
Adjustments for items unpaid by seller		*Adjustments for items unpaid by seller*	
210. City/town taxes to		510. City/town taxes to	
211. County taxes to		511. County taxes to	
212. Assessments to		512. Assessments to	
213.		513.	
214.		514.	
215.		515.	
216.		516.	
217.		517.	
218.		518.	
219.		519.	
220. TOTAL PAID BY/FOR BORROWER		520. TOTAL REDUCTIONS AMOUNT DUE SELLER	
300. CASH AT SETTLEMENT FROM/TO BORROWER		**600. CASH AT SETTLEMENT TO/FROM SELLER**	
301. Gross amount due from borrower (line 120)		601. Gross amount due to seller (line 420)	
302. Less amounts paid by/for borrower (line 220)	( )	602. Less reductions in amount due seller (line 520)	( )
303. CASH (☐ FROM) (☐ TO) BORROWER		603. CASH (☐ TO) (☐ FROM) SELLER	

L. SETTLEMENT CHARGES

		Paid From Borrower's Funds at Settlement	Paid From Seller's Funds at Settlement
700.	**TOTAL SALES/BROKER'S COMMISSION** based on price $ @ % =		
	Division of Commission (line 700) as follows:		
701.	$ to		
702.	$ to		
703.	Commission paid at Settlement (Money retained by broker applied to commission $ ____)		
704.	Other sales agent charges		
705.	Additional commission		
	800. ITEMS PAYABLE IN CONNECTION WITH LOAN		
801.	Loan Origination Fee %		
802.	Loan Discount %		
803.	Appraisal Fee to		
804.	Credit Report to		
805.	Lender's Inspection Fee		
806.	Mortgage Insurance Application Fee to		
807.	Assumption Fee		
808.			
809.			
810.			
811.			
	900. ITEMS REQUIRED BY LENDER TO BE PAID IN ADVANCE		
901.	Interest from to @ $ /day		
902.	Mortgage Insurance Premium for months to		
903.	Hazard Insurance Premium for years to		
904.	years to		
905.			
	1000. RESERVES DEPOSITED WITH LENDER		
1001.	Hazard insurance month @ $ per month		
1002.	Mortgage insurance month @ $ per month		
1003.	City property taxes month @ $ per month		
1004.	County property taxes month @ $ per month		
1005.	Annual assessments month @ $ per month		
1006.	month @ $ per month		
1007.	month @ $ per month		
1008.	month @ $ per month		
	1100. TITLE CHARGES		
1101.	Settlement or closing fee to		
1102.	Abstract or title search to		
1103.	Title examination to		
1104.	Title insurance binder to		
1105.	Document preparation to		
1106.	Notary fees to		
1107.	Attorney's fee to (includes above items numbers;)		
1108.	Title insurance to (includes above items numbers;)		
1109.	Lender's coverage $		
1110.	Owner's coverage $		
1111.			
1112.			
1113.			
	1200. GOVERNMENT RECORDING AND TRANSFER CHARGES		
1201.	Recording fees: Deed $; Mortgage $; Release $		
1202.	City/county tax/stamps: Deed $; Mortgage $		
1203.	State tax/stamps: Deed $; Mortgage $		
1204.			
1205.			
	1300. ADDITIONAL SETTLEMENT CHARGES		
1301.	Survey to		
1302.	Pest inspection to		
1303.			
1304.			
1305.			
1306.			
1307.			
1400.	**TOTAL SETTLEMENT CHARGES** (enter on lines 103, Section J and 502, Section K)		

The above settlement statement is hereby approved, the disbursements indicated are authorized, and settlement may be completed by settlement agent.

Borrower _____ Seller _____

Appendix 247

SCHEDULE OF REAL ESTATE OWNED

PLEASE COMPLETE IN FULL DETAIL

This schedule of other real estate owned is to be attached to and made a part of my Loan Application and Financial Statement dated _____, for property at _____

title of which is to be in names of _____

(If percentage of ownership is less than 100% indicate % amount and complete all columns using only your percentage of ownership.)

Property Address	*	No. of Units	A. Acquisition Date B. Acquisition Cost	Name and Address of Lender on C. 1st Mortgage D. Junior Lien	Loan Number	Market Value	Balance 1st Mtg	Balance Junior Liens	Monthly Cash Flow					Cash Flow
									(1) Monthly Rental Income	(2) Monthly Taxes & Insurance	(3) Monthly Operating Expenses	Monthly Loan Payments		Column #1 Less Columns 2, 3, 4 & 5
												(4) 1st Mortgage	(5) Junior Liens	
1.			A. B.	C. D.										
2.			A. B.	C. D.										
3.			A. B.	C. D.										
4.			A. B.	C. D.										
5.			A. B.	C. D.										
6.			A. B.	C. D.										
7.			A. B.	C. D.										
Attach additional sheets if necessary					TOTAL	$	$	$	$	$	$	$	$	$

* Indicate if property is: R = Rental   S = Sold
PS = Pending Sale
L = Vacant Land
PR = Primary Residence

REMARKS: The undersigned declare, under the penalty of perjury, that the statements, information and representations set forth herein are true and correct.

Signed _____ (Date) _____

Signed _____ (Date) _____

Glossary

ADJUSTABLE RATE MORTGAGE (ARM). A mortagage loan with an interest rate that may change during the term according to a set market.

AMORTIZATION. A gradual decrease in debt made according to a set schedule of installment payments. In most circumstances, the amount of interest owing on the outstanding balance is deducted from the total monthly payment and the remainder is applied to the principal, until the principal is paid in full.

APPRAISED VALUE. For lending purposes, the appraised value of your home is an opinion by the appraiser based on information about the house and on the appraiser's knowledge of the area. For VA loans the appraisal is called a CRV, or a Certificate of Reasonable Value, and for FHA loans it is a Conditional Commitment. For conventional, FHA, and VA programs the appraised value is determined using a Uniform Residential Appraisal Report. The estimate of value can be calculated by using one or more of three methods: the reproduction or costs approach, the income approach (for investment properties), and the sales comparison approach. The value used to determine the maximum loan amount is the lesser of the appraised value or the sales price.

ASSUMABILITY. The transfer of property and debt from one borrower to another. Under most circumstances, the original borrower is still liable for the debt unless the assumptor is proven credit-worthy and a release of liability is approved through the lender.

BALANCE SHEET. A statement of the financial condition of a business or individual, including assets, liabilities, capital and net worth on a given date. It is part of the required financial statement, along with two years of federal tax returns, for borrowers who are self-employed or who receive income from a business.

BALLOON PAYMENT. The last payment of a balloon mortgage loan after periodic installments of principal and interest. The balloon payment results from the collection of principal and interest payments that don't fully amortize the loan. Usually it is a lump sum due at the end of the term.

BIWEEKLY MORTGAGE. A mortgage loan with payments collected biweekly, which reduce the principal balance sooner by applying twenty-six payments a year to the debt instead of only twelve.

BUILDING PERMIT. A permit issued by local authorities to construct, remodel or remove a specific structure on a chosen lot according to approved plans and specifications. Most lenders require a building permit, a building contract, a cost breakdown, a description of materials and a set of plans to apply for a construction loan.

BUYDOWN. A set amount of money put aside in a third party account, usually by the seller builder or lender, to be applied to the interest of the mortgage loan for the period of time specified in the buydown agreement. The purpose is to allow the borrower to qualify at a lower buydown rate, thus offering more attractive financing to potential buyers. Because of restrictions by agencies and investors (FHA, VA, FHLMC and FNMA), lenders have guidelines for qualifying for a buydown.

CAP. A limit to the increases or decreases in the monthly payment or in the interest charged on an adjustable rate loan. Usually, there are two caps, one for the periodic changes (monthly, biannual, or annual), which occur at the change date and one for the life of the loan.

CASH FLOW. The net income from an investment property or business—the income after deductions for expenses.

CASH-OUT REFINANCE. A new mortgage loan that pays off existing liens on a property and allows cash back to the borrower from the equity in the same property. Limitations on the amount of the loan-to-value ratios exist for owner-occupant borrowers. Most lenders don't offer cash-out refinances to investors.

CERTIFICATE OF OCCUPANCY (C OF O). A signed certificate issued by local authorities at the completion of the construction of a building or at the completion of a remodeling project allowing the dwelling to be inhabited. It is requirement for closing escrow and disbursing the permanent, or take-out, financing.

CERTIFICATE OF REASONABLE VALUE (CRV). The VA version of the appraisal issued by the local VA office upon receipt and review of the URAR completed by the VA appraiser. The new LAPP system used by the VA allows the lender to use a staff VA-approved appraiser and issue a CRV.

CHANGE DATE. A set time when your adjustable rate mortgage payment may increase or decrease according to terms of the agreement. The amount of change is determined by the market index and the amount of margin set at the close of the loan and is limited by the cap.

CLOSING. The signing of legal documents, the disbursement of funds, and the delivery of a deed necessary to complete a purchase or refinance transaction.

CO-BORROWERS (ALSO CALLED CO-MORTGAGORS). People who agree to add their income and credit history to the loan applications to help qualify the borrowers. For the FHA, their income after their total expenses may be used to help qualify the co-borrowers need not be relatives, just logically associated. For the VA, a co-borrower may be used but the amount of guaranty is determined by the veteran's share of ownership in the property. For conventional loans, the co-borrower must occupy the property if the loan-to-value ratio is over 90 percent, but they need not be relatives. In most cases, the co-borrower must execute all loan papers and is liable for the payment of the loan equally with the borrower.

CONDITIONAL COMMITMENT. The term used for FHA loans for the estimate of value placed on the property by the appraiser. The conditional commitment to insure a loan is subject to the final credit approval by a D.E. underwriter or by the FHA (direct agency approval), who then issue a firm commitment. The lender then disburses the loan funds, closes escrow, and pays the mortgage insurance premium. A Certificate of Insurance is issued to the lender by the FHA after receiving written proof of the entire transaction.

CONDOMINIUM. The term used for ownership of a unit in a multi-family development. The owner usually owns the interior space and surfaces, walls, ceilings, and floors and a share of the land under the unit including all common areas for general use of the owners. Title to the common area is expressed as a fraction of that area, for example, $\frac{1}{34}$th interest in the common areas owned by the XYZ Homeowner's Association for a thirty-four unit development.

CONSTRUCTION LOAN. See Interim financing.

CONVENTIONAL LOANS. The group of loans originated by lenders that are not insured or guaranteed by government programs (FHA, VA), but that may be purchased by FNMA, FHLMC, or other investors in these types of loans.

CONVERSION OPTION. An agreement between the lender and the borrower to convert an adjustable rate mortgage loan to a fixed rate loan during a preset period (or conversion window) at the option of the borrower. The new rate is normally determined by the market at the time of the conversion and the new terms are set in the original agreement (promissory note).

CONVERTIBLE ADJUSTABLE RATE MORTGAGE (CARM). An adjustable rate mortgage loan that contains a conversion option in the agreement. Usually, during a set period of time (several months to several years) the rate of the mortgage can be changed to a fixed rate loan or to another variation of an adjustable rate loan, based on a prearranged factor (current fixed rate plus a margin).

COST BREAKDOWN. A form completed by the builder or contractor constructing a new home or remodeling an existing home that details the costs of each part of the construction in order to arrive at the total construction costs. Most lenders require this form, along with the building permit, a description of materials, the contract and the plans and specifications, when you apply for a construction loan.

DEED OF TRUST. The security instrument used to secure the promissory note with real property in some states. The title is actually conveyed to a third party (the trustee—usually a title company or an attorney) on the condition that the trustee will reconvey title to the mortgagor (borrower) upon payment in full to the mortgagee (lender or beneficiary) or will sell the land and repay the debt should the mortgagor default.

DEPARTMENT OF HOUSING AND URBAN DEVELOPMENT (HUD). A government agency established by the Housing and Urban Development Act of 1965 to administer housing and urban development programs, including the Federal Housing Administration.

DEPOSIT RECEIPT. A term used for a type of contract to purchase property, which includes a receipt for the earnest (good faith) money deposit received by the seller. This contract is legally binding for the term, amount, and conditions stated when executed by all parties.

DEPRECIATION. The loss in value of a piece of property or permanently attached improvement to the property due to age, physical deterioration, or economic conditions. The allowable depreciation on federal income tax returns can reduce the tax liability of an investor and is considered in the analysis of the net income of a self-employed borrower.

DESCRIPTION OF MATERIALS. The form prepared by the builder or contractor that details the supplies and materials that will be used to construct or remodel a home. This form, along with the cost breakdown, the contract and the plans is required to apply for a construction loan.

DISCOUNT POINTS. A one-time charge (one point equals 1 percent of the principal loan amount) by the lender and collected at closing to increase the yield on the mortgage loan as compared to the other loans on the secondary market.

DOWN-PAYMENT. The difference between the sales price of a home and the amount the lender will loan.

EQUITY. For lending purposes, the difference between the value of your property and the value of the liens against the property.

ESCROW ACCOUNT. See Impound account.

FEDERAL HOME LOAN BANK BOARD (FHLBB). The agency that supervises and regulates federally chartered savings institutions, the Residential Trust Corporation (RTC) and the Federal Home Loan Mortgage Corporation (FHLMC, or FreddieMac). The twelve district offices of the Federal Home Loan Bank monitor the savings and lending rates and publish the cost of funds in each district, an index used to determine the changes in many adjustable rate mortgages.

FEDERAL HOME LOAN MORTGAGE CORPORATION (FHLMC, OR FREDDIE MAC). A private corporation authorized by Congress to buy and sell conventional loans through participation sales certificates secured by pools of like loans. FHLMC also sells Government National Mortgage Association (GNMA) bonds to finance the purchase of government loans.

FEDERAL HOUSING ADMINISTRATION (FHA). A part of the U.S. Department of Housing and Urban Development created by the National Housing Act of 1934 to offer long-term, fully amortized, low-down-payment, federally insured loans to homebuyers.

FEDERAL INCOME TAX FORM 1040. The cover sheet or summary form for your individual income tax returns. The starting point for analyzing the net income for an individual borrower who is self-employed. The 1040 and all accompanying schedules and attachments should be included in a complete loan package for an investor or any borrower who receives income from a business.

FEDERAL NATIONAL MORTGAGE CORPORATION (FNMA, OR FANNIE MAE). A private corporation created by Congress to establish a secondary market source for the purchase and sale of conventional, FHA and VA loans.

FIRM COMMITMENT. The FHA form issued by a D.E. underwriter or by the local FHA office accepting the credit and appraisal portion of a loan package and committing FHA insurance upon proof of an acceptable closing.

GENERAL CONTRACTOR. A person who is licensed by the state to supervise the construction of a new dwelling or the renovation of an existing dwelling according to an agreement between the landowner and the contractor. The general contractor may hire employees or subcontract work to other contractors for completion, but is ultimately responsible for the completion of the project by a certain date for a certain amount.

GOVERNMENT NATIONAL MORTGAGE ASSOCIATION (GNMA, OR GINNIE MAE). A corporation created by Congress to administer the mortgage-backed securities programs using government loans guaranteed by GNMA.

GRADUATED PAYMENT MORTGAGE (GPM). A mortgage loan in which the monthly payments start lower so the borrower can qualify and gradually increase over three to five years to a level payment. The result of inadequate interest payments in the first years can result in negative amortization, in which the unpaid interest is added on to the principal, resulting in a balance (when the payments level off) that is actually more than the beginning balance.

HOME EQUITY LOAN OR LINE OF CREDIT. A shorter term (one to five years) mortgage loan in second position to the first mortgage loan with voluntary advances during a predetermined period and repayment either during the line of credit period or in monthly installments until paid in full.

HOMEOWNER'S ASSOCIATION (HOA). A group of residents in a single family, condomium, or planned unit development organized to provide maintainence for the common areas and community facilities for the common enjoyment of the residents.

HOMEOWNER'S WARRANTY PROGRAMS (HOW). An extended warranty program offered by builders (beyond the normal one-year warranty) that protects the homeowner from damages caused by defects in the building of the home. If a builder will provide one of the approved ten-year homeowner's warranties, an FHA buyer can get a maximum FHA loan on a home completed within the last year that did not have FHA inspections during its construction.

HOUSING EXPENSE. The total of monthly charges of principal, interest, property taxes, fire and flood insurance, mortgage insurance, homeowner's association dues, or any special assessments due monthly in connection with owning a home.

IMPOUND ACCOUNT. An account for the collection and disbursement of property taxes, fire and flood insurance premiums, and other property assessments due to protect the interests of the lender and the homeowner. An impound account is required on all FHA and VA loans and most conventional loans with over an 80 percent loan-to-value ratio. Also called an escrow account.

INCOME STATEMENT. Also called a profit and loss statement. A list of income and expenses for a certain period of time (usually quarterly) resulting in a net income or loss figure. The income statement, along with the balance sheet, is required for self-employed borrowers in addition to the federal tax returns for the previous two years.

INDEX. In mortgage lending, the term for the market used to determine the periodic adjustments in the interest rate. The index can be your district cost of funds as determined by the Federal Home Loan Bank, the one-year Treasury bill average, or any other measure of the market used in your area.

INSTALLMENT LOANS. Loans that have a set term and a fixed monthly installment payment and that usually amortize over the term. There are variations to the installment loan, but usually this term refers to a loan with regular payments monthly as opposed to variable rates or payments. Common examples are home improvement loans, auto loans, and other consumer loans.

INTERIM FINANCING. Also called a construction loan. Short-term (usually six months to one year) financing used to complete a construction project. The owners usually obtain a take-out loan or permanent financing to pay off this debt.

INVESTOR. In discussing mortgage loans, the term investor can have two separte meanings. For loans traded on the secondary market the trader is sometimes called the investor, the person or organization who buys and sells mortgage loans. For qualifying for a mortgage loan, the term means any person who owns property for investment purposes.

LAND CONTRACT. Commonly, a contract for the purchase of unimproved land with the title remaining with the seller or developer until the terms have been met.

LIFE CAP. The limit that the interest rate can increase or decrease over the term of the loan on an adjustable rate mortgage loan.

LINE OF CREDIT. An open-end loan with terms to include advances and periodic repayments of principal and interest or, initially, interest only. In the case of a home equity line of credit, the loan is secured by your property and becomes a second lien.

LOAN-TO-VALUE RATIO. Expressed as a percentage the loan amount as compared to the lesser of the sales price or appraised value of the home. The difference between the loan amount and the value is the down payment required.

MARGIN. A set percentage, which, when added to the index on an adjustable rate mortgage loan, will determine the new rate of interest to be charged at each change date, subject to the change date caps and the life cap.

MORTGAGE INSURANCE (MI OR SOMETIMES PMI). Insurance that protects the lender against a loss due to a default on the loan. It is required on conventional loans with a loan-to-value ratio of over 80 percent. The cost of the MI is collected by the lender at the closing or added to the principal loan. The amount of the insurance varies by the loan-to-value ratio, from 81 to 95 percent, and varies by the type of loan (fixed or adjustable) according to the coverage that the lender and investor require. Private mortgage insurance is offered through several companies, such as Mortgage Guaranty Insurance Corporation (MGIC).

MORTGAGE INSURANCE PREMIUM (FHA MIP). The phrase used for the insurance premium charged by the FHA for an insured loan. The amount of the premium may be paid in cash at the closing or may be financed by the lender and added to your principal loan.

MORTGAGE. The security instrument in some states that secures the loan using your property. Some states use a mortgage, some use a deed of trust, and some use a trust deed, depending on the state's laws.

MORTGAGEE. The lender or creditor in a mortgage transaction, sometimes called the beneficiary.

MORTGAGOR. The borrower or debtor in a mortgage transaction.

NEGATIVE AMORTIZATION. Also called add-on interest. The monthly addition of unpaid interest to principal, which results in an increase instead of a decrease in the principal balance. This can happen on any type of graduated payment mortgage or adjustable rate loan when the beginning monthly payment is too low to cover all the interest due and the unpaid portion is added monthly to the principal.

NONRECURRING CLOSING COSTS. Those costs that are paid at the closing of an escrow to the lender, the title company, the attorney, the appraiser and the credit agency and that will only occur at the closing.

NOTICE OF COMPLETION. A form completed and recorded by the contractor or builder to notify subcontractors and the local authorities that mechanic's liens can be filed.

ORIGINATION FEE. The loan origination fee charged by the lender for the paperwork involved in the preparation of a mortgage loan package. Usually from 1 to 2.5 percent of the loan amount.

PERMANENT LOAN. Also called a take-out loan. The permanent financing used to pay off a construction loan or reimburse the builder for construction costs at the completion of a project. Usually a thirty-year or fifteen-year, fixed or adjustable rate FHA, VA, or conventional mortgage loan secured by the completed improvements and property.

PITI. The term used for the principal, interest, taxes and insurance paid monthly on a mortgage loan.

PLANNED UNIT DEVELOPMENT (PUD). For residential lending purposes, a development plan for a subdivision with restrictions on the use of the areas owned in common and conditions for the use of the individually owned lots. Many planned unit developments contain single-family residences, duplexes, condominiums and common areas owned by a homeowner's association. The purpose of the PUD is to regulate conforming features of a residential development, including schools, roads, service areas, and even commercial development.

PLANS AND SPECIFICATIONS. The drawings created by an architect, engineer or designer showing the plot plan, floor layout, electrical design, plumbing, doors, windows, roofing, foundations and including a description of the application of the materials.

PLOT PLAN. A drawing showing the layout of the improvements (dwellings, structures) on a piece of land: the dimensions, the connections to utilities, and driveways, landscaping, and fencing included in the construction project.

PORTFOLIO. The term used to describe the loans held by banks, savings and loans, life insurance companies, pension and trust funds, and savings banks that are not currently traded on the secondary market. Usually portfolio loans are nonconforming or unconventional in nature; often they are either jumbo first mortgage loans (large loans over FHA, VA, FHLMC and FNMA loan limits) or first or second mortgage loans that have higher or lower yields than other loans sold on the secondary market.

PRELIMINARY TITLE REPORT. A title search of the property prior to a committment to insure or an issuance of a title policy. The commitment to insure along with the survey or the preliminary title report will reveal any legal limitations to the use of the property, including any ingress or egress restrictions, taxes owed, existing liens, mineral rights and water rights, and will allow a lender to determine the quality of the legal title.

PREPAID INTEREST. The amount of interest owed at the closing for a mortgage loan for the use of the principal from the date of the closing to the first payment due date.

PREPAIDS. A term used to decribe the items other than nonrecurring closing costs that are commonly paid for at the closing. They include property taxes, fire and flood insurance, private mortgage insurance and any other assessments on the property. The amount of prepaids can be placed in an impound account for FHA, VA, and some conventional loans over 80 percent loan-to-value, or can be used to pay taxes and insurance due at the closing with future payments paid by the borrower.

PREPAYMENT PENALTY. A fee for the privilege of paying a portion or all of the principal mortgage amount in advance of the due date. Normally, the prepayment penalty is due only during the first one to five years of the mortgage loan and only on conventional portfolio loans.

PRIMARY FINANCING. A term for the first mortgage lien on real property, as opposed to any secondary financing or second liens. It has first position on the title, after property taxes and special assessments or homeowners association dues are paid.

PROFIT AND LOSS STATEMENT. Another term for the income statement used to calculate the net business income of a self-employed borrower. The balance sheet and the profit and loss statement, in addition to the federal income tax returns, are the financial statements required by lenders from borrowers who are self-employed.

PROMISSORY NOTE. The document that states the borrower's promise to pay and lists the terms, the principal amount, the interest to be charged and any special features that affect the terms. The promissory note, completed and executed properly, meets the Uniform Commercial Code requirements of a negotiable instrument, eligible to be traded on the secondary market. A promissory note secured by the property with a Deed of Trust, Mortgage or Trust Deed has a value (yield) that can be traded.

PROPERTY TAXES. A lien against your property prior to any mortgages for the payment of local, municipal and state taxes. These make up the primary tax base for most state revenues. Rates may vary by state, county, city or region.

PURCHASE AGREEMENT. Also called a purchase contract. A term for the contract between the buyer and seller to purchase real property.

REAL PROPERTY. Land and anything attached, including dwellings, structures, trees, mineral rights, water rights, and any interest or rights to future improvements.

REALTOR. A member or associate member of the National Association of Realtors. A broker or agent who represents clients in the buying and selling of real properties.

RECONSIDERATION OF VALUE. An attempt to change the value of a property as determined by the appraiser. Usually, the borrower or realtor presents to the lender documented evidence (sales of comparable homes in the same area as the subject) that the value should be increased. Since loan amounts are based on the lesser of the sales price or the appraised value, a reconsideration of value is especially important for transactions in which the borrower is unable to contribute the additional money necessary to make up the difference between a low appraised value and the sales price.

REFINANCING. The origination of a new loan using the proceeds to pay off existing liens and using the same property as security.

RELEASE OF LIABILITY. The agreement issued from a lender authorizing the termination of one borrower's personal liability for a debt and transferring the liability to an assumptor who has been proven credit-worthy.

RESIDUAL. For mortgage loan purposes, the amount of a borrower's monthly income that remains after deducting all of the obligations and debts he or she pays on a monthly basis. A common measure of the qualifications of a borrower for FHA and VA loans.

REVERSE ANNUITY MORTGAGE (RAM). A mortgage loan from a lender to a borrower that utilizes the equity in a single-family dwelling to pay the borrower a set monthly amount. These are commonly available today for persons over sixty-two who own their home free and clear, who meet the guidelines and who wish to draw on the equity in their home. The FHA's test program, called the Home Equity Conversion Reverse Annuity Mortgage #255, is available in some areas.

SALES CONCESSION. Items of value contributed by the seller, the builder, or another third party to induce the borrower to purchase the property.

SECONDARY FINANCING. In relation to mortgage loans, this term has two meanings. When speaking of home equity loans, it refers to a mortgage loan in second position to the first mortgage and used to draw on the equity in your property. It is also used to describe a second loan originated at the time of purchase to reduce the down-payment requirement and increase the loan-to-value ratio. For example, a home with a value of $100,000, a first mortgage of $80,000 and secondary financing of $10,000 (a carry-back note) has a combined loan-to-value (CLTV) of 90 percent and a loan-to-value (LTV) of 80 percent.

SECONDARY MARKET. A term used for the marketplace where loans secured by real property, either first mortgages or second mortgages, are traded. A loan that can be sold in this marketplace must meet the standards set by prudent lenders and by the agencies who insure and guaranty these loans, thus creating a need for uniform lending practices.

SERVICING. The procedure for collecting of mortage loan monthly payments and disbursing net funds to the owners of the loans. The servicing agent pays the net interest funds and monitors, or in some cases pays, the property taxes, fire and flood insurance, private mortgage insurance and any other assessments to protect the security of the loan.

SUBCONTRACTOR. The company or person who contracts with the general contractor or builder to perform a portion of the labor or supply materials.

SUBORDINATE FINANCING. A term used to describe the second lien or any lien that is subordinated, or subject, to the first lien.

TAKE-OUT FINANCING. Also called permanent financing. A common phrase used by lenders for the permanent mortgage loan that pays off the construction loan or reimburses the builder at the completion of the project. Usually a thirty-year or fifteen-year loan with a fixed or adjustable interest rate amortized with regular monthly installments and using the completed improvements and property as security.

TITLE INSURANCE POLICY. An agreement between the insured (the lender and borrower) and the insuror (the title company) to reimburse the insured for any loss caused by a defect in the title to the real property by undisclosed liens, lack of access to the property or any other limitation to the use and sale of the property.

TRUST DEED. A form used in some states to transfer a title to real property to a trustee (third party) for the purpose of conveying title to the borrower (mortgagor) upon repayment of the debt or, in the case of foreclosure, disposing of the property and repaying the lender (mortgagee). Other forms, such as a deed of trust or a mortgage instrument, are used in some states.

TRUSTEE. The third party in a deed of trust or trust deed who holds title to the property for the benefit of the lender (mortgagee or beneficiary).

UNIFORM RESIDENTIAL APPRAISAL REPORT (URAR). The forms completed by the VA, the FHA and the conventional appraisers for appraising residential properties. The form allows for the replacement costs method, the income approach (for income properties) and the sales comparison approach for arriving at the estimate of market value.

VA FUNDING FEE. The amount collected and remitted to the Veterans Administration at the closing for a VA loan. The amount varies by the loan-to-value ratio.

VACANCY FACTOR. The percentage of the gross rental income alloted to a potential loss from vacancies, usually from 5 to 25 percent of the rents, depending on the area. This deduction must be made to arrive at net rental income or cash flow.

VETERANS ADMINISTRATION, DEPARTMENT OF VETERAN AFFAIRS (VA). An agency of the Federal Government created by the Serviceman's Readjustment Act of 1944 to administer services to qualified veterans, including the guaranty of low-down-payment, long term home loans.

W-2S. The four-part form issued by your employer to notify you and the IRS of your total earnings for each year. Your completion of the W-4 form will determine how much is withheld from your earnings for federal and state income taxes. The total taxes, both federal and state, and the total FICA (Social Security) is indicated, as well as your social security identifying number and if applicable, your federal employee identifying number. The employer is required to send you your copies of this form by the last day in February and you are required to notify your current and previous employers of any change of tax status or address throughout the year.

Index

Adjustable rate loans   127
Amortization schedule   126
Applicable   85
Assumability
   FHA   59
   VA   70
   Conventional   82
Bonus income   93
Borrowed funds   103
Building contract   224
CAPS   128
Child support/alimony   95
Closing   51, 111
Closing costs   28–40, 145
Co-barrowers/co-signers   105
Commission income   93
Condominiums   61
Construction loans   189–200
Concersion option   131
Conventional maximum loan
    amounts   74
Credit Analysis
   FHA   62
   VA   71
   Conventional   79, 90
Description of materials   195
Discount points   65
Equity loans   153
Expenses   120
FHA loans   7, 55
FHA maximum loan amount   23, 56
FHA mortgage insurance
    (MIP)   58
Fixed rate loans   124
For sale by owner   43
Gifts   102
Graduated payment loans 133

Home equity lines of credit
   158
Income   8, 73, 92
Interest/dividend   94
Lender's role   48
Loan approcal   107, 110
Loan interview   84, 86
Loan to value
   FHA   57
   VA   69
   Conventional   75
Military income   98
Negative amortization   132
Note receivable income   94
Overtime   92
Portable mortgages   138
Prepaid costs   179
Prepayment penalty   150
   FHA   59
   Conventional   82
Private mortgage insurance   77
Property requirements
   FHA   59
   VA   71
   Conventional   78
Ratios   21
Residuals   21, 72
Realtor's role   41
Rreduced document loans   81
Refinance   141, 152
Rental properties   94, 179–187
Retirement income   97
Reverse annuity mortgages   137
Sales concessions   76
Schedule C income   99
Schedule E income   171, 172, 182
Second job   93
Second/vacation   167–177

Secondary financing   102, 151, 153
Secondary market   5
Self-employed barrower   99
Servicing   112
Social security   98
Stocks and bonds   104
Time deposits   103
Timeshares   173
Tips/gratuities   93
Trust income   97
Types of lenders   45

Unemployment/public assistance   96
VA loans   8
VA benefits   96
VA eligibility   66
VA funding fee   25, 69
VA loan guaranty   66
VA maximum loan amount   67
Wage earner income   92

DIXIE LEE BUTLER has over 25 years experience in the housing loan field and currently is the owner of Mortgage Lending Seminars, a firm specializing in training lending personnel to process mortgage loans. She has been a lending training specialist and FHA Direct Endorsement Underwriter for several mortgage lenders and a contract underwriter for Mortgage Guaranty Insurance Corp. Ms. Butler resides in Reno, Nevada.

Order Today!

Exceptional Real Estate Titles . . .

The Real Estate Investment Advisor: The '90s Guide to Buying and Selling Real Estate, G. Timothy Haight & Daniel D. Singer, $18.95

Buying More House For Less Money: How to Make Sure You Get Your Money's Worth, Ceil Lohmar, $9.95

For Sale By Owner: A No-Nonsense Guide to Getting the Best Price for Your House, Ceil Lohmar, $9.95

Encyclopedia of Real Estate and Finance: Over 1,000 Terms Defined, Explained and Illustrated, James Newell & Albert Santi, $24.95

Mortgage Manual: Q&As on FHA, VA and Conventional Mortgage Loans, 4th Edition, Albert Santi, $19.95

Real Estate Finance: Everything You Need to Know About the Dollars & Sense of Financing Real Estate, A. G-Yohannes, $21.95

The Investor's Self-Teaching Seminar — Your Home as Your Best Investment, Robert W. Richards & Grover C. Richards, $19.95

USE ORDER FORM ON NEXT PAGE TO ORDER!

ORDER FORM

Quantity	Title	Price

Payment: MasterCard/Visa/American Express accepted. When ordering by credit card your account will not be billed until the book is shipped. You may also reserve your order by phone or by mailing this order form. When ordering by check or money order, you will be invoiced upon publication. Upon receipt of your payment, the book will be shipped. Please add $3.50 for postage and handling for the first book and $1.00 for each additional copy.

Subtotal	
IL residents add 7% tax	
Shipping and Handling	
Total	

Credit Card # _____

Expiration Date _____

Name _____

Address _____

City, State, Zip _____

Telephone _____

Signature _____

Mail Orders to:

PROBUS PUBLISHING COMPANY

1925 N. Clybourn Avenue

Chicago, IL 60614

or Call:

1-800 PROBUS-1